The Future of Historically Black
Colleges and Universities

The Future of Historically Black Colleges and Universities

Ten Presidents Speak Out

edited by
Carolyn O. Wilson Mbajekwe

McFarland & Company, Inc., Publishers
Jefferson, North Carolina, and London

LIBRARY OF CONGRESS CATALOGUING-IN-PUBLICATION DATA

The future of historically black colleges and universities : ten
    presidents speak out / edited by Carolyn O. Wilson Mbajekwe.
        p.   cm.
    Includes bibliographical references and index.

    ISBN-13: 978-0-7864-2565-5
    ISBN-10: 0-7864-2565-2 (softcover : 50# alkaline paper) ∞

    1. African American universities and colleges.   2. African
    Americans—Education (Higher)   I. Wilson Mbajekwe, Carolyn O.
    LC2781.F88 2006
    378.73089'96073--dc22   2006010926

British Library cataloguing data are available

Cover photograph ©2005 Photodisc

Manufactured in the United States of America

*McFarland & Company, Inc., Publishers
    Box 611, Jefferson, North Carolina 28640
    www.mcfarlandpub.com*

To the memory
of Dr. Mary McLeod Bethune,
who devoted her life
to the struggle for racial advancement

ACKNOWLEDGMENTS

A study of this scope would not have been possible without the support and cooperation of many individuals. First and foremost, I am grateful to the featured college presidents for graciously allowing me to interview them about African American higher education and their careers in black college leadership. The presidents provided support and encouragement at every stage of this project and were exceedingly generous with their time and knowledge. They have made the production of this book a truly remarkable and rewarding experience for me. For years to come, the insights and perspectives in this book will stand as an indispensable resource for helping us to understand the role of historically black colleges in American higher education in the new century, the daily functioning of the institutions, and the future roles of the black colleges.

I also thank the numerous presidential special assistants for their wonderful cooperation for this project. For their professional competence in coordinating the interview sessions, resolving scheduling conflicts, and handling critical post-interview logistics, I am deeply indebted to Evola Bates of Jackson State University, Cynthia Buskey of Savannah State University, Beverley Crane of Morehouse College, Jacqueline Curtis of Norfolk State University, Tracey Foxworth of the United Negro College Fund, Adrienne Harris of Morehouse College, Delores C. Mitchell of Bowie State University, Yvonne Skillings of Spelman College, and Karen Watkins of Xavier University of Louisiana.

As always, I am thankful to my graduate school professors Leroy

Davis, Leslie M. Harris, and James L. Roark for all they have done over the years to encourage my intellectual growth and development. I must also acknowledge my undergraduate professors Michael M. McCormick, David F. Godshalk, and Jeanne M. McNett, who nurtured my early intellectual interests and pointed me in the direction of graduate school. I am also grateful to Daryl M. Scott, who introduced me to the wonderful world of historical research.

While working on this book, I received much support and encouragement from my colleagues in the department of history and political science at Elizabeth City State University: Flora B. Brown, Kwabena Boansi, Glen Bowman, Rebecca Seaman, Shaun Stokes, and Margery Coulson-Clark. My department chair in particular, Flora B. Brown, has been a wonderful source of encouragement, as has Jennifer Keane-Dawes, dean of arts and humanities at Elizabeth City. Good family friends such as Ambassador and Mrs. Bismarck Myrick, Chris and Myrna Kennerly, Uche Egemonye and Koppen Ashy, Kharen Fulton, and Bob and Margaret Crews provided great inspiration.

I remain indebted to my family and childhood community for inspiring me and for instilling in me from birth an appreciation for the great value of historically black institutions. From the earliest days of my youth I knew the importance of historically black colleges and universities, for I was born and raised in Mayesville (Sumter County), South Carolina, the birthplace of Dr. Mary McLeod Bethune, the founder of Bethune-Cookman College and one of the most influential African American women in United States history. My family's neighbors and closest friends were the grandnieces and grandnephews of Dr. Bethune. As a child, I spent many hours with my neighbor, listening to her regale me with stories about her legendary "Aunt Mame." Only the sounds of my mother's voice beckoning me to supper, homework or a household chore could tear me away from the old woman's feet. That is how I came of age — a bright-eyed child sitting at the feet of the elders, soaking in stories about great black leaders and important black institutions.

Over the years we have watched with pride as other Sumter County natives, working in the tradition of Dr. Mary McLeod Bethune, have gone out into the world and made their mark in institutional leadership in general, and in higher education leadership in particular. Their ranks include Dr. Lucy J. Reuben, former provost and vice chancellor of North Carolina Central University; Frank L. Matthews, the founder and publisher of *Black Issues in Higher Education*, the nation's leading minority-focused higher education news magazine; Dr. Lois T. Green, former associate vice chancellor of Elizabeth City State University; poet Nikki Finney, associate professor of creative writing at the University of Kentucky; Dr. Marla F. Frederick, assistant professor of African and African American Studies and of the Study of Religion at Harvard University; Eugene F. Kennedy, former mayor of Seat Pleasant, Maryland, and founder of the Maryland Black Mayors Association; and Rev. Dr. Clyde Anderson, an executive with the United Methodist Board of Global Ministries. And my family members, through the roles they played (and still play) in the local Baptist Church, fraternal lodges, and community organizations, have demonstrated the virtues of leadership and self-help. Growing up in this small, tight-knit community with its strong work ethic and devotion to family, education, community institutions — a place where young people were taught the importance of responsibility — I learned how to be black and to be proud of my blackness long before I went away to graduate school and started reading all those fancy books about the politics of identity. In the spirit of that great Sumter County, South Carolina, tradition, this book is dedicated to the memory of Dr. Mary McLeod Bethune.

Lastly, but most importantly, I am indebted to my husband Patrick Uchenna, my dear friend and intellectual partner. Without the unflinching support of Patrick, this book would not exist. For at one critical point when conceptual problems and scheduling conflicts forced me to consider abandoning this project, he encouraged me to pick up the pieces and carry on. Patrick and our sons, Bosah Arinze and Nnamdi Edward, warm my heart and inspire my soul.

TABLE OF CONTENTS

PREFACE

There is presently a dearth of literature and scholarship on the impacts of twenty-first century changes and transformations on historically black colleges and universities. For instance, virtually nothing has been written about how the American-based movement for diversity in higher education, as well as the larger trends of globalization and internationalization, are affecting traditionally African American–serving institutions. Equally glaring is the absence of the views and perspectives of the presidents of black colleges from most discussions about American higher education in the new era in general, and minority higher education in particular.

In an effort to fill this void in our knowledge about black higher education, between 2002 and 2004 I conducted interviews and held in-depth discussions with ten of the nation's leading black college presidents. The purpose of the study was to give these presidents an opportunity to express their views on many aspects of black higher education in contemporary America.

In their own words, the presidents provide answers to questions that until now have never been raised by scholars of black higher education. They describe the important historical role black colleges and universities played in American higher education before the era of desegregation; define the mission of historically and predominantly black institutions in a society emphasizing racial and cultural diversity; and reveal how the national movement for diversity is affecting developments at their respective institutions. Moreover, the presidents discuss

1

the impact of breakthroughs in technology on research and teaching at historically black colleges; their priorities and challenges in fundraising and development; their views on university-community outreach; and finally, their visions for the future of traditionally African American–serving higher education institutions.

It is my sincere hope that this book will enhance the understanding of scholars, educators, policy makers, and others who carry the critically important responsibility of developing programs and strategies to ensure higher education access and opportunity for *all* Americans by securing the viability of the nation's colleges and universities.

INTRODUCTION

In recent times much has been written about the state of the American university in the twenty-first century. Much of the present dialogue focuses on the complex changes and transformations American colleges and universities are undergoing in response to a plethora of powerful and far-reaching social, economic, demographic, and technological forces. The various processes driving this change system include the breaking down of racial, ethnic, religious, and gender-based legal barriers to group and individual advancement, the welding of world communities through the processes of globalization and internationalization, the development of new technologies, and the emergence of a high-tech, knowledge-centered economy.[1] Most often these changes are considered for their direct implications for the quality and quantity of higher education available to American students and conditions of higher education access in America. But even more significantly they are considered for the critical issue of how colleges and universities approach their traditional mission of research, teaching, and service.[2]

While the literature on the American university in the twenty-first century is most insightful and informative, it has two major shortcomings. First, virtually nothing has been written about the impact of contemporary social and structural changes, transformations, and pressures on the nation's historically black colleges and universities. Second, the literature overlooks the views and opinions of the men and women who lead black institutions. To date, no scholar has examined the perspectives of the presidents and other high-ranking administrators who sit at the helm of historically black colleges and universities and who shoulder the critical responsibility of conceptualizing and articulating the mission and vision of these institutions in the new era.

This book is intended to bridge the gap in our knowledge of traditionally African American–serving higher education institutions. It presents the views, thoughts, opinions, perspectives, experiences, and ideas of ten presidents of the nation's historically black colleges (both retired and currently serving) on the position of traditionally black institutions in the changing world of higher education in the twenty-first century. The aim is to portray historically black colleges and universities from the viewpoints of the presidents, with the goal of helping us to better understand the challenges and opportunities facing black institutions, and how their leaders are responding to the environment of higher education in the new century.

In straightforward and candid fashion, the presidents share their views on a wide variety of issues. These topics range from the presidents' understanding of the important past contributions of historically black colleges to their concept of how the history and heritage of the black colleges inform the schools' present mission. Other topics include the effect of the changing technological environment on research, teaching, curriculum, and faculty of historically black colleges; how the presidents define diversity in higher education; and how they are responding to the diversity movement within America, as well as the twin phenomena of globalization and internationalization.

The presidents also discuss their fundraising priorities, the challenges they face in this particular area, and the strategies they are employing to obtain alumni, federal, corporate, and foundation support for their schools. Additionally, the presidents give insight into their understanding of service and university-community engagement, and discuss programs they are sponsoring to foster development in their local communities.

The ten presidents profiled in this study reflect the great diversity that characterizes historically black college leadership in the twenty-first century. The presidents hail from diverse backgrounds, espouse different outlooks, and inherited distinctive institutional legacies. As a group they represent six private institutions and four public. Their student bodies range from 550 to 8,200. Their curriculums encompass the broad scope of higher education, from liberal arts programs at the undergraduate level to comprehensive master's and doctoral level programs. Some of the presidents are themselves graduates of historically black colleges, while others attended predominantly white institutions. Some came to their present position from within the black college administrative ranks, while others came from administrative posts at predominantly white institutions. One, in fact, left the presidency of a predominantly white institution to take on her present role at a historically black college. Another was chief academic officer of a large west-coast public system. The vast diversity of the personal and professional backgrounds of the featured presidents poses a strong counter to widely held notions about the homogenous nature of black college leadership.

The extraordinary breadth and caliber of their professional experience and the reach of their influence make these presidents key spokespersons for black higher education and historically black colleges. They are in the forefront of the national dialogue on race and higher education in America, presenting papers, leading workshops, and participating on national commissions and researches. One of the presidents featured in this book is a former United States assistant secretary for post-secondary education. Another is the president and chief executive officer of the United Negro College Fund, the nation's oldest and most influential black higher education consortium. Another is currently the longest sitting university president in America — black or white — with 35 years of service, and four currently serve on the White House Board of Advisors on Historically Black Colleges. Another is the past president and chief executive officer of the National Association for Equal Opportunity in Higher Education (NAFEO), a consortium of 103 historically black colleges, and recently retired from his third college presidency. Still another is the author of a highly acclaimed book on race and education and served on a presidential commission on race, while another is a former president of the National Science Foundation. In their collective wisdom the men and women featured in this book are exemplary of the broad depth of personal and professional experiences and expertise needed to guide the traditionally black institutions through this time of transformation.

These presidents are united in purpose — helping the nation's historically black colleges and universities survive in the new millennium by successfully adapting to the changing conditions of higher education. This shared commitment among the presidents stems from their understanding of the historical forces that shaped and defined the development of African American higher education and its relationship to the larger black political struggle for freedom, justice, and equality.

Higher education institutions for African Americans emerged in the aftermath of the Civil War and the wake of Reconstruction.[3] The first institutions to emerge were the private colleges. The private schools were established under the supervision of a number of groups and organizations, including northern white missionaries, black church groups, and black communities. Of the northern white religious groups, organizations such as the American Missionary Association, the American Baptist Mission Society, and the Methodist Episcopal Church were leaders.[4] The efforts of African American church groups to establish institutions of higher education were spearheaded by the African Methodist Episcopal Church, the Colored Methodist Episcopal Church, and the Baptist Church. Other private institutions resulted from the efforts of visionary individuals such as Booker T. Washington, James Shepard, James C. Price, Mary McLeod Bethune, and Elizabeth Evelyn Wright.[5] The advent of the public system of higher education for African Americans was a byproduct of the Second Morrill Act of 1890. The Act provided land-grant colleges for blacks in states where land-grant institutions existed for whites.[6]

During their formative years, which coincided with the period of American history known as Redemption, an era characterized by widespread racial repression, black institutions faced numerous challenges to their growth and development. African Americans were politically disfranchised, forced into the economically exploitative sharecropping and tenant cropping system, excluded from public facilities and institutions by mandate of Jim Crow segregation laws, denied equal opportunity in education, and subjected to horrendous racial violence.[7] The educational impact of this contentious state of race relations was that African American elementary and secondary education in the South was extremely underdeveloped. This, in turn, hindered the growth and development of black higher education institutions as generations of African Americans who were potentially capable of completing college-level work were denied the opportunity to obtain the prerequisite secondary training. The culture and environment of the post–Civil War South adversely affected the development of African American higher education institutions in more direct ways, ranging from assigning black institutions the limited role of educating African Americans exclusively to starving black institutions of funding.[8]

This was the environment in which higher education institutions for African Americans were founded. Yet the black college story abounded with profound ironies. For in spite of all the limitations placed on the development of black colleges, these institutions that had been started to preserve segregation and inequality (at least in the minds of whites who imposed segregation and Jim Crow) turned out to be the tools that undermined segregation and inequality.

First and foremost, throughout the Jim Crow period, the black colleges provided the only available means of higher education access to generations of African Americans. The role black institutions played in providing higher education access was critical to black progress. As historian Adam Fairclough points out in his groundbreaking study *Teaching Equality: Black Schools in the Age of Jim Crow*, because slave-owners during the slavery period prohibited black literacy, African Americans would come to believe strongly that education was the key to freedom, liberation, and uplift.[9] Because of this belief in the empowering quality of knowledge, the acquisition of education became the focal point of the black *political* struggle for justice and equality. And all debates about how to uplift the race (for example the early twentieth century debate between Booker T. Washington and W.E.B. Du Bois) always revolved around the question of what was the best educational strategy to accomplish the goal of race advancement.

Yet coming into Emancipation African Americans still had a long road to travel in order to reach their goal of obtaining empowerment through education. When the Civil War erupted in 1861 at least 90 percent of all African Americans were illiterate, and only 28 percent had received college- or university-level training from any American institution.[10] And in the whole of the country there were only three institutions—all in the North—established for the express purpose of providing higher education to blacks. By 1925, however, sixty years later, there were no fewer than one hundred higher education institutions for blacks, with most located in the South, and only 16 percent of African Americans were incapable of reading or writing.[11] In 1928 there were 12,000 students enrolled in black colleges. By 1941 the number of African Americans enrolled in these institutions had increased to 37,000. Just nine years later, in 1950, on the eve of *Brown v. Board of Education*, this number had doubled to 74,000.[12] The black college was single-handedly responsible for increasing the educational opportunities available to young blacks. By raising the level of education in the black community, black colleges made vital contributions to the African American political struggle for justice and equality.

Reflecting on the important role black institutions played in providing higher education access to African Americans, Walter E. Massey, president of Atlanta's Morehouse College, states: "They provided a professional and educated class at a time when it was very difficult for any class to be educated in any other way."[13] Michael L. Lomax, president and chief executive officer of the United Negro College Fund and former president of Dillard University, maintains, "Black colleges and universities have provided access to education for African Americans. That has been the number one important role that we played, certainly since the nineteenth century when African Americans were excluded from every level of educational opportunity, till the twentieth century where, at least for the first half of it, historically black colleges remained the number one opportunity for post-secondary education for African Americans."[14] Carolynn Reid-Wallace, former United States assistant secretary for post-secondary education and former president of Nashville's Fisk University, posits: "Without these institutions, up until literally the early seventies, large numbers of the educated population that we now know would not exist."[15] Norman C. Francis, president of Xavier University of Louisiana and currently the longest sitting university president in America, similarly states: "America would not have had the professional cadre of African Americans that it has today and has enjoyed over these many years had it not been for black colleges."[16]

In addition to performing the political work of providing higher education access to African Americans, scholars have identified numerous other ways the black colleges contributed to the black fight for equality. One important contribution the institutions made was that they imbued African American students with an empowering black cultural identity that countered then dominant white supremacist ideas about the origins of black people and the contributions of black people to the world. During the early 1920s when the common currency among whites was that American blacks descended from an inferior race, Leo Hansberry, a professor of history at Howard University, was teaching black students about the "glories" of the African ancestral past.[17] Hansberry's efforts at Howard culminated in the formation of the first African studies program at a college or university in America. Of his works, Hansberry remarked: "No institution is more obligated and no ... school is in a better position to develop [an African diaspora] program [than] Howard.... This is the area in which Howard has the most promising and immediate opportunity to distinguish itself as a leader in the general cause of public enlightenment."[18]

Students studying history at Virginia State College in the 1930s under Rayford Logan received similar instruction in the history of Africa.[19] A "Pan-African perspective has always been an integral part of the value-cluster" of black institutions, writes one scholar.[20] As early as

1895, Atlanta University hosted a conference on Africa, and in 1912 Tuskegee Institute convened an "International Negro Conference."[21] Walter E. Massey, a student at Morehouse in the 1950s, recalls that during his student days the "Morehouse curriculum ... was very much infused with the history of black people.... There was a particular emphasis on it because it was recognized that these were the only institutions that were likely to teach the history."[22] Massey remembers Morehouse offering courses such as "Black Religion," "Black History," and "African Affairs."

The black college served as the nexus for much of the African American progressive political activism of the early twentieth century. As Fairclough points out, many of the leaders of black colleges, especially the presidents of these institutions, were actively involved in a wide variety of civil rights, social justice, and human welfare organizations.[23] A range of black college presidents, including Robert Moton, John Hope, Charles S. Johnson, and Mary McLeod Bethune, figured prominently among the membership and leadership of organizations such as the National Association for the Advancement of Colored People, National Urban League, Southern Regional Council, Young Men's Christian Association, Southern Women for the Prevention of Lynching, National Council of Negro Women, and League of Women Voters.[24]

Benjamin E. Mays, president of Atlanta's Morehouse College from 1940 to 1967, personified the social activist tradition prevalent among black college leaders of the early to middle twentieth century. Mays played an important role in the founding of the Southern Regional Council. He also served on the Board of Directors of the NAACP, chaired the National Sharecroppers and Rural Advancement Fund, and was a major figure in other social justice organizations, such as the Southern Conference for Human Welfare and the American Crusade to End Lynching.[25] Mays always told his students that even though African Americans lived in a segregated world, they did not have to *accept* segregation in their hearts.[26]

Many of the aforementioned social justice groups often met on the campuses of black colleges as black institutions were the only place in the segregated South where African Americans and forward-looking whites could gather and dialogue without fear of reprisal from white southerners. The Atlanta-based Commission on Interracial Cooperation, for instance, held most of its meetings at the Atlanta University Center.[27] In 1952 Morehouse College president Benjamin E. Mays made the following observation: "If there is held an institute of human relations in Tennessee where people can come together as Americans and as Christian citizens, this institute must be held at Fisk, LeMoyne, or Lane.... There is no other institution in Tennessee where such an institution could be held with complete freedom.... If the Negro and white peoples are to get together in Georgia and discuss their common problems on the basis of complete equality, the meeting must be held on the campuses of the Negro private colleges.... These colleges (black colleges) set the pace in these areas for the colleges of the south.... The freedom which is inherent in the private Negro colleges does not exist on the campuses of the white colleges of the South.... The private Negro colleges are citadels of freedom and democracy."[28]

In so many ways, as Benjamin E. Mays observed, the environment of the black college personified the democratic ideal in higher education. In the wake of the Nazi insurgence in Europe many Jewish scholars fled to the United States, where they sought employment in white northeastern colleges and universities. Finding the doors of white northeastern colleges barred by the lock of anti–Semitism, many of these Jewish scholars turned South, where they found employment opportunities in black higher education institutions.[29] Similarly, from the founding of black institutions to the present, Anglo-Americans were represented on the faculties and administrative staffs of the various institutions. And during the entrenched years of Jim Crow segregation, black foreign students (African and West Indian) who would have been excluded from white institutions freely enrolled at black colleges and universities. A cadre of African leaders ranging from Nnamdi Azikiwe of Nigeria and Kwame Nkrumah of Ghana received their undergraduate education and training at black colleges and universities.[30]

As Henry R. Ponder, former chief executive officer of the National Association for Equal Opportunity in Higher Education and former president of Talladega, Fisk, and Benedict colleges, states: "Diversity has always been at the heart of everything we do."[31] The claim recently made by one scholar that historically black institutions are only beginning to embrace diversity is outlandish and demonstrates a gross ignorance of the history of black colleges.[32] The black colleges pioneered the idea of diversity in higher education.

Finally, the black college environment instilled within its students feelings of race pride and race consciousness, which in turn led to greater self-esteem and self-confidence. The very existence of the schools stood as symbols of the "highest level of black achievement," undercutting stereotypes that African Americans were intellectually inferior to whites and therefore incapable of running complex institutions.

African Americans who taught and worked in colleges for blacks towered as positive role models in the eyes of their students, proving that if given the opportunity blacks could become professors, deans, college presidents, social scientists, physicians, attorneys, and so on. If blacks occupied the lowest rung on the social ladder, the lives and accomplishments of these professional blacks seemed to say, it was not because of biological inferiority but because institutionalized and entrenched racism blocked their path to progress.

The remarks and observations of black college alumni impress these points. In ripe old age when asked about the highlights of her school experience at Scotia College, Dr. Mary McLeod Bethune replied: "My contact with the fine young Negro teachers ... who gave me confidence in the ability of Negro women ... and gave me the incentive and made me feel that if they could do it I could do it, too."[33] The eminent sociologist St. Clair Drake wrote of his experience as a student at Hampton in the late 1920s: "I received a good liberal education plus training to teach high school. I also absorbed the service to the race values and learned to appreciate Negro history, music, and folklore. It never occurred to me that what I was getting was inferior."[34] Going on to earn the doctorate at the University of Chicago, Drake added: "I never felt handicapped there by having gone to Hampton."[35] Carolynn Reid-Wallace, former president of Fisk University and a student at Fisk in the late 1950s, asserts: "These schools [black colleges] ... offered to large numbers of people opportunities to study and to come to discover who they are.... I had no idea, no clue that I could one day become the president of a university, that I could one day make my mark on society.... The historically black institutions enabled you to understand your worth, your power, your potential, and your strength. They ennobled individuals to go forth and to be full citizens."[36]

Marie V. McDemmond, president of Norfolk State University, remembers her undergraduate institution, Xavier University of New Orleans, as a place where "you were told that you could do anything.... You were never given any doubt that you could not succeed.... No matter how poor you were or whatever ... it was expected for you to do well."[37] Walter E. Massey, who attended Morehouse College during the administration of the legendary Benjamin E. Mays, recalls the college as a place where students were told that "you can do whatever you are inspired to do if you work at it and that we at Morehouse are going to hold you to very high standards ... standards perhaps even higher than those you will have to compete with in the non–African American world because you must be better than everybody else.... As a Morehouse man that is what you have to strive for."[38] Earl S. Richardson, president of Morgan State University, remembers the faculty and administrators of his alma mater, Maryland State College (the forerunner of the University of Maryland Eastern Shore), as individuals who "made you think you were somebody."[39] Henry Drewry, a senior advisor to the Mellon Foundation and a 1948 graduate of Talladega College, states: "What we had on that campus — the education, the support — outweighed what the outside world could do."[40]

In addition to African Americans who taught and worked on campus, the black college environment gave students exposure to black leaders and role models from the wider community. At weekly chapel, or campus-wide assemblies, students could hear blacks who were leaders in other fields (educators, politicians, business leaders, journalists, social workers, theologians, and so on) speak on issues pertinent to African Americans.[41] Oftentimes, campus assemblies featured black personalities from outside the United States. In the fall of 1954, William V.S. Tubman, the president of Liberia, then the only independent nation in black Africa, visited the Atlanta University Center, where he addressed an overflowing crowd at Sisters Chapel at Spelman College. Edward McIntyre, who was a junior at Morehouse at the time and who would go on to become Mayor of Augusta, Georgia, recalls of Tubman's visit: "My feeling was a feeling of pride and uplifting ... because here was a black president of a country.... It gave you a sense of saying, this can happen one day, maybe, in America.... It was overwhelming."[42] Walter E. Massey, who was also a student at Morehouse at the time, remembers Tubman's visit as the "most memorable" chapel experience of his student days. "The fact that the president of what was then a very important and thriving nation was on campus was very memorable."[43]

Throughout the period of segregation, African Americans themselves recognized the ironies, contradictions, and paradoxes of their situation. On the one hand, they recognized that because the colleges were designated to educate blacks exclusively they seemed to hinder African Americans from entering mainstream society. But on the other, they recognized that the schools had also been instrumental in pushing the race forward. The black higher education institutions had trained generations of black leaders, and fostered the growth and development of a rich, unique, dynamic, and empowering black culture and identity.

Throughout his illustrious life and career, W.E.B. Du Bois, the preeminent African American scholar and activist of the early twentieth century, repeatedly spoke about the paradoxes of the black situation, and especially that of the black college.[44] Because of the ironies of segregation as it related to the role of black higher education institutions in the struggle for racial equality, Du Bois "feared that the fight against segregation would ... undermine the unique contributions of black Americans and warned against basing a challenge to segregation on the inferiority of separate Negro institutions."[45] By the early 1930s as the Great Depression wore on, and Du Bois began to turn away from his assimilationist-integration view of racial uplift, he argued that the appropriate educational strategy for blacks to achieve equality in America was to fight against compulsory or enforced segregation — not because separate black institutions were inferior to white ones, but because segregation was unconstitutional — and at the same time to fight for the growth and expansion of black institutions. Du Bois wanted African American higher education leaders to agitate to bring black institutions to parity with white institutions, while simultaneously working to make both historically black and traditionally white institutions more inclusive. This strategy was premised on the school of thought we now know as "cultural pluralism" or "multiculturalism."[46] Indeed, historian David Levering Lewis posits that Du Bois' writings from the mid–1920s contain an "embryonic vision ... of multiculturalism."[47]

An examination of African American thought on educational strategies of racial uplift in the age of Jim Crow shows that the idea of cultural pluralism as the best program for racial equality and empowerment was also expressed in the speeches and writings of a number of Du Bois' contemporaries. These include intellectuals Alain Locke, Carter G. Woodson, Kelly Miller, Mary Church Terrell, and educators John Hope and Mordecai Johnson.[48]

In the summer of 1936 Kelly Miller, a professor at Howard University, wrote an article in the *Journal of Negro Education* in which he argued that the use of "race-specific strategies" was a program African Americans needed to consider in their quest for empowerment. Miller argued:

> The Catholics operate catholic institutions for the development of the peculiar type of character and qualities demanded by the Catholic church. If Jews support and operate their own institutions to cultivate their own geniuses and perpetuate their own tradition, if Baptists, Methodists, and Presbyterians undertake the extra expense of operating purely denominational schools for the sake of developing peculiar tenets of these several sects, why should not the Negro even without the compulsion of segregation favor and foster institutions of higher learning that cater to the talent and genius of the race?[49]

As early as 1916 Alain Locke gave a lecture that outlined his vision of racial progress. Locke stated that he saw "culture-citizenship" as "the goal of race progress and race adjustment." "Culture-citizenship," he argued, "must come in terms of group contribution to what becomes a joint civilization."[50] And in his study of African American life in Washington, D.C., from 1930 to 1960, Donald Earl Collins shows that the "combining of desegregation and multiculturalism as one strategy" was one tactic District blacks embraced in their struggle to achieve empowerment and equality.[51]

Thus throughout the early 1950s, as the legal struggle against segregation in education was coming to a head and America stood on the cusp of great and mighty change, and the argument was being made in certain quarters that black institutions were inferior to white institutions and were negatively affecting black progress, and therefore integration and assimilation into white institutions was the best recourse for the race, African American educators and intellectuals were celebrating the achievements of black institutions and openly acknowledging their role in advancing the race. In 1952 Frederick D. Patterson, the president of Tuskegee Institute, confidently stated that the black college had been an important "spearhead" for African American progress in America.[52] One year earlier, in 1951, when an official of the Rockefeller General Education Board asked for his thoughts on the long-term destiny of colleges for African Americans in light of the changing nature of race relations, Rufus E. Clement, the president of Atlanta University, responded in straightforward fashion: "Segregation or no segregation, Atlanta University and the Negro colleges will be needed.... The vast majority of Negroes prefer Negro colleges.... In these colleges Negroes are at home.... They have their fraternities, their football games, their loyalties, their friends."[53]

The dilemma black educators faced on the eve of *Brown v. Board of Education* was not whether to uphold their institutions. Rather, the dilemma was how to move forward without losing their institutions; how to carve out a space in the new and emerging environment of desegregation and cultural opportunity for African Americans that would both protect and expand the economic and cultural interests of black institutions. By debating about the future of black colleges African Americans were also debating about their history, their culture, their freedom, as well as the future of the race.

African American educational leaders wanted equality but they did not necessarily think that equality was only achievable through assimilationist integration. In the minds of many, equality was associated with cultural pluralism: ending enforced segregation and thereby removing the stigmas associated with black institutions; bringing institutions once designated for blacks to parity with institutions established for whites; and encouraging diversity within both white and black institutions.

One moment where such ideas were expressed was the 1952 Howard University national conference on "The Courts and Racial Integration in Education," convened one year *before* NAACP lawyers went before the United States Supreme Court to argue the case that would come to be known as *Brown v. Board of Education*. Though a historic event, or moment, in African American history, the conference has been overlooked by scholars of the black experience. The purpose of the meeting was to provide a forum for those working in the fight against segregation to discuss strategies for breaking down Jim Crow segregation in schools, ways to implement desegregation should the court ban segregation, and what desegregation could mean to educational institutions then serving African Americans exclusively.[54] The conference was attended by nearly 400 of America's leading African American civil rights activists, scholars, attorneys, social scientists, labor leaders, college presidents, federal officials, and journalists. The attendees were black and white and hailed from every region in the country.[55]

At this meeting, Benjamin E. Mays, president of Morehouse College and then the most important and influential African American higher education leader in the nation, told the audience:

> when integration comes ... the Negro and white colleges will be judged on their merits.... Those that meet the standards of excellence in scholarship, character, and equipment will survive and those that do not meet these standards will not survive.... No college will survive because it is a Negro college and no college will go out of existence because it is a Negro college.... The college will be judged on its ability to provide good education to all the people.[56]

Frederick D. Patterson, president of Tuskegee Institute and founder of the United Negro College Fund, asserted:

> the future of the private Negro college under a system of integration is that of becoming an integral part of the whole of private education.... It shall do this, as private education remains a part of the whole of all higher education in America.[57]

Rufus B. Atwood, president of Kentucky State College and an officer of the Association of Negro Land Grant Colleges, posited:

> It is hopefully envisioned that in a matter of time Negro students will be admitted in all of the state's institutions that now serve white students only, and white students will be admitted into what is now the institution for Negroes.... We are directing our efforts to have what is now the state's Negro college become an integral part of the state's system of higher education.[58]

Other African American higher education leaders present, including Mordecai Johnson, president of Howard University, Horace Mann Bond, president of Lincoln University, and Martin D. Jenkins, president of Morgan State College, expressed similar views.[59]

Even though the *Brown* verdict rejected the cultural-pluralism paradigm of desegregation advocated by African American higher education leaders at the 1952 Howard University conference, the black higher education leadership class continued to push for its multicultural vision of college desegregation. Throughout the 1950s and 1960s black college leaders such as Benjamin E. Mays, Frederick D. Patterson, and Rufus B. Atwood wrote treatise after treatise and delivered speech after speech defending the continued existence of traditionally African American higher education institutions.[60] Led by Benjamin E. Mays, these black college presidents made the goal of shifting the national dialogue on the meaning and aim of collegiate desegregation from one based on integrating African Americans into previously all-white institutions to one that emphasized building black colleges up to the level where they could attract white students and subsequently enter the mainstream of higher education the central point of their post–*Brown* careers.[61] African American educators wanted black colleges to find new missions not defined by segregation; increase their curricular offerings to meet the changing manpower needs of the economy; and be in the vanguard of innovation and advancement in higher learning. In other words, black college leaders wanted their institutions to adapt and adjust to the changing environment of higher education in the new era, not fade into oblivion.

Throughout his illustrious career Benjamin E. Mays repeatedly called for a "two-way street" approach to integration. With a deep commitment to the values of producing outstanding leaders, service, personal integrity, and academic excellence, he endeavored to build Morehouse College into a first-rate institution that would showcase the great potentials of historically black colleges.[62] Walter E. Massey asserts that Benjamin E. Mays, like many black college presidents of the desegregation era, "believed that historically black institutions could do both ... that the schools could maintain their heritage and predominant flavor and vision; but could maintain that while having it open, and by having a large number of students who were not African American."[63] According to Massey, Mays did not see it as "either/or."[64]

In 1953, as the social, economic, and demographic changes wrought by World War II and NAACP litigation were converging to pull the first props from under the system of segregation, Charles S. Johnson, the president of Fisk University, told a large audience gathered for the Annual United Negro College Fund Convocation:

> In this transition, these Negro colleges are not beggar institutions waiting for an opportunity for their students to tip quietly into the back of the class-rooms of white colleges.... The colleges themselves and their products have something of great value, and, we believe even magnificence to contribute to the entire process.[65]

In short, the African Americans who led black colleges through the profound and far-reaching changes and transformations of the 1950s saw desegregation as a vehicle to move their institutions from the margins to the center of higher education. African American educators believed that growing and expanding the colleges for blacks, rather than integrating them out of existence or separating them from the mainstream, would be the best educational solution to the problems of blacks and the best strategy to achieve justice and equality of opportunity for African American students. But most importantly, they believed strongly that in the immediate post-segregation period and beyond the colleges established for African Americans could play a critical role in rebuilding the nation along the true democratic ideals.

The story of black college presidents in the era of desegregation reconceptualizes our understanding of African American thought on the meaning of desegregation and its implications for historically black institutions. And more importantly, their story cuts at the heart of what Lisa Delpit calls the "debilitating myth," that is, the widespread belief that "the reason black people fought so hard for desegregation is that deep down they agreed with the larger society's view that without access to white culture, white teachers, white schools, and white leadership, black people could never adequately educate their children, nor hope to create a decent future for their race."[66]

Earl S. Richardson, president of Morgan State University, maintains that for African Americans of the 1950s and 1960s "integration was not about closing schools.... It was about desegregating all schools.... It was about bringing blacks into the mainstream so they would have a choice of white or black institutions ... and it was the same for bringing whites to black institutions so they had a choice."[67] But mainstream

America, Richardson notes, "misinterpreted what integration was all about…. They decided that what integration meant was to destroy part of what was supposed to be integrated."[68]

The efforts of Benjamin E. Mays and other black college leaders to grow and expand their schools into the new era of integration and cultural opportunity for African Americans tells us much about black thought on crucial questions of race, empowerment, equality, and identity as America stood in the midst of great and mighty change. Their struggles open a window onto understanding not only nuances of the black experience as it pertains to the development of higher education per se, but also the wider, multidimensional nature of black culture, and the often contradictory and always complex ways in which educational ideology informed and influenced black interpretations of freedom and equality. This is the vision of black colleges in a post–*Brown v. Board of Education* America that the current generation of black college presidents inherited.

The present generation of black college presidents is working to actualize the vision of black colleges handed down by Benjamin E. Mays and other black college leaders of the mid-twentieth century. Building on the traditional values of leadership, service, and academic excellence, these presidents are working to move historically black institutions to the grand heights envisioned by Benjamin E. Mays, Frederick D. Patterson, Rufus B. Atwood, and other black college leaders of the mid-twentieth century. Morehouse College president Walter E. Massey, for instance, states that Morehouse has followed and tried to maintain the legacy of Benjamin E. Mays in regard to his quest for black colleges to embrace a standard of excellence that transcends race.[69] While the efforts of the present generation have resulted in numerous success stories, black colleges and their leaders as a whole face major challenges in their quest for excellence.

All of the presidents interviewed for this book maintain that one of the major challenges facing black colleges is related to availability of resources. Historically black colleges and universities, like predominantly white institutions, need solid financing in order to offer high-quality academic programs and maintain modern campus infrastructure. As Carolynn Reid-Wallace reminds us, a fancy mission statement or statement of priority means nothing if an institution lacks the necessary financial resources.[70] "If you do not have the money," she says, "all of the rhetoric in the world will not get you where you need to be."[71]

Historically black colleges and universities lag seriously behind predominantly white institutions in this area. When the *Chronicle of Higher Education* recently reported the nation's top 300 colleges and universities in terms of endowment value, only four black colleges—Howard, Hampton, Morehouse, and Spelman—were listed.[72] Most telling, Howard University, the black college claiming the largest endowment ($312 million), lags far behind 130 predominantly white institutions. Moreover, it has been pointed out that the combined overall endowment value for all 103 historically black institutions is only $1.6 billion, and the combined endowment value of Morehouse, Spelman, Howard, and Hampton accounts for nearly 45 percent of that total.[73] Having inadequate endowment funds limits the resources black colleges are able to channel toward key areas such as per pupil spending and annual operating budget.

The sources of the problems of black colleges in the area of financing are numerous. First and foremost, alumni generate the vast majority of philanthropy to higher education institutions. While paltry alumni giving is a problem for all colleges and universities in America, it is a special problem for black institutions. Unlike the graduates of majority colleges, the graduates of historically black institutions generally have not been able to amass vast personal wealth and establish links within the corporate community.

Michael L. Lomax, president of the United Negro College Fund and former president of Dillard University, asserts that the "biggest difference between alumni philanthropy at black colleges in comparison to white colleges is that black institutions do not have as strong a base of donors."[74] William Gray, former president of the United Negro College Fund, describes the situation this way: "Black colleges by the very nature of their constituency, operate very close to the line.... They simply do not have alums who have had access to capital accumulation; they generally don't have multimillionaires to draw from."[75] Another problem is that many historically black institutions lack the high-tech advancement infrastructure and manpower necessary to aggressively seek alumni support ("it takes time and resources to gain the resources," says Lomax). Historian of education Marybeth Gasman also points out a greater inclination on the part of African Americans to give to black churches, fraternities and sororities rather than black colleges. These factors combine to make paltry alumni giving a serious problem at black higher education institutions.[76]

Corporate, foundation, and non-alumni individual support comprise other key sources of philanthropy for American colleges and universities. Several studies show that black colleges lag far behind white schools in such support. Far too often mainstream corporations, foundations, and private citizens tend to associate black higher education institutions (regardless of how sound the academic programs) with perceptions associated with African Americans generally: inferior and incompetent. Because of this thinking, corporate and foundation contributions to black institutions pale in comparison to what is given to majority white institutions. One of the presidents featured in this book speaks of what he sees as "some resistance in the corporate community to treating historically black institutions on a par with majority institutions." "We have a long way to go in getting the corporate world to understand the importance of what we do," another insists.

Black college presidents often find themselves in the position of constantly fighting longstanding public perceptions of their institutions. Marie V. McDemmond, president of Norfolk State University, states that it "is still very hard for traditionally black colleges and universities to prove their worth in the circles of American higher education."[77] Likewise, Earl S. Richardson of Morgan State University posits that "people do not give to things they do not understand and appreciate."[78] Morehouse College president Walter E. Massey asserts that the challenge for the president of a black college is to position the school as an "institution in which your donors and supporters want to invest because they see it as a important contributor to society ... rather than giving a handout as a form of charity to an institution that perhaps deserves support but would not survive or barely survive without the charity.... It is ... moving from being seen almost as a welfare case to one in which the donor wants to invest because when people give on the basis of charity they give small amounts of money ... but when they see it as an investment they give large amounts of money."[79]

Paralleling the situation in the corporate and foundation sectors, research indicates that black institutions are not receiving their fair share of federal funds. In the fiscal year 2002 black post-secondary institutions received less than 10 percent of all federal money earmarked for higher education.[80] Even with a recent 5 percent increase in federal support to black institutions, the overall federal outlay still totals less than 10 percent.[81]

In light of these circumstances, the task of fundraising has proven most daunting for the presidents of black colleges. One of the presidents featured in this book remarks that she had no idea it would be so hard to acquire funding for black institutions. Indeed, the pressures associated with fundraising have been the primary reason for high turnover rates of black college presidents. A recent report shows that in the past two years, more than two dozen black colleges—roughly a quarter of all black institutions—have lost presidents.[82] The majority of the presidents cited the pressure to raise money as their main reason for leaving.[83] These constraints notwithstanding, historically black colleges and universities will remain viable only if they can successfully raise the funds necessary to pay for qualified faculty, cutting-edge technology, and modern physical plants.

Another challenge confronting historically black colleges and universities is their lack of visibility in higher education media and public relations circles. The reason for this is twofold. First, the content of mainstream higher education news publications is generally slanted towards majority white institutions. Little or no attention is paid to the happenings at traditionally black institutions. Because of this consistent ignoring of black colleges there is a major vacuum in the knowledge of many Americans—of all races—about predominantly African American serving institutions. Carolynn Reid-Wallace, former president of Fisk University, contends that black colleges are "doing some remarkable things but nobody knows about it."[84] In a similar vein, Earl S. Richardson, president of Morgan State University, states that there is a prevailing ignorance in the minds of many Americans about the workings of historically black institutions.[85] This gap in the visibility of black institutions in the national media and public relations community has led many black college presidents, including Beverly Daniel Tatum of Spelman, Calvin W. Lowe of Bowie State, Marie V. McDemmond of Norfolk State, and Earl S. Richardson of Morgan State to make raising the profile of their respective institutions a key goal.

The second aspect of the visibility problem is that far too often the scant news that is reported about black colleges is negative in nature. The only stories readers of the nation's leading mainstream higher education news publications encounter about traditionally black institutions are ones that highlight the so-called "crisis" of black colleges: stories about black schools experiencing management problems, losing accreditation, or facing financial bankruptcy. And while it is true that some black colleges struggle with such issues, to focus exclusively on these problems presents an incomplete picture of black institutions. Some black colleges, like some white colleges, have their problems and their struggles, but the institutions are still going about their mission of educating young people, reaching out to the community, and being in the forefront of curricular advancements. And many are doing excellent work. The mainstream media's focus on the "problems" of black colleges is doing a major disservice to these institutions. What is needed is a *balanced* focus on black institutions. We need news stories about what black institutions are accomplishing in spite of not having the multibillion dollar endowments most white colleges enjoy.

For instance, in recent times journalists writing for the nation's leading mainstream higher education news magazines have made a fetish out of the financial difficulties Clark Atlanta University is experiencing. Yet how many of these journalists have ever mentioned that Clark Atlanta has the first and still the only American Library Association–accredited school of library studies in Georgia and therefore has trained the lion's share of Georgia's librarians—black and white? Or how many have noted, for that matter, that the *Princeton Review* recently included Clark Atlanta University in its listing of the 100 best colleges in the southeastern United States?[86] And while writers for mainstream higher education news publications deluge us with story after story about the troubles of Morris Brown, they have avoided telling us that for many years Morris Brown sponsored numerous programs geared toward empowering the local community. Norfolk State University president Marie V. McDemmond insists that black colleges are generally not "noted for the treasures they are."[87] According to Earl S. Richardson of Morgan State University there is a great need for "educating the public on the value nuances of historically black colleges."[88]

Finally, another problem confronting black colleges is continued ambivalence over their existence. While this problem is not as great as it was in the 1970s during the immediate post–Civil Rights Movement era, remnants of it still emerge from time to time. In light of the fact that black colleges educate only 18 percent of African Americans enrolled in higher education, and recent courts rulings have extended the life of affirmative action in higher education admissions at majority-white institutions, questions frequently arise as to the continued need for black institutions. In his 2001 book *Is There a Conspiracy to Keep Black Colleges Open?* sociologist Gerald A. Foster argues that the continued existence of black institutions is a roadblock to black progress.[89] The argument, as scholars of education Roebuck and Murty write, is that "in a society that is striving for racial integration, the further duplication of physical facilities, academic programs, and services within a racially segregated, two-tiered higher education system is counterproductive financially, philosophically, and pedagogically."[90]

This lingering ambivalence over the continued existence of black institutions is a direct result of a major vacuum in collegiate desegregation policy. It has been 50 years since the Supreme Court ruling in *Brown v. Board
of Education* outlawed racial segregation in the elementary and secondary
schools of the nation. The verdict of the court in *Florida ex. rel. Hawkins
Board of Control* (1956) extended the concept of desegregation to higher
education, which in turn was reinforced by Title VI of the 1964 Civil Rights
Act.[91] Yet in the half-century since these court rulings and legislative acts
mandated desegregation, legislatures, the judiciary, and others who write
and influence policy affecting higher education in American have failed to
clearly and cogently spell out what college desegregation means, what strategies are required to achieve it, and what criteria measure its observance.[92]
But most importantly, legislatures and the judiciary have failed to define
the meaning and implications of desegregation for the colleges originally
established for African Americans. The works of numerous scholars of black
education, most notably Russell W. Irvine and Jacqueline Jordan Irvine, M.
Christopher Brown II, and Charles V. Willie, remind us of this vacuum.[93]
The problem, these scholars and analysts argue, is that most legal mandates
pertaining to desegregation are "full of ambiguous concepts," laden with
vague and ambivalent legal jargon, void of clear and straightforward meaning.[94] Confusion in terminology has prevented clarity of concept, which in
turn has made it patently impossible to interpret the law with the goal of
gleaning insights that could lead to the formulation of meaningful policy.

In his study *The Quest to Define Collegiate Desegregation*, M.
Christopher Brown writes: "Higher education is still without a prevailing legal standard that clearly articulates what it means for postsec-
ondary education to be desegregated or to have dismantled dual
educational structures."[95] The judiciary, Brown contends, has failed to
"establish a legal mandate that resolves the following issues: What is
meant by desegregation? What policies constitute compliance...?"[96]

In a similar vein Irvine and Irvine assert:

> What constitutes a desegregated school environment? Is desegregation the
> same as integration? What is a necessary and sufficient racial mix to be con-
> sidered a desegregated situation? These are questions for which there are no
> easy, readily available answers.[97]

Charles V. Willie maintains that a "similar feature" of court cases
and legislation decreeing desegregation is "the absence of a clear
definition of desegregation and little, if any, guidance by the court."[98]
Other scholars have expressed related views.[99]

This vacuum, scholars and analysts of desegregation and black colleges argue, has created a situation in which the black colleges have been left — literally — in limbo, surrounded by confusion and disagreement over their mission and purpose in a post–*Brown* America. Black colleges since the era of civil rights, Bowles and De Costa maintain, have been caught "between two worlds."[100] This situation has spawned much ambivalence and uncertainty in the minds of Americans of all races about the value and importance of black higher education institutions. This ambivalence, they reason, is a major factor behind reluctant, tepid, and unequal public support of black colleges. Earl S. Richardson of Morgan State University states that "there are still those in the public sector who when they hear *historically black college* throw up a wall…. For them it conveniently denotes segregation."[101] This combination of ambivalence and unequal support tends to complicate plans to grow and develop historically black colleges, which in turn makes it difficult to establish programs of long-term strategic planning.[102] As Charles V. Willie writes, "It is time for the court and the legislature to say what they mean and mean what they say" with regard to the implications of desegregation for black colleges.[103] The viability of black colleges in the new millennium will depend on these critical constituencies reaching consensus.

Despite these challenges, the leaders of historically black colleges and universities continue to soldier on, working to make the vision of Benjamin E. Mays a reality. All of the presidents interviewed for this book state emphatically that there is no conflict between the existence of historically black institutions in the twenty-first century and the national emphasis on diversity and multiculturalism. America is a highly pluralistic society, and historically black colleges and universities, like women's colleges, schools with strong religious backgrounds, and similar colleges with a specific racial or ethnic heritage, enhance diversity in higher education.

Among the distinctive features of their heritage and mission, most black colleges include the emphasis on collaborative rather than competitive learning, the maintenance of a nurturing and individualizing environment, the emphasis on the history, the culture, and the contributions of African Americans, and the focus on service to the community. All of the presidents agree that institutions of traditionally black higher education should preserve these features of their heritage and mission. While serving as president of Dillard University, Michael L. Lomax embraced "a heritage quality" to his vision for the institution.[104]

Marie V. McDemmond of Norfolk State University adds: "I think historically black colleges and universities should preserve their heritage and historic mission."[105]

Yet while recognizing the strengths of the heritage and historic mission, the presidents also recognize that we live in a global society, and that historically black colleges and universities must prepare their students to live and work in this society. The colleges, the presidents state, must adapt and adjust to the changing environment of higher education in the twenty-first century. As they see it, in order for black colleges to be successful in the new millennium, the institutions must undertake the task of both preserving past strengths and becoming relevant to the new era. The institutions must merge what Walter E. Massey of Morehouse College calls the "best features of their heritage and mission" with the vast opportunities and advances of the present.[106] They must identify those core values that according to Calvin W. Lowe, president of Bowie State University, go "beyond value to black folks ... but that have intrinsic value" to all people.[107] In other words, black colleges must use the values and strengths of the past as a foundation for future success in the wider world of higher education. As Lowe describes it, black college leaders must "look to our history and our traditions as a guide, not as an anchor."[108]

Part of becoming relevant to the new millennium means that black colleges must have access to what United Negro College Fund president Michael L. Lomax calls the "cutting edge of technology and science and the ability to communicate across cultures and across geographies that purely are elements of the new millennium."[109] It is here, in this quest for excellence, that as Carolynn Reid-Wallace posits, "what it means to be a historically black institution in the twenty-first century is not unlike what it means to be a majority white institution in the twenty-first century."[110] Like all colleges, historically black institutions are trying to maintain the competitive curriculum, strong faculty, outstanding and diverse student body, and stable financial base crucial to success in higher education in the new millennium. This is where the mission and vision of all colleges and universities in America — regardless of racial or religious background or heritage — merges.

For their part, the presidents featured in this book are making efforts that are truly noteworthy. In keeping with the legacy of Benjamin E. Mays, the presidents view the pursuit of academic excellence as their foremost priority. Accordingly, they are placing great emphasis on curricular development. Several of the presidents argue that the success of the black college in the area of curriculum development is largely dependent on the institutions resolving themselves to the fact that they "cannot be everything to everybody." With this observation in mind, the presidents are consolidating programs in their existing areas of strength, dismantling outmoded or duplicate programs, and establishing new programs to meet the needs of the changing economy.

At traditional liberal arts institutions such as Morehouse College, Spelman College, and Fisk University the presidents are working to enhance their already rigorous academic programs. Similarly Xavier University is reinforcing its strengths in the areas of mathematics and science around a strong liberal arts core. Another notable example is Dillard University under the leadership of Michael L. Lomax. After assuming the presidency of Dillard, Lomax hired a range of new and nationally prominent faculty who worked collectively and in conjunction with an outstanding provost to completely revamp the curriculum. Their efforts resulted in an academic program capable of competing with the best in the nation.

The historically black colleges are also keeping pace with the technological trends of the economy by increasing their programs and strengths in science and technology. This is especially true of the larger institutions. Since becoming president of Norfolk State University, Marie V. McDemmond has consolidated nine schools into five, with a heavy focus on mathematics, science, and technology. Norfolk State University has added both undergraduate and graduate programs in engineering, and has started a graduate program in computer science.[111] Several other institutions, including Savannah State University, Morgan State University, and Bowie State University, have also added new programs in engineering, computer science, and information science.

While making every effort to prepare students for life and work in the American society of the twenty-first century, the presidents also recognize that their students must be able to live and function in the global society of the new millennium. In light of that recognition, the presidents are placing a great deal of emphasis on globalization and internationalization as curricular components. Dillard University has a Global Studies program, which provides oversight for international curricular infusion. Spelman College has an International Affairs Center and a highly acclaimed Japanese Studies Program. Xavier University of New Orleans maintains a Center for Intercultural and International Programs. Morehouse College is home to the Andrew Young Center for International Affairs. Savannah State University sponsors an International Education Center. Norfolk State University employs a dean for internationalization.[112]

Moreover, many of the colleges maintain study-abroad programs and student exchanges and partnerships with international universities. Dillard University has an exchange program with several Asian and African universities. Savannah State University has an exchange program with universities in China and Ghana, and is developing one with a university in the Virgin Islands. Norfolk State University offers a joint Master's of Social Work program with a university in St. Croix.[113]

In addition to maintaining competitive academic programs with emphasis on internationalization and globalization, historically black colleges and universities are also making significant contributions to the production of knowledge. Many of the institutions have helped advance the science of knowledge by expanding their research infrastructure through the creation of centers and institutes where faculty and students engage in cutting-edge research and study. At North Carolina A&T State University, an institution with a legacy and tradition of excellence in science and technology training, faculty and students engage in research in several institutes and centers, including the Center for Aerospace Research, the Center for Electronics Manufacturing, and the Center for Energy Research and Technology. The university's research sponsors range from NASA to the United States Department of Agriculture and from the Department of Defense to the National Science Foundation and the Department of Transportation. At Norfolk State University, the Center for Materials Research is a hub for graduate work and research in the sciences. Savannah State University is home to a nationally recognized research program in marine sciences.[114]

Like Benjamin E. Mays and other members of the mid-twentieth century generation of black college leaders, the presidents featured in this book have built their quest for academic excellence around a commitment to diversity. Numerous studies have shown that diversity is a vital aspect of learning and education.[115] However, much of the present dialogue on diversity in higher education focuses on diversity in the context of majority white institutions. There is virtually no dialogue on diversity as it pertains to the nation's historically black colleges and universities. Hence, there is a widely held assumption among Americans of all personal and professional backgrounds that historically black colleges and universities are not diverse institutions. As Carlton E. Brown, president of Savannah State University, asserts, "People often make the assumption that historically black colleges and universities are all black."[116] Conversations with the presidents of black colleges, however, reveal a picture that is quite different.

Several of the featured presidents point out that although historically black colleges may be majority African American the institutions are in reality very diverse. This diversity, they argue, stems from the great internal variation within the black community. Diversity is manifested by the fact that even though the students are predominantly black they come from different religious backgrounds, different socioeconomic strata, different geographic backgrounds and so on. Walter E. Massey, the president of all-male Morehouse College, asserts that "one has to move beyond the obvious framings of diversity: race, gender, and ethnicity ... you must also look at what diversity means at an individual level.... What we tell our students is that you look among your student body here and though you are still predominantly African American and male, you try to look at the diversity that exists.... You come from all over the nation, all over the world in fact."[117]

Beverly Daniel Tatum, president of all-female Spelman College, says: "There are lots of ways to think about diversity.... You can think about diversity in terms of sexual orientation.... You can think about diversity in terms of the black experience within the context of color differences.... You can think about diversity at a women's college in terms of who is in a sorority, who is not in a sorority.... There are a lot of ways of speaking about the diversity of the community."[118] Massey and Tatum add another dimension when they point out that at their respective institutions (Morehouse and Spelman Colleges), the majority of their students have been in predominantly white schools and communities all their lives. For such students, according to Massey, "four years at a predominantly black institution is not the same as white students who have been in a predominantly white environment all of their lives going to a predominantly white institution and encountering people of color."[119]

The diversity of historically black colleges resulting from differences within the black community has been greatly enhanced by the sustained efforts of the presidents to recruit more broadly among non–African American populations. The most recent census has identified Hispanics as one of the most rapidly growing ethnic communities in America. Many of the presidents interviewed for this study speak of making concerted efforts to recruit within the Hispanic community. Several state that their drive to recruit among this population is based on a recognition that the challenges Hispanics face in higher education are similar to those faced by African Americans. Marie V. McDemmond of Norfolk State University maintains that her institution has a "very large push to diversify" its student population with special emphasis on the recruitment of Hispanics, a significant population group in the Hampton Roads area.[120] Norfolk State University has a Hispanic lab and a Hispanic recruiter who actively visits Hispanic communities. The University is also a member of the Hispanic Association of Colleges and Universities—the only historically black college or university with membership in this organization.[121]

During her tenure at Fisk University, Carolynn Reid-Wallace also made special efforts to reach out to the Hispanic community. Reid-Wallace states that one of her strategies was to engage Hispanic communities by frequently speaking to Hispanic leaders and educators about Fisk. As a sign of her dedication to building a bridge to the Hispanic community, Fisk offered free computer technology courses to Hispanic students.[122] Savannah State University boasts a significant number of Hispanic students, and the university's radio station was the first in the area to offer Hispanic programming. Other presidents, including Calvin W. Lowe of Bowie State University, speak of significant recruitment efforts among Hispanics.

In addition to the recruitment and enrollment of Hispanic students, the presidents also speak of efforts to recruit and enroll foreign-born black students, primarily from Africa and the West Indies. As previously stated, the historically black colleges and universities of America have a long and extensive relationship with Africa. African students have been enrolled at black colleges since the founding of the institutions in the late nineteenth and early twentieth centuries. The tradition continues. All of the presidents interviewed for this study speak of having African students enrolled in their institutions. In similar vein, all of the presidents state that their respective institutions have significant enrollment of students from the West Indies.

The Asian population is another ethnic community whose presence is increasing on the campuses of historically black colleges and universities. Norfolk State University reports the enrollment of several Asian students. At Xavier University of Louisiana, 25 percent of the enrollment in the college of pharmacy is non-black, with a significant part of the non-black population being Asian.[123] In addition to the enrollment of Hispanic students, foreign-born black students, and Asian students several of the presidents report significant enrollment of students from Europe. A noteworthy example of international enrollment at a historically black college is Savannah State University, which enrolls students from forty-seven countries.

Diversity within the black college community is also manifested at the faculty level. As earlier noted, since the era of their founding historically black colleges and universities have been models of racial diversity at the faculty level. When the schools were initially established many had predominantly white faculties and administrative boards. Several had white presidents even into the mid-twentieth century. True racial diversity at the faculty level remains a distinctive feature of the black colleges. At Xavier University of New Orleans the teaching faculty is roughly 53 percent white.[124] Numerous other historically black colleges report similar numbers. In addition to white Americans, faculties of Asian, African, Hispanic, and European backgrounds add to the diversity of institutions of traditionally black higher education.

When all these factors are taken into consideration, it becomes apparent that historically black colleges and universities are very diverse institutions. In fact, they are far more diverse than their white counterparts. Carlton E. Brown of Savannah State University, for instance, points to the fact that his institution has more non-black students and faculty than the University of Georgia has non-white students and faculty.[125] Indeed, Savannah State University boasts the most diverse faculty in the University System of Georgia.

Another strategy the presidents have used to promote institutional diversity is forming partnerships with majority research universities. Dillard University maintains a teaching exchange program with Emory University and an exchange forum with the University of Colorado at Boulder. Xavier University has major partnerships with Tulane University, the University of New Orleans, and Louisiana State University.[126] Both Morehouse and Spelman collaborate with the Georgia Institute of Technology. Norfolk State University partners with Old Dominion University.[127] Numerous other presidents report partnerships and collaborations with majority institutions.

The presidents state that the end result of diversity in higher education is to help students understand and appreciate cultures others than the one in which they were raised. "To help people accept differences … and not trying to acclimate everybody to one ethnic or cultural bias," that is the end result of diversity, Marie V. McDemmond of Norfolk State University maintains.[128] This understanding and appreciation of diverse cultures is a prerequisite for successful living in the highly pluralistic American society of the twenty-first century. Once students acquire this understanding and appreciation, the presidents hope, the long-term impact of having diversity at the college level will be the emergence of what Morehouse College president Walter E. Massey calls a "less prejudiced and discriminatory society."[129]

Finally, the current generation of black college presidents is continuing the legacy and tradition of service championed by Benjamin E. Mays. Marie McDemmond's constant exhortation to students at Norfolk State University is that "service to our community is paramount." She adds, "What I say to students, I say it in graduation speeches, convocation speeches, everything, is that you have an obligation, because you have made it this far, to go back and educate those in your community, those from where you have come, be it family, neighbors, or whatever." Walter E. Massey speaks of inspiring the present generation of Morehouse College students with the ideals of service he heard roll off the lips of Benjamin E. Mays at Mays' famous chapel talks during Massey's student days. Carolynn Reid-Wallace passed on to her students the message of service she received from her teachers at Fisk University in the 1950s.

The teachings of the presidents have translated into concrete programs and initiatives. Many of the schools maintain centers that coordinate institutional activities to uplift and promote positive change within the community and instill within students a commitment to the idea of service. At Morehouse College, the Emma and Joe Adams Public Service Institute weaves the school's community outreach initiatives into a cohesive thread. The Spelman College Center for Leadership and Civic Engagement empowers students to promote change in not only the local community but the world. Outreach programs at Bowie State University are coordinated through the school's Maryland Center.[130]

The specific ways the presidents are using the resources of their respective institutions to help find solutions to the problems and challenges faced by local communities are manifest. Xavier University, in partnership with Tulane University, sponsors the National Center for the Urban Community, which spearheads renewal efforts in urban communities of New Orleans. Morgan State University and Jackson State University also support urban renewal programs.[131] Several of the colleges, including Savannah State University, Norfolk State University, Jackson State University, and Bowie State University, maintain small business entrepreneurial centers to foster economic growth and development in local communities. Bowie State University partners with Prince George's County in an SAT Preparatory Saturday Academy.[132]

Spelman College students participate in Habitat for Humanity projects. Students from Xavier University tutor in the local community. Dillard University participates in the Campus Kitchen Food Drive. Students from North Carolina A&T State University installed a computer laboratory in a public housing complex.[133] When Carolynn Reid-Wallace assumed the presidency of Fisk University one of the first things that she did was to remove the fences that separated the college campus from the local community. Her goal was to make the campus more welcoming to locals.[134] Because of the good works of the presidents and students, the historically black colleges and universities are making vital contributions to efforts to solve problems and challenges that afflict communities across the country.

As for the overall progress of black colleges and universities in their quest for excellence, the record speaks for itself. Historically black colleges and universities constitute only 3 percent of all colleges and universities in America, but they carry the lion's share of the responsibility of educating students from underrepresented population groups. Institutions of traditionally black higher education produce 28 percent of all bachelor's degrees, 15 percent of all master's degrees, and 17 percent of all first professional degrees earned by African Americans.[135] And nationally, 85 percent of all African American physicians, 75 percent of all African American PhDs, 50 percent of all African American engineers, and 46 percent of all African American business executives received either their undergraduate or graduate level training at a historically black college.[136] Several of the presidents featured in this book preside over institutions that have single-handedly led the trajectory of black college success.

Xavier University of Louisiana, for example, ranks first in the nation in the number of African American students earning undergraduate degrees in both the biological/life sciences and the physical sciences. Xavier is also a national leader in educating African American students in psychology, computer science, and mathematics. Moreover, Xavier carries the distinction of placing more African Americans into medical school than any other college or university in the nation.[137] Morehouse College was the first historically black college to produce a Rhodes Scholar. North Carolina A&T State University trains a disproportionate share of African American engineers. Fisk University ranks in the top ten percent of colleges and universities nationally whose graduates go on to earn the PhD in the sciences. Bowie State University is a national leader in the overall production of African Americans with master's degrees in computer science and information sciences. The Morgan State University ROTC program ranks second nationally (West Point ranks first) in the production of African American generals.[138]

A recent study revealed that of the top twenty four-year colleges and universities producing African American students who go on to enroll in PhD programs, twelve of the top twenty are historically black colleges.[139] Among the twelve are institutions such as Fisk University, Talladega College, Morehouse College, and Spelman College. Describing the productivity of black colleges in successfully educating African American students, Norman C. Francis, president of Xavier University of Louisiana, states: "It is not a chicken and an egg situation. It is just a practical where is the productivity coming from and the answer to that is that it is disproportionately coming from black colleges."[140] In terms of providing higher education access and opportunity to minority students, the contributions of historically black higher education institutions are second to none.

These factors make it imperative that the American public embrace historically black colleges and universities and support programs and initiatives geared toward helping the institutions reach their highest potential. Efforts to improve the overall standard of education in America must consider the vital contributions made and being made by black institutions. And from a larger perspective, finding an appropriate policy program to enhance historically black colleges is fundamental to developing an overall national plan for solving the many problems that challenge America's minority communities, especially problems of poverty and inequality.

If America is to remain in the vanguard of global economic growth, production, and prosperity it must support the institutions that have made possible the current national success. Benjamin E. Mays and his contemporaries held a grand vision for black colleges coming into the new era of integration and cultural opportunity for African Americans. The men and women who currently lead historically black colleges and universities are continuing the work begun by Mays and other African American educators of the mid-twentieth century. The present challenge is for America to hold up the hands of those who hold up the historically black colleges and universities.

Notes

1. Dan H. Wishnietsky, *American Education in the Twenty-First Century* (Bloomington: Phi Delta Kappa Educational Foundation, 2001); Philip G. Altbach and Robert Oliver Berdahl (editors) *American Higher Education in the Twenty-First Century: Polit-*

ical, Social, and Economic Challenges (Baltimore: John Hopkins University Press, 1999); Steven Brint (editor), *The Future of the City of Intellect: The Changing American University* (Stanford: Stanford University Press, 2002); James J. Duderstadt, Farris W. Womack, Patricia W. Ingraham (editors), *The Future of the Public University in America: Beyond the Crossroads* (Baltimore: John Hopkins University Press, 2003).

2. *Ibid.*

3. For a comprehensive survey of the general development of black education see James D. Anderson, *The Education of Blacks in the South, 1860–1935* (Chapel Hill: University of North Carolina Press, 1988); For specific discussions of the origins and development of higher education institutions for African Americans, see, J.E. Browning and J.B. Williams, "History and Goals of Black Institutions of Higher Learning," in Charles V. Willie and R.R. Edmonds (editors), *Black Colleges in America* (New York: Teachers College Press, 1978); Dereck J. Rovaris, *Mays and Morehouse: How Benjamin E. Mays Developed Morehouse College, 1940–1967* (Silver Spring: Beckham House Publishers), 24–55; Dwight Oliver Wendell Holmes, *The Evolution of the Negro College* (New York: Teachers College, 1934); Institutional histories of African American institutions include: Horace Mann Bond, *Education for Freedom: A History of Lincoln University, Pennsylvania* (Princeton: Princeton University Press, 1976); Clarence A. Bacote, *The Story of Atlanta University: A Century of Service, 1865–1965* (Atlanta: Atlanta University Press, 1969); Maxine D. Jones and Joe M. Richardson, *Talladega College: The First* Century (Tuscaloosa: University of Alabama Press, 1990); Mildred D.G. Gallot, *A History of Grambling State University* (Lanham: University Press of America, 1985); Joe M. Richardson, *A History of Fisk University, 1865–1946* (Tuscaloosa: University of Alabama Press, 1980); Clarice Thompson Campbell, *History of Tougaloo College* (Doctoral Dissertation, University of Mississippi, 1970); Walter Dyson, *Howard University, The Capstone of Negro Education, A History: 1867–1940* (Washington, DC: The Graduate School Howard University, 1941); Edward A. Jones, *A Candle in the Dark: A History of Morehouse College* (Valley Forge: The Judson Press, 1967); Leedell W. Neyland and John W. Riley, *The History of Florida Agricultural and Mechanical University* (Gainesville: University of Florida Press, 1963); Florence M. Read, *The Story of Spelman College* (Princeton: Princeton University Press, 1961); George C. Wright, "The Founding of Lincoln Institute." *Filson Club Quarterly* 49:57–70.

4. Rovaris, 38–39.

5. Works on the individual founders of black colleges include: Louis R. Harlan, *Booker T. Washington: The Wizard of Tuskegee* (New York: Oxford University Press, 1983); Joyce Ann Hanson, *Mary McLeod Bethune and Black Women's Political Activism* (Columbia: University of Missouri Press, 2003); J. Kenneth Morris, *Elizabeth Evelyn Wright, 1872–1906: Founder of Voorhees College*, 1983.

6. Edward Danforth, Eddy Jr., *Colleges for Our Land and Time: The Land-Grant Idea in American Education* (New York: Harper Brothers, 1956), pp. 102–102, 257–259; John E. Sullivan, *A Historical Investigation of the Negro Land-Grant College from 1890 to 1964* (Ed.D. Dissertation, Loyola University, 1969); Frederick Rudolph, *The American College and University: A History* (New York: Random House, 1962).

7. Noteworthy among general works on American race relations after slavery are: C. Vann Woodward, *The Strange Career of Jim Crow* (New York: Oxford University Press, 1955); Rayford W. Logan, *The Negro in American Life and Thought: The Nadir, 1877–1901* (New York: Dial Press, 1954); Leon F. Litwack, *Trouble in Mind: Black Southerners in the Age of Jim Crow* (New York: Knopf, 1998); Otto Olsen(editor), *Reconstruction and Redemption in the South* (Baton Rouge: Louisiana State University Press, 1980); Joel Williamson, *The Crucible of Race: Black/White Relations in the American South since Emancipation* (New York: Oxford University Press, 1984).

8. Rovaris, 32; Jean Preer, *Lawyers v. Educators: Black Colleges and Desegregation in*

Public Higher Education (Westport: Greenwood Press, 1982); M. Christopher Brown, *The Quest to Define Collegiate Desegregation* (Westport: Bergin & Garvey, 1999).

9. Adam Fairclough, *Teaching Equality: Black Schools in the Age of Jim Crow* (Athens: University of Georgia Press, 2001), 3.

10. Brown, 2.

11. Rovaris.

12. Fairclough, 35–36.

13. Carolyn O. Wilson Mbajekwe interview with Walter E. Massey, 29 August 2002.

14. Carolyn O. Wilson Mbajekwe interview with Michael L. Lomax, 26 August 2002.

15. Carolyn O. Wilson Mbajekwe interview with Carolynn Reid-Wallace, 12 September 2002.

16. Carolyn O. Wilson Mbajekwe interview with Norman C. Francis, 16 October 2002.

17. Michael R. Winston, *Howard University Department of History, 1913–1973* (District of Columbia: Howard University Department of History, 1973); Joseph E. Harris, ed., *Pillars in Ethiopian History: The William Leo Hansberry Notebooks, Volume I* (District of Columbia: Howard University Press, 1974).

18. William Leo Hansberry, in Joseph E. Harris, ed., *Pillars in Ethiopian History: The William Leo Hansberry Notebooks, Volume I* (District of Columbia: Howard University Press, 1974).

19. Kenneth Robert Janken, *Rayford W. Logan and the Dilemma of the African American Intellectual* (Amherst: University of Massachusetts Press, 2001).

20. Drake, St. Clair, "The Black University in the American Social Order," *Journal of the American Academy of Arts and Sciences* 100(3) 1971: 837.

21. *Ibid*, 837.

22. Carolyn O. Wilson Mbajekwe interview with Walter E. Massey.

23. Fairclough, 39.

24. Leroy Davis, *A Clashing of the Soul: John Hope and the Dilemma of African American Leadership and Black Higher Education in the Early Twentieth Century* (Athens: University of Georgia Press, 1998); Joyce An Hanson, *Mary McLeod Bethune and Black Women's Political Activism*; Marybeth Gasman, *Charles S. Johnson: Leadership Beyond the Veil in the Age of Jim Crow* (Albany: State University of New York Press, 2003).

25. Orville Vernon Burton, "Foreword" to Benjamin E. Mays, *Born to Rebel: An Autobiography* (Athens: University of Georgia Press, 2003).

26. Mays, *Born to Rebel: An Autobiography*.

27. *Ibid*, 72.

28. Benjamin E. Mays, "The Negro Private College Leads the Way," *The Pittsburgh Courier*, 14 June 1952.

29. See PBS documentary *From Swastika to Jim Crow*.

30. Nnamdi Azikiwe, *My Odyssey: An Autobiography* (New York: Praeger, 1970); Kwame Nkrumah, *Ghana: The Autobiography of Kwame Nkrumah* (New York: Nelson, 1957).

31. Carolyn O. Wilson Mbajekwe interview with Henry R. Ponder, 26 February 2003.

32. Serbrenia J. Sims, *Diversifying Historically Black Colleges and Universities: A New Higher Education Paradigm* (Westport: Greenwood Press, 1994), 1.

33. Mary McLeod Bethune, "Self-Revelations" in Audrey Thomas McCluskey and Elaine M. Smith (editors), *Mary McLeod Bethune: Building a Better World, Essays and Selected Documents* (Bloomington and Indianapolis: Indiana University Press, 1999).

34. Drake, "The Black University in the American Social Order," 833–834.

35. *Ibid*, 834.

36. Carolyn O. Wilson Mbajekwe interview with Carolynn Reid-Wallace.

37. Carolyn O. Wilson Mbajekwe interview with Marie V. McDemmond, 11 September 2002.

38. Carolyn O. Wilson Mbajekwe interview with Walter E. Massey, 29 August 2002.

39. Carolyn O. Wilson Mbajekwe interview with Earl S. Richardson, 30 October 2003.

40. Drewry quoted in Bailey C. Ruby, "Proud Past, Uncertain Future: Some Historically Black Colleges are Fighting for their Lives," *Detroit Free Press Online*, 21 February 2003.

41. Fairclough, *Teaching Equality*; p. 37; Carolyn O. Wilson interview with Walter E. Massey; Carolyn O. Wilson Mbajekwe interview with Michael L. Lomax; Carolyn O. Wilson Mbajekwe interview with Carolynn Reid-Wallace.

42. McIntyre quoted in Jonathan Ernest, "An Unofficial Guest," *Augusta Chronicle*, 23 September 2001.

43. Carolyn O. Wilson Mbajekwe interview with Walter E. Massey, 29 August 2002.

44. For an examination of the thought of W.E.B. Du Bois on the ironies of segregation as it related to the position of African American higher education institutions, see Jean Preer, *Lawyers v. Educators: Black Colleges and Desegregation in Public Higher Education* (Westport: Greenwood Publishing, 1982), 5–6, 21–26; David Levering Lewis, *W.E.B. Du Bois: The Fight for Equality and the American Century, 1919–1963* (New York: Henry Holt and Company, 2000), 311–314; 345.

45. Preer, 2.

46. The process of cultural pluralism in education involves allowing historically white institutions and historically black institutions to coexist (so as to perpetuate the culture, traditions, and identity of both cultural groups), with both institutions enjoying full, equal, and unhampered access to the nation's economic resources, and with members of both cultural groups freely and voluntarily (if they so desire) participating in each other's institutions. In short, cultural pluralism in education endeavors to make historically white and historically black institutions economic, political, and cultural equals. Cultural pluralism can be seen as being synonymous with *multiculturalism*, which is defined as the incorporation and inclusion of minority groups, and their cultures and histories into the institutions of the dominant society. A key component of cultural pluralism and multiculturalism is *multicultural education*, which aims for the inclusion of other cultures in the school curriculum. See: Donald Earl Collins, *"A Substance of Things Hoped For:" Multiculturalism, Desegregation, and Identity in African American Washington, 1930–1960* (PhD Dissertation: Carnegie Mellon University, 1997); Speech by Joseph Fernandez, "Linking Desegregation to Multicultural Education," from *The 40th Anniversary of Brown v. Board of Education Conference*, 17 May 1994; James Banks, "The Canon Debate, Knowledge Construction, and Multicultural Education," *Educational Researcher* 22 (June/July 1993): 4–14.

47. Lewis, *The Fight for Equality and the American Century*, 138.

48. See: Johnny Washington, *Alain Locke and Philosophy, A Quest for Cultural Pluralism* (Westport: Greenwood Publishing, 1986); Carter G. Woodson, *The Mis-Education of the Negro* (Washington: Associated Publishers, 1933); Kelly Miller, "The Reorganization of the Higher Education of the Negro in Light of Changing Conditions," *Journal of Negro Education* 5 (July 1936); Mary Church Terrell, *A Colored Woman in a White World* (New York: Arno Press, 1940).

49. Kelly Miller, "The Reorganization of the Higher Education of the Negro in Light of Changing Conditions," *Journal of Negro Education* 5 (July 1936).

50. Donald Earl Collins, *"A Substance of Things Hoped For:" Multiculturalism, Desegregation, and Identity in African American Washington, 1930–1960* (PhD Dissertation: Carnegie Mellon University, 1997).

51. *Ibid.*

52. Frederick D. Patterson comments at the Howard University conference on "The Courts and Racial Integration in Education," Washington, DC, 18 April 1952.

53. Rufus E. Clement remarks to official of the General Education Board, 18 July 1951, box 39, folder 355, General Education Board Papers, Rockefeller Archive Center.

54. Proceedings of the Howard University conference on "The Courts and Racial Integration in Education" can be found in *The Journal of Negro Education* Volume XXI (summer 1952).

55. *Ibid.*

56. *Ibid*, 352.

57. *Ibid*, 369.

58. *Ibid*, 359.

59. Proceedings, "Howard University Conference on the Courts and Racial Integration in Education."

60. Carolyn O. Wilson Mbajekwe, "Black Colleges after *Brown:* Benjamin E. Mays, Frederick D. Paterson, and the Quest for a Cultural Pluralism-Based Definition of Collegiate Desegregation (PhD Dissertation: Emory University, 2006).

61. *Ibid.*

62. Dereck J. Rovaris, *Mays and Morehouse: How Benjamin E. Mays Developed Morehouse College, 1940–1967* (Silver Spring: Beckham House Publishers); Benjamin E. Mays, *Born to Rebel: An Autobiography* (New York: Scribner, 1971); Lawrence Edward Carter, Sr., *Walking Integrity: Benjamin E. Mays, Mentor to Generations* (Atlanta: Scholars Press, 1996).

63. Carolyn O. Wilson Mbajekwe interview with Walter E. Massey, 29 August 2002.

64. *Ibid.*

65. Charles S. Johnson speech at the 10th Annual United Negro College Fund Convocation, San Francisco, California, 12 January 1953, box 157, folder 10, Charles S. Johnson Papers, Amistad Research Center.

66. Lisa Delpit, "Foreword" to Michelle Foster, *Black Teachers on Teaching* (New York: New Press, 1997).

67. Carolyn O. Wilson Mbajekwe interview with Earl S. Richardson, 30 October 2002.

68. *Ibid.*

69. Carolyn O. Wilson Mbajekwe interview with Walter E. Massey, 29 August 2002.

70. Carolyn O. Wilson Mbajekwe interview with Carolynn Reid-Wallace, 12 September 2002.

71. *Ibid.*

72. "Endowments at Colleges and Universities, 2001–2002" *The Chronicle of Higher Education*. The html version of this report can be found at: http://chronicle.com/stats/endowments/endowment_results.php3.

73. See: June, Audrey Williams. "Man With a Mission: On the eve of his retirement, the president of the United Negro College Fund reflects on the purposes and challenges of black institutions," *The Chronicle of Higher Education*, 7 November 2003.

74. Carolyn O. Wilson Mbajekwe interview with Michael L. Lomax, 26 August 2002.

75. Andrea Jones, "Hard Times Harder on Black Colleges," *The Atlanta Journal-Constitution*, 7 November 2003.

76. Marybeth Gasman, *Fund Raising from Black-College Alumni: Successful Strategies for Supporting Alma Mater* (Washington, DC: Council for the Advancement and Support of Education, 2003).

77. Carolyn O. Wilson Mbajekwe interview with Marie V McDemmond, 11 September 2002.

78. Carolyn O. Wilson Mbajekwe interview with Marie V McDemmond, 11 September 2002.

79. Carolyn O. Wilson Mbajekwe interview with Walter E. Massey, 29 August 2002.

80. Bob Kemper, "Black Colleges' Hopes Unmet," *Atlanta Journal Constitution*, 20 June 2004.

81. *Ibid.*

82. Megan Scott, "Fund raising Weighs on Black-College Presidents," *The State Newspaper*, 01 September, 2002.

83. *Ibid.*

84. Carolyn O. Wilson Mbajekwe interview with Carolynn Reid-Wallace, 12 September 2002.

85. Carolyn O. Wilson Mbajekwe interview with Earl S. Richardson, 30 October 2002.

86. See Clark Atlanta University website, home page, http://www.cau.edu.

87. Carolyn O. Wilson Mbajekwe interview with Marie V. McDemmond, 11 September 2002.

88. Carolyn O. Wilson Mbajekwe interview with Earl S. Richardson, 30 October 2002.

89. Gerald A. Foster, *Is There a Conspiracy to Keep Black Colleges Open?* (Dubuque: Kendall/Hunt Publishing Company, 2001).

90. Julian B. Roebuck and Komanduri S. Murty, *Historically Black Colleges and Universities: Their Place in American Higher Education* (Westport: Praeger, 1993).

91. M. Christopher Brown, II, *The Quest to Define Collegiate Desegregation: Black Colleges, Title VI Compliance, and Post-Adams Litigation,* 1–10.

92. *Ibid,* xvii–xviii.

93. Brown, The Quest to Define Collegiate Desegregation: Black Colleges, Title VI Compliance, and Post-Adams Litigation; Charles V. Willie, "Foreword" to M. Christopher Brown, The Quest to Define Collegiate Desegregation: Black Colleges, Title VI Compliance, and Post-Adams Litigation; Russell Irvine and Jacqueline Irvine, "The Impact of the Desegregation Process on the Education of Black Students: Key Variables," The Journal of Negro Education 52(40) 1983: 410–422.

94. Brown, *The Quest to Define Collegiate Desegregation.*

95. Brown, p. xvii.

96. *Ibid.*

97. Irvine and Irvine, p. 411.

98. Charles V. Willie, "Foreword" to M. Christopher Brown, *The Quest to Define Collegiate Desegregation.*

99. Williams, "Public Policy and Black College Development."

100. Frank Bowles and Frank A. DeCosta, *Between Two Worlds: A Profile of Negro Higher Education* (New York: McGraw-Hill, 1971).

101. Carolyn O. Wilson Mbajekwe interview with Earl S. Richardson, 30 October 2002.

102. Williams, "Public Policy and Black College Development."

103. See Willie statement in "Foreword" to M. Christopher Brown, *The Quest to Define Collegiate Desegregation.*

104. Carolyn O. Wilson Mbajekwe interview with Michael L. Lomax, 26 August 2002.

105. Carolyn O. Wilson Mbajekwe interview with Marie V. McDemmond, 11 September 2002.

106. Carolyn O. Wilson Mbajekwe interview with Walter E. Massey, 29 August 2002.

107. Carolyn O. Wilson Mbajekwe interview with Calvin W. Lowe, 2 April 2002.

108. *Ibid.*

109. Carolyn O. Wilson Mbajekwe interview with Michael L. Lomax, 26 August 2002.

110. Carolyn O. Wilson interview with Carolynn Reid-Wallace, 12 September 2002.

111. Carolyn O. Wilson Mbajekwe interview with Marie V. McDemmond, 11 September 2002.

112. Carolyn O. Wilson Mbajekwe interview with Michael L. Lomax, 26 August

2002; Carolyn O. Wilson Mbajekwe interview with Norman C. Francis, 16 October 2002; Carolyn O. Wilson Mbajekwe interview with Walter E. Massey, 29 August 2002; Carolyn O. Wilson Mbajekwe interview with Carlton E. Brown, 13 March 2003; Carolyn O. Wilson Mbajekwe interview with Marie V. McDemmond, 11 September 2002.

113. Carolyn O. Wilson Mbajekwe interview with Michael L. Lomax, 26 August 2002; Carolyn O. Wilson Mbajekwe interview with Carlton E. Brown, 13 March 2003; Carolyn O. Wilson Mbajekwe interview with Marie V. McDemmond, 11 September 2002.

114. Carolyn O. Wilson Mbajekwe interview with James C. Renick, 30 May 2002; Carolyn O. Wilson Mbajekwe interview with Marie V. McDemmond, 11 September 2002; Carolyn O. Wilson Mbajekwe interview with Carlton E. Brown, 13 March 2003.

115. See, William E. Kirwan, "Diversity in Higher Education: Why It Matters," in Frank W. Hale, Jr. (editor), *What Makes Racial Diversity Work in Higher Education* (Sterling: Stylus Publishing, 2004), xxi–xxiv; Raymond F. Bacchetti and Stephen S. Weiner, "Diversity is a Key Factor in Educational Quality and Hence in Accreditation," *The Chronicle of Higher Education* (May 8, 1991), 37, A48.

116. Carolyn O. Wilson Mbajekwe interview with Carlton E. Brown, 13 March 2003.

117. Carolyn O. Wilson Mbajekwe interview with Walter E. Massey, 29 August 2002.

118. Carolyn O. Wilson Mbajekwe interview with Beverly Daniel Tatum, 28 February 2003.

119. Carolyn O. Wilson Mbajekwe interview with Walter E. Massey, 29 August 2002.

120. Carolyn O. Wilson Mbajekwe interview with Marie V. McDemmond, 11 September 2002.

121. *Ibid.*

122. Carolyn O. Wilson Mbajekwe interview with Carolynn Reid-Wallace, 12 September 2002.

123. Carolyn O. Wilson Mbajekwe interview with Norman C. Francis, 16 October 2002.

124. *Ibid.*

125. Carolyn O. Wilson Mbajekwe interview with Carlton E. Brown, 13 March 2003.

126. Carolyn O. Wilson Mbajekwe interview with Michael L. Lomax, 26 August 2002; Carolyn O. Wilson Mbajekwe interview with Norman C. Francis, 16 October 2002.

127. Carolyn O. Wilson Mbajekwe interview with Walter E. Massey, 29 August 2002; Carolyn O. Wilson Mbajekwe interview with Beverly Daniel Tatum, 28 February 2003; Carolyn O. Wilson Mbajekwe interview with Marie V. McDemmond, 11 September 2002.

128. Carolyn O. Wilson Mbajekwe interview with Marie V. McDemmond, 11 September 2002.

129. Carolyn O. Wilson Mbajekwe interview with Walter E. Massey, 29 August 2002.

130. Carolyn O. Wilson Mbajekwe interview with Walter E. Massey, 29 August 2002; Carolyn O. Wilson Mbajekwe interview with Beverly Daniel Tatum, 28 February 2003; Carolyn O. Wilson Mbajekwe interview with Calvin W. Lowe, 2 April 2002.

131. Carolyn O. Wilson Mbajekwe interview with Norman C. Francis, 16 October 2002; Carolyn O. Wilson Mbajekwe interview with Earl S. Richardson, 30 October 2002; Carolyn O. Wilson Mbajekwe interview with Ronald F. Mason, March 7, 2003.

132. Carolyn O. Wilson Mbajekwe interview with Calvin W. Lowe, 2 April 2002.

133. Carolyn O. Wilson Mbajekwe interview with Beverly Daniel Tatum, 28 February 2003; Carolyn O. Wilson Mbajekwe interview with Norman C. Francis, 16 October 2002; Carolyn O. Wilson Mbajekwe interview with Michael L. Lomax, 26 August 2002; Carolyn O. Wilson Mbajekwe interview with James C. Renick, 30 May 2002.

134. Carolyn O. Wilson Mbajekwe interview with Carolynn Reid-Wallace, 12 September 2002.

135. Figures quoted in John K. Waddell, "Black Colleges Fill Vital Need," *Richmond Times-Dispatch,* 24 October 2004. For additional facts and figures on the productivity of the nation's historically black higher education institutions see: American Association of University Professors, "The Historically Black Colleges and Universities: A Future in the Balance," *Academe,* January–February (1996) 49–58. HTML version available at: Http://eric-web.tc.columbia.edu/hbcu/report.html; U.S. Department of Education, "Historically Black Colleges and Universities and Higher Education Desegregation," March 1991. Http://www.ed.gov/about/offices/list/ocr/docs/hq9511.html.

136. American Association of University Professors, "The Historically Black Colleges and Universities: A Future in the Balance," *Academe,* January–February (1996) 49–58. "HTML version available at Http://eric-web.tc.columbia.edu/hbcu/report.html.

137. Carolyn O. Wilson Mbajekwe interview with Norman C. Francis, 16 October 2002; For further discussions of Xavier University's record of excellence in educating minorities see, Michael A. Fletcher, "Small Black College Nurtures Achievement," *The Washington Post,* Saturday, 10 May 1997, p. A01; Pearl Stewart, "Why Xavier Remains No. 1," *Black Issues in Higher Education,* July 19, 2002; Anthony Walton, "The Eye of the Needle: Katherine Drexel," *Notre Dame Magazine,* October 2004.

138. Carolyn O. Wilson Mbajekwe interview with Walter E. Massey, 29 August 2002; Carolyn O. Wilson Mbajekwe interview with James C. Renick, 30 May 2002; Carolyn O. Wilson Mbajekwe interview with Carolynn Reid-Wallace, 12 September 2002; Carolyn O. Wilson Mbajekwe interview with Calvin W. Lowe, 2 April 2002; Carolyn O. Wilson Mbajekwe interview with Earl S. Richardson, 30 October 2002.

139. "Top 100 Degree Producers," *Black Issues in Higher Education,* 3 June 2004.

140. Carolyn O. Wilson Mbajekwe interview with Norman C. Francis, 16 October 2002.

I. The Private Historically Black Colleges

1

BEVERLY DANIEL TATUM

President, Spelman College

Dr. Beverly Daniel Tatum took office in August 2002 as the ninth president of Spelman College, Atlanta, Georgia. Spelman is one of only two historically black, all-female, four-year, liberal arts institutions in America. The college enjoys national prominence as the premiere institution for the education of black women. Tatum was formerly the acting president of Mount Holyoke College in South Hadley, Massachusetts. She joined Mount Holyoke College in 1989 as an associate professor in the Department of Psychology and Education, and after moving up to the rank of professor and department chair was appointed dean of the college and vice president for student affairs at Mount Holyoke in 1998. Prior to serving at Mount Holyoke, Tatum was an assistant and then associate professor of psychology at Westfield State College and a lecturer at the University of California at Santa Barbara.

A nationally recognized authority on race in America, Tatum's academic expertise is in the study of racial identity development in teens, the impact of race on the classroom environment, and the experiences of African American families in predominantly white communities. She is the author of the highly acclaimed book "Why Are All The Black Kids Sitting Together in the Cafeteria? And Other Conversations About Race," which was at the center of the national dialogue about race after its publication in 1997. The success of the timely book made Tatum a much sought after featured lecturer on the subject of race relations, and landed her a seat as a partic-

43

ipant in the first Town Hall Forum of President Clinton's Initiative on Race.

A fourth generation college professor, Tatum was raised in Bridgewater, Massachusetts, where her father was the first African American faculty member at Bridgewater State College where he served in the education department. Tatum earned the bachelor's degree in psychology at Wesleyan University, where she graduated magna cum laude *in 1975, and received the doctoral degree in clinical psychology from the University of Michigan, Ann Arbor, in 1984. She earned the master's degree in religious studies from Hartford Seminary in 2000. Her commitment to Spelman College is to continue the institution's tradition of excellence and achievement. When talking to young women about Spelman College, Tatum states: "If you want to be at the center of the educational experience, rather than on the margin, you want to be at Spelman."*

I am the ninth president of Spelman College and I have inherited the legacy of the strong leadership of my eight predecessors. Spelman is the premiere institution for the education of black women and it is fiscally sound, which is a blessing. We have an endowment of approximately $250 million. While that is certainly not enough to meet all our needs, it is sufficient to provide solid financial footing for the institution and that has been important. The sense of history and mission has been continuous so that Spelman is an institution with a clear focus in terms of what it is that we are trying to accomplish. And that is valuable.

The priorities of presidents of American colleges and universities, be they predominantly black or white, are the same in the sense of preparing talented young women and men for leadership in the

Beverly Daniel Tatum (courtesy Spelman College Office of Public Relations/Communications).

twenty-first century. There are a lot of problems that need to be solved and this is the generation that we hope will be able to solve some of them. So we need to prepare them to be able to think critically, to communicate their ideas with clarity and to be ready to give back to their communities.

I came to Spelman College from Mount Holyoke College, which is a predominantly white institution for women, and I was educated at Wesleyan University as an undergraduate, and at the University of Michigan as a graduate student. But my point here is that if I were talking about Wesleyan or Mount Holyoke, I would still say the goal is to prepare students for ethical leadership, to be able to think critically, to communicate ideas clearly, and to be able to give back to their communities. But, clearly the capacity to do that with African American students is enhanced at historically black colleges and universities, where you have a specialized population. And as I like to say when I am talking to young women about Spelman, if you want to be at the center of the educational experience, rather than on the margin, you want to be at Spelman.

When I was working at Mount Holyoke College, it was our goal to prepare all of our students. It was not that we said we were going to do it especially for white students and not for others. But the reality of predominantly white institutions is that the nature of the history, the staffing patterns, curriculum, all those things, is such that even in the best case, the reality is that you do not do it as effectively for some people as you do it for others. So clearly historically black colleges and universities are specializing in a particular population. But the goal, I think, in terms of preparing students for leadership is the same, though one might also say that at historically black colleges and universities the leadership that you are particularly interested will lead to the betterment of the African American community.

The Mission of Spelman College in the Twenty-First Century

Historically black colleges vary in terms of the mission and the kinds of students that they attract. But with particular reference to Spelman, the goal and the mission of the institution continues to be relevant. The opportunities for black women today are certainly greater than they were in 1881 when Spelman was founded. The kinds of oppor-

tunities that we see available to women of African descent currently
were certainly not even on the table in 1881. However, it is still the case
that black female students are not necessarily going to be at the center
of the educational experience at other places. And it is still the case that
racism and sexism can hinder a young black woman's aspirations and/or
the opportunity to achieve her goals.

Having said that, Spelman College is a place that is organized with
the sole purpose of helping her achieve those goals, and has specialized
in doing so since 1881, almost 125 years. That continues to be important. If you look at the role of women in general, not specifically African
American women or women of African descent, but if you look at the
role of women in general in bringing about social change, I think women
have a unique role to play. Or maybe a unique perspective, a gendered
perspective that is important and certainly the experiences of black
women need to be celebrated and highlighted as we think about preparing leaders for the twenty-first century.

The mission statement of Spelman is an enduring one. The mission statement says, "An outstanding historically black college for
women, Spelman promotes academic excellence in the liberal arts and
develops the intellectual, ethical and leadership potential of its students.
Spelman seeks to empower the total person, who appreciates the many
cultures of the world and commits to positive social change." That is
our mission, and so, I do not have to invent one. It is clear that that is
what we want to do.

But how do we operationalize that mission in the next decade? What
I would say is that we need to focus on maintaining our tradition of academic excellence. At this moment in history that means thinking carefully about how we are going to attract and retain the best faculty at a
time when many of our faculty are starting to retire, and when we are
also competing for the talents of faculty of color, African American faculty in particular, with institutions that are offering higher salaries and
lower course loads. It is not the case that we only want to hire African
American faculty, but certainly we want to maintain a significant representation of faculty of color on our campus because we want our students to see themselves reflected in the professoriate. So that is one
thing.

Academic excellence also means thinking about student excellence.
We have a very strong student body, and Spelman is a very competitive
institution. We have this year 4,500 applicants for 525 slots. So it is not
that we do not have good students interested in Spelman. But it is the

case that some of those students will choose not to come to Spelman because we have not offered them the same level of financial aid that places like Harvard, Yale, Stanford, Duke and other places can make available to them. So as we think about academic excellence, we have to think about resources, both for faculty and for students. We want to maintain a cutting-edge curriculum that requires resources for curriculum development, and we want to have a strong library. All of that falls under the rubric of academic excellence.

Also at the heart of our mission is the idea of leadership development and civic engagement. Leadership development and civic engagement are the things that we have been very involved in for a long time. But, that is part of our challenge. Our students are engaged in lots of service outreach and so we think about civic engagement as really important, but we want to think in a synergistic way about what kinds of leadership opportunities and experiences our students need for the twenty-first century.

There are things that have been in place here a long time and are fairly common as many schools have these kinds of programs; for instance, tutoring in the local schools and working with Girls Inc. or the YWCA. But there are other kinds of things that are curricularly connected, like for example Spelman students majoring in Spanish are working as translators in the local hospital and Spelman students who are taking a sociology course on survey research methods are using these methods in the local community to do these assessments for a local health center. You hear a lot of talk now about health disparities in the African American community, and we have students interested in exploring public health issues as part of our curriculum. So there are those kinds of things going on.

We tend to focus on community service, community outreach, and children in the local neighborhood, and that is important. But I am also quite interested in having our students think about global understanding in the twenty-first century. We are not just citizens of the United States; we are citizens of the world. We need to have a better understanding of that global picture. One of the things that Spelman does which I think is really wonderful is a first-year seminar that all first-year students take called, "The African Diaspora and the World," which focuses on having an understanding of at least people of African descent around the world and the various issues that have shaped our experiences. So focusing on leadership from a global perspective is important.

We also want to focus on improving our environment in terms of upgrading facilities and working to enhance the development of the community surrounding Spelman. We want to be visible as an excellent institution. We think we have a lot to talk about and we want to make sure that the higher education community knows what is going on here at Spelman. We want to make sure that what we are doing here is visible and we want to focus on our infrastructure to be sure that we have the technology we need and the human capacity to accomplish the goals that we are trying to accomplish. So that is a kind of broad stroke of what it is that I expect to be working on in the coming years.

I talk about Spelman as being nothing less than the best, that I want students who come to Spelman to be able to say, "Yes, this place is built for me." There are not very many places that a black woman can step on a campus and say, "This place is built for me." So we want to acknowledge and celebrate that "Yes, this place was built for you." But we want those students to say, "This place was built for me and it is nothing less than the best." That I am not having to settle for second best when I make this choice. I can have the same kind of opportunities that I would have had at one of those other institutions that would have offered me a lot of financial aid, and that I can have not only those opportunities here, but also the unique opportunity of really experiencing myself at the center of the education and becoming part of that Spelman network of 13,000 talented African American women around the globe who are doing important things in the world.

Diversity: Creating an Inclusive Learning Environment

Diversity is an important aspect of higher education in the twenty-first century and Spelman is certainly a diverse community. That diversity manifests itself in terms of religion, in terms of socio-economic status, and in terms of ethnicity, even within the racial category of black, because of course there is ethnic variation in terms of domestic US citizens versus international students from the Caribbean or Africa. So there are lots of different ways to think about diversity. You can think of diversity in terms of sexual orientation. You can think about diversity in terms of the black experience again within the context of color differences. You can think about diversity at a women's college in terms of who is in a sorority or who is not in a sorority. There are lots of ways of speaking about the diversity of the community. Not to mention geographic origin, those people who are from rural or urban communities. There are those who came from mostly black communities and those who have chosen to come to a historically black college because they have spent most of their lives in white schools. There is a lot of diversity that can be examined and understood that can be a source of dialogue.

One of my initiatives as the new president has been to introduce a dialogue project which is designed to help students develop the skills to be able to engage with one another across lines of difference of the various sorts I just enumerated in order to talk about important social issues. For example, to have students of different class backgrounds talking about issues related to class and the distribution of resources in the United States. Or international students talking with American domestic students about foreign policy issues. Or to have students of varying sexual orientations talking to each other about heterosexism in our society, or to have Muslim and Christian students dialogue. Spelman was founded by Christian missionaries, and we have as our motto, "our whole school for Christ," and yet we have Muslim students and Bahai students and faculty of various religious traditions. How do we engage in mutually respectful ways across lines of religious difference, for example? So, there are lots of ways to look at diversity and I think our students should be encouraged to do so.

Even in the context of a historically black college, I think you can create opportunities for cross-racial dialogues. For example, Spelman College is a women's college that is historically black. But, we are not far away from Agnes Scott College, which is also a women's college, though predominantly white. Even prior to my arrival there have been opportunities for dialogue between Agnes Scott students and Spelman students, which I think is useful for both institutions. Not to mention also gender issues and how those might be explored with our brother institution Morehouse College.

In general, anybody who wants to diversify their institution can think about how welcoming that institution is. Do students who are coming to that institution see themselves reflected in important ways? When I was at Mount Holyoke I talked about what I called the "ABCs" as being important to creating inclusive environments. The "A" stands for affirming identity. That, in order to affirm identity, we have to acknowledge that all students, wherever they may be, and however they define themselves, want to see important dimensions of their identity reflected in the environment — whether that is in terms of the faces of the faculty, or staff that work there, in terms of the curriculum that is offered, in terms of the kinds of social opportunities that the institution provides, in terms of the kinds of speakers that get invited. There are many ways to affirm the multiple identities of our students.

To use an example at a historically black college, I have mentioned that we have religious diversity here at Spelman. In December, as we were approaching Christmas, which of course is the big holiday that everybody is attending to, it was also the season of Ramadan. And we also have Muslim students at Spelman, so one of the things I felt that was important institutionally was to indicate some formal acknowledgement that Ramadan was taking place. And that meant that Muslim students were fasting from sunrise to sunset and that it is common during the season of Ramadan to host a special meal, especially towards the end of it, as a breaking the fast called "Iftar." And so one of the things that I did was to host an Iftar meal at the President's house and invite the Muslim students on campus to attend, and any Muslim faculty or staff members who were here. I myself am not a Muslim, but they were very appreciative of the gesture, and it was a way of signaling to the community that we know you are here. That is just a small example, but I think institutions need to think about who is in the community, or who do you want to be in the community? And how are you going to signal to them that you recognize that they may have needs that differ from other students and how are those needs going to be responded to? That is all about affirming identity.

At the same time, you want to "B," which is build community. And you want to find ways to bring all the disparate members of the community together and assure a sense of what it means to be a student at that institution. When I was at Mount Holyoke, it was about what does it mean to be a Mount Holyoke woman. At Spelman, the question is, what does it mean to be a Spelman woman? There is more than one way to be a Spelman woman. But we want to have everybody feel connected to this powerful mission that we have as the oldest historically black college for women. And so let's think about how we are going to make that real for people and how everyone can feel included in that mission.

And then the "C" of the ABCs is cultivating leadership. We want the students who come to our campuses, whether they are coming to Spelman, or to Mount Holyoke or to Wesleyan, or wherever they are coming, they are coming into an environment different from the one that they left. To use Spelman as an example, I would say approximately half of the first-year students I greeted in September came here from predominantly white communities. The other half came from mostly black communities but each of them has entered into an environment different from the one they left. And so, one of the issues in terms of cultivating leadership is about creating opportunities for students to really learn how to deal effectively with people different from themselves and in situations different from the ones they grew up in. And the only way that you can do that is by intentionally creating structured opportunities for them to practice doing such. That is part of the dialogue project that I have been talking about where you help students learn how to facilitate groups talking about difficult issues across lines of difference. When you create such opportunities, they are able to really learn those skills. It is an important skill to be able to interact with somebody different from yourself and most students do not come to college with that skill already well developed. But you want them to leave with that skill developed, so you have to create the opportunities for them.

Promoting Positive Change

I am a fourth generation college professor. And I say that because I have grown up in a family where education is very important. It has just been part of my socialization since birth, that it is important to be educated, and that education is a tool for personal and community development. And it is more important than anything else. That was certainly a message, that if you do not do anything else, get your education. So I enter my role as a college president with that message well engraved.

Throughout my career, I would say certainly in the last ten years, I have been very intentional about the choices that I have made as it relates to expanding my sphere of influence in terms of promoting positive change. I was a classroom professor for a long time and I enjoyed that. And certainly, I influenced my students. But at a certain point, I began to think about how I could expand my own sphere of influence, in terms of the issues that I was concerned about, and mostly that had to do with antiracism education. So I started doing workshops and lots of speaking engagements with teachers, kindergarten through high school as well as in higher education, about teaching about racism in the classroom. That was an important way to expand my sphere of influence because as a teacher you influence students, but if you influence other teachers then you really expand your sphere.

And then I started hearing from teachers that "we think these are great ideas, but it is our principals or our college presidents, or our school superintendents that really need to hear this message." And I started speaking to those people, to expand that sphere of influence. And then I found myself not being able to accept all the speaking engagements that were coming my way. So I decided to write down what I was saying, and I wrote my book, *Why Are All The Black Kids Sitting Together in the Cafeteria? And Other Conversations About Race,* as a way of further expanding that sphere. And then right about the time that the book was published, I was offered the opportunity to be dean of the college at Mount Holyoke. Initially I was not interested in being a *college* administrator because I thought that it would be boring, to be perfectly honest, and I liked teaching very much. But it was suggested to me that if I became dean of the college at Mount Holyoke, I could take the ideas that I had written about in my book and apply them in a way that would not only influence what happened at Mount Holyoke, but these ideas might be a model for other institutions.

The "affirming identity, building community, and cultivating leadership ideas" were ideas that I had developed at Mount Holyoke and applied them at Mount Holyoke, in terms of developing programs and really trying to create a truly improved learning environment for all students there. And we were conducting research about the effectiveness of that strategy. But at the same time I was administering these programs at Mount Holyoke, I was also writing about them and speaking about them at higher education conferences and other organizations as a way of exporting those ideas. And then I got the opportunity to be president of Spelman. And in thinking about being president of Spelman, one of the things that was very clear to me was not only was Spelman a wonderful opportunity to influence the 2,000 black women who are here as students and who look up to their president, but also because of Spelman's national profile it would be an opportunity to expand one's sphere of influence in terms of expanding the audience with whom you have an opportunity to interact. And even though I have been here only eight months, I can see that I was right about that.

Institutional Priorities

At any institution technology is obviously really important. Technological advances are rapid and we want our students to be knowledgeable and literate in terms of that advancing technology. However, for historically black colleges that is a particular challenge because of the expense of that technology. So staying current when you do not have lots of dollars to stay current with is a challenge. So that is one thing, the technology. But increasingly the cutting edge of the curriculum is interdisciplinarity; interdisciplinarity in terms of social sciences, humanities, the arts and the sciences. The whole model of traditional departmental boundaries I think is increasingly challenged. And I think that perhaps because of the longevity of faculty members and sometimes the longevity of presidents at historically black colleges, there maybe a conservative tendency in terms of curricular innovation. And that is important to think on and so that may be one of the challenges that might be unique for historically black institutions. Though as I said, you see it most critically around the area of technology.

And I think that increasingly leadership development is important. I think that if you look at recent scandals, for instance, the Enron scandal, you see evidence of the collapse of leadership. There are many examples of leadership failure. And I think that people of color in general, African Americans in particular, have served in some ways as the social conscience of our nation. You can look at the leadership provided by somebody like Martin Luther King, Jr., but not just him. There are many other great examples like Marian Wright Edelman for instance, who is a Spelman alumna. If you look at the people who are really speaking up about issues of social justice, they are not exclusively African American, but African American voices have been, for many decades, at the center of those conversations. And I think that it is important for us to maintain that social consciousness, and not succumb to the glitter of potential wealth, which is not to say that money is not important. But we want to understand that our goal in life is not only self-preservation, but it is also the preservation of a larger community.

Spelman College: A Legacy of Training Leaders for America

You name any area or field of endeavor and you can point to the contributions and achievements of Spelman alumnae. Spelman, in particular, has had a very strong track record in the sciences, and has been one of the leading producers of African American women entering medical school. So if you look at health disparities and health care providers, and increasing the number of African American health care providers, certainly, that has been a major contribution. You can also look at

Ambassadors Ruth Davis and Aurelia Brazeal in terms of the world of foreign policy. You can look at somebody like Marian Wright Edelman and her commitment to the nonprofit sector and the welfare of children. You can look at somebody like Bernice Johnson Reagon, the founder of Sweet Honey in the Rock, and her use of the arts in the name of social justice. You can look at writers like Tina McElroy Ansa or Pearl Cleage, or Alice Walker. Spelman alumnae are making contributions in all walks of life; artists of all kinds, scientists, inventors, Wall Street executives and so on. I can think of alums like Kimberly Davis who is a highly placed executive at JP Morgan Chase or Jeri Devard at Verizon.

Four Generations of Black College Leadership

I am the child of two Howard University graduates, and certainly they are proud of that education. When I was going off to college, my mother lobbied for Howard University as a potential choice for me. I had other things in mind and certainly wanted to chart my own path. So that was about my own desires, and independence and making a different choice. But certainly, many of the people that I admire were educated at historically black colleges. So I understood that was an important dimension.

I have mentioned that I am a fourth generation college professor. My grandmother and grandfather on my father's side both taught for a time at Tuskegee Institute. That grandfather actually attended Tuskegee and then taught there. My grandmother attended Spelman for a period of time then transferred to Atlanta University and graduated from there. She went on to Tuskegee where she taught for a period of time, and then the two of them ran a Catholic school known as the Cardinal Gibbons Institute in Maryland, which has been described as the "Catholic Tuskegee." It closed during the Depression years. And before that her father, my great-grandfather, was the first Head of the School of Architecture at Howard University. So there has just been a long history in my family of being associated with institutions of higher education. I was born in Tallahassee, Florida, when my father was teaching at Florida A&M. And so this is to say that I certainly have always had an appreciation for the value of these institutions.

I visited Spelman on January 28, 2002. That was my first visit ever to the campus. And I came because I knew I had been nominated for the presidency and I wanted to see the campus and get a feel for it, to see if it was a place that I thought I might like to be. And when I came to the campus I was very impressed with the students. I did not tell anybody that I was coming because I wanted an anonymous visit. So I came and walked around. I paid attention to the students I saw. I walked into Sisters Chapel, which is the landmark building on campus. Then I went to admissions and I picked up a brochure. And on the back of the brochure was the statement of the mission. And I was quite taken with that mission statement.

It was the statement I referred to earlier about being an outstanding historically black college for women focused on their total empowerment: the intellectual, the moral, the ethical leadership, the commitment to preparing women to be positive change agents, and the notion of academic excellence and liberal arts. I am a big fan of a liberal arts education. And so I read that statement. But the statement that I read not only spoke of the mission, but it also talked about how when you step on the Oval, which is the middle of the campus, and walk through the campus Arch, which is what you do at graduation, you join this Spelman sisterhood of powerful women making positive change in the world. And then the statement talked about being an outstanding institution committed to the liberal arts, committed to the leadership development of students—all those things that I consider valuable in terms of my own commitments in higher education. And then there was a sentence that said, "This is your heritage and your calling." And I said: "It is."

2

WALTER E. MASSEY

President, Morehouse College

Dr. Walter E. Massey is the ninth president of his alma mater, Morehouse College. Located in Atlanta, Georgia, Morehouse is the nation's largest liberal arts college for men. Morehouse College is an institution with a long, rich legacy and tradition. Under the leadership of the legendary Benjamin E. Mays, who served as president from 1940 to 1967, and his commitment to the values of producing outstanding leaders, service, personal integrity, and academic excellence, the college grew from its origins as a strong southern institution into a national institution that meets the standards of excellence set by the finest colleges and universities in the land. Morehouse has always been a national leader in the overall production of African American students who go on to earn the PhD, and it is one of only four historically black colleges that has a chapter of Phi Beta Kappa.

A member of the class of 1958, Massey's return to Morehouse follows a long and successful career in higher education leadership in which he served in a wide range of executive positions: provost and senior vice president for academic affairs at the University of California; vice president for research at the University of Chicago; director of the Argonne National Laboratory; and director of the National Science Foundation. Massey has also served as dean of the college and full professor of physics at Brown University.

Under Massey's able leadership, Morehouse College continues to rise to new heights of academic excellence. The College has enhanced its *academically rigorous liberal arts curriculum through the addition of several centers and research enterprises, including the Leadership Center, the Morehouse Research Institute, and the Andrew Young Center for International Affairs. The College has also broadened its global curriculum, expanded foreign study, and increased the recruitment of students from abroad.*

Morehouse is a wireless environment and was recently ranked among Yahoo's 100 most wired undergraduate college campuses. In 1993, Morehouse became the first historically black college or university to produce a Rhodes Scholar. In 2001 when it produced a second Rhodes Scholar, Morehouse was one of only three undergraduate, liberal arts colleges in the nation to produce a Rhodes that year. The year 2003 witnessed Morehouse produce a third Rhodes Scholar. This time the college was the only higher education institution in the state of Georgia to win a Rhodes.

Massey emphasizes that although Morehouse is predominantly black, and all male, it is still an institution that values diversity. Diversity at Morehouse College, he maintains, is manifested in the fact that students hail from different cultural backgrounds, different religions, different classes, and different economic and social strata. Before students can appreciate the

diversity of the larger world, Massey asserts, they must first recognize and appreciate the diversity within their own racial group.

A native of Hattiesburg, Mississippi, Massey received his doctoral degree in physics in 1966 from Washington University, St. Louis, Missouri. He is also the recipient of several honorary degrees from institutions including Washington University, Amherst College, and Yale University.

When most people talk about the state of black colleges in the twenty-first century, there is a tendency to assume that all historically black colleges and universities are alike or similar, and that they face basically the same challenges. But asking what are the most important challenges

Walter E. Massey (courtesy Morehouse College).

facing historically black colleges is like asking what are the most important challenges facing colleges in the South. Just as southern institutions are not all the same, historically black colleges are not all the same. So, to understand what it means to be a historically black college in the twenty-first century, one must first differentiate among HBCUs because different colleges are following different paths into the future.

Probably the greatest differentiator among HBCUs is public versus private institutions. For example, public, historically black schools in most states in the South are under mandates to broaden their applicant pool to, in fact, become more similar to historically white institutions. I do not know what will happen in that regard but, ultimately, public black colleges and universities will become different kinds of institutions than they have been in the past, and than they are today.

Among private, historically black schools, I think you will see more differentiation in the future. Some will remain small, local or regional institutions whose missions will probably not change very much. They will be focused on providing access to higher education for students who would have difficulty pursuing a degree elsewhere because of financial or academic requirements they could not meet.

Then there will be another group of private, black institutions, and I count Morehouse among them, that will simply evolve into national and international institutions that will be compared with other first-rate colleges and universities, regardless of their historic origin. The distinguishing feature of the institutions in this group will be that we are historically, traditionally, and probably will remain overwhelmingly African American in enrollment, but not exclusively. In that regard, I do not see for Morehouse or for other institutions like us a major change in the twenty-first century. Our ongoing relevance or importance will be clearly answered by our success.

Having made these distinctions, I will say that, generally, historically black colleges and universities face the same challenges that most other colleges and universities face, and those include maintaining academic excellence, competing for the best students, and building a sound and stable financial base. In addition to these basic challenges, HBCUs face the additional challenge of preserving the best features of their heritage and mission, while not becoming mired in the past. Historically black institutions cannot assume that their tradition, historic heritage, and mission will allow them to be successful in the future. They must be willing to adapt to the changing environment of higher education in the twenty-first century.

Mission Is Critical

Some people in the higher education community seem to hold the view that there is a conflict between academic excellence and institutional heritage. They argue that because an institution's primary clientele is students from a particular, minority community this limits the excellence that institution can achieve. I do not subscribe to that notion. In my view, there is no real conflict between excellence and heritage, but I do believe that one has to be careful in the language used in articulating how to achieve this balance, because the two can *appear* to conflict. That is why HBCUs must carefully choose what their missions are and try to speak to obtaining those missions, but not try to be everything to everyone.

As president of Morehouse, I inherited a very clear mission. My predecessors, particularly, Dr. Benjamin E. Mays, had a strong commitment to producing leaders for society. Coupled with the notion of leadership was a strong commitment to service, to giving back to the community. And always, these commitments were carried out in the context of academic excellence.

With this mission in mind, Dr. Mays moved Morehouse from being a very good southern institution to being an outstanding national institution. He was adamant that Morehouse would be able to compete favorably with other institutions with a strong academic standing. Over the years, Morehouse has followed Dr. Mays' mission and worked to maintain his legacy. In fact, my vision for Morehouse in the twenty-first century is quite similar to his— that is, that Morehouse will be one of the very finest, undergraduate liberal arts colleges in the nation — period — and the college of choice for African American men.

The Challenge of Diversity

Having clearly defined their missions, one of the first concerns of all institutions— including HBCUs— is the issue of diversity. I think the efforts to diversify American campuses generally are good, quite noteworthy, in fact. Most institutions now recognize the educational value of students encountering others of different backgrounds, cultures, and races. The study the University of Michigan developed in preparation for its defense of its affirmative action program demonstrated this quite strongly. The end result of diversity at the college level should be an improved educational experience, because that is what colleges are about, first and foremost. But in the long run, one would also hope the end result of diversity on college campuses would be a less prejudiced and discriminatory society.

At Morehouse, we give careful consideration to the question of institutional diversity as part of our strategic planning process: Exactly what does diversity means at a historically black, still predominantly black, all-male institution? Our answer is to approach diversity from the point of view of Roosevelt Thomas, a management consultant who has written a number of books on the subject. Thomas argues that while looking at diversity in any corporation, institution or society, one has to move beyond the obvious framings of diversity, such as race, gender, and ethnicity, and also look at what diversity means at an *individual* level.

When they come to Morehouse, the majority of our students have been educated in predominantly white institutions all their lives. For these young men, the experience of four years at a predominantly black institution is not the same as for white students who have been in a predominantly white environment all of their lives and go to a predominantly white institution where they encounter people of color. So, we tell our students that while they may look at their fellow Morehouse students and see all men and mostly African Americans, they should also try to see the diversity that exists beyond those classifications. The fact is that our students come from all over the nation, and all over the world. Our students come from different cultural backgrounds, different religions, different economic and social class strata, and so forth. We challenge our students to learn to recognize and appreciate the diversity within others, a distinction we hope they will carry on to the larger world.

Speaking of the larger world, we also recognize that we need to give our students a more global educational experience, so we have strategies for achieving diversity in that way. For example, we have a number of international students, and we are recruiting more broadly than we have in the past in places where there are large numbers of students of African descent. We also provide students with opportunities to live and study abroad in all parts of the world. The other way we achieve diversity is not through direct recruiting per se, but by being the kind of institution that is attractive to all students. So, we are getting more applications from non-black and non–American students because they simply see Morehouse as a good institution and many of them want to have the experience of not being in the majority for once in their lives.

The Liberal Arts Curriculum

As I said earlier, different historically black colleges and universities will pursue different missions, and those different missions will call for different approaches to curriculum development. Large state universities like Florida A&M, for example, will have a very different curriculum from institutions like Tugaloo College.

For Morehouse and other liberal arts colleges, the challenge is how to preserve the commitment to a liberal education at a time when there is so much emphasis on professionalism. This is a particular concern for historically black colleges, but also for most schools that have many first-generation college students, or students who come from low-income backgrounds. In those situations, parents and students have as their goal for an education to find a career and a job. So, sometimes they see a commitment to a liberal education, for which you are required to take courses that do not seem relevant to a particular job, as not particularly meaningful.

At Morehouse, we have a strong commitment to remaining a liberal arts college. All of our students, regardless of their major, must take courses from our core curriculum, which provides them with an introduction and immersion into the traditional liberal arts disciplines: religion, philosophy, science, mathematics, history, foreign languages, and the social sciences. We do not offer online degree programs at Morehouse College and, except as supplements to our on-campus offerings, we have no plans to do so. We feel very strongly that having a residential experience on or near the campus is very important for the kind of liberal arts education we want to provide.

Retaining Good Students

In the area of student retention, counseling and advising is the greatest challenge confronting historically black colleges and universities. Economics is an equally critical factor. At most HBCUs, the income level of the majority of students is such that it is very challenging for them to complete their education without working, or without taking out excessive loans. And this begins to affect their class performance.

In every study we have done at Morehouse, we have found that the primary cause for student attrition is financial. So, we are trying to work with students and their parents to plan financially for four or five years. We also counsel them on taking the right courses in the right sequence so that they can graduate in four, or at least five, years. And we advise them on how to balance the work experience, if they must work, with the college experience so that they do not wind up in their third year or so and realize they will have to stay around longer than they can afford to because they have not taken the right courses, or their loans have maxed out. It really is a matter of working very closely with the students and counseling them on how to plan their academic careers.

Effective counseling is also critical to ensuring that HBCUs can increase the number of African American students going on to graduate and professional programs. Institutions must make students aware, very early in their college careers, what will be required to go to graduate school. They need programs, including training, counseling and coaching, to help students prepare to take the various exams: the Graduate Record Exam, the Law School Admission Test, and the Medical College Admission Test. And, they need enough people either on the faculty or visiting to give lectures about what it is like to be a member of a given profession.

Along with retention, we, at Morehouse, also place great emphasis on preparing our students for graduate and professional training. The largest number of our majors is in the division of science and mathematics, the second largest is in business and economics, and then the social sciences and humanities. Morehouse still sends more African American males to medical school than any other college, and a significant number of our graduates go on to graduate school in the sciences. In 2003, we were recognized by the *Wall Street Journal* as one of the nation's top 30 feeder schools for sending students to leading law, business and medical school programs.

Faculty Development

All HBCUs face important concerns regarding faculty, perhaps the most important of which is competing in the open market to hire and retain them. To attract the best faculty, institutions have to pay competitive salaries. There is no particular market for good faculty for historically black institutions, although Morehouse, and I am sure many other HBCUs, are able to attract a significant number of alumni who want to come back to teach out of a sense of loyalty and commitment.

We attract outstanding faculty to Morehouse by paying competitive salaries and providing professional development support —funds either for release time to do research and scholarship, or to take sabbaticals or short time off for visits at other institutions. We also support our faculty in seeking external scholarships and fellowships, such as the Fulbright and others. And we have offices that assist faculty in obtaining research and scholarship grants.

If a college or university is not able to pay competitive salaries, then that institution must try to seek out individuals who have a commitment to the kinds of institutions that historically black colleges are. Quite often, that recruitment is done through networks rather than advertising in standard journals. Alumni are very important in this regard in identifying individuals and helping to recruit them, and inviting them to campus to give talks and lectures so that they can see the kind of experience they would have as a member of the faculty. We want faculty who will enjoy being a part of the Morehouse community.

Information Technology

In addition to diversity, and student and faculty recruitment and retention, information technology infrastructure is a critical area of concern for historically black colleges and universities in the twenty-first century. One has to give it a very high priority — not just in technology in the classroom, but also in the administration of the institution, including registration and class management. Students expect it, the faculty expect it, and technology does make an institution much more productive, so it has to be a very high priority.

I advise being selective in one's investments in information technology. One of the big mistakes that some schools have made is to try to invest broadly in all aspects of technology. The problem is, the technology changes so fast that an institution can become trapped in equipment and software that is obsolete. Being selective means asking the right strategic questions. The key is to focus on the one or two things that are most important for an institution's mission and the kind of students it has, and to invest in those areas.

Over the past eight years, Morehouse has invested a great deal in technology enhancement. Our campus is completely wired with high-speed fiber optic networks, and we also have a wireless environment. In addition, we have invested a great deal in computer equipment for classrooms and availability in the dormitories. Not only have we spent money on the technology, but also on training, which is perhaps as important as the infrastructure itself.

Institutional Advancement

Fundraising and development is another major challenge facing historically black colleges and universities. There actually are two different kinds of challenges in this regard — one internal, the other external and historic. The internal challenge is resources — the need to spend and invest the appropriate amount of money to achieve results. Most HBCUs have not had the resources to have a professional, fully staffed development office, nor the technology that is required to operate one. The external challenge is to position the institution as one in which donors and supporters want to invest because they see it as an important contributor to society, as opposed to a charity to which they give a handout. When people give on the basis of charity, even to institutions deserving of support, they give small amounts of money. But when they see an institution as an investment, they are more likely to give larger amounts of money.

In this regard, Morehouse fares well in comparison to small, liberal arts colleges, primarily because we are more national than most small, liberal arts colleges, meaning that our student body is much more national, our alumni more national, and much of our sources of support comes from large cities such as New York, Chicago and Los Angeles. We belong to the Associated Colleges of the South, which is a group of about 19 very good, southern liberal arts colleges, including Davidson, the University of Richmond, Furman, and Rhodes. Morehouse and Spelman are the only historically black college members and, as I said, Morehouse competes fairly well for fundraising when compared to this group. Where we do not compare as well is with fundraising among our alumni.

Morehouse is in the middle of a capital campaign. We have invested more resources into our professional development offices so that we can make contact with our alumni, both in person through the Internet and other ways. We also have more events where we bring alumni back to campus, and we hold more events around the country where we take the show on the road, so to speak, to them. Generally, we are developing more sophisticated methods of identifying alumni who have the resources to contribute generously. It is not a very difficult problem to address in terms of what needs to be done; it is a matter of having the organization in place and the resources to support it, to implement the strategies we put in place.

At Morehouse, we also do fairly well with corporate fundraising. Until recently, we had not adequately tapped government resources, but we now have hired a lobbyist in Washington — a strategy used by most of the successful schools. We also have a very active office that alerts faculty to opportunities to apply for grants and assists them in grant writing.

HBCUs can also obtain resources by forming partnerships with other institutions — including other historically black colleges and minority-serving institutions, as well as traditionally white institutions. At Morehouse, we have an almost 25-year relationship with Georgia Tech through a 3–2 program in engineering. Of course, we are members of the United Negro College Fund and several other consortia. The benefits of these partnerships are immense. We share programs or resources, but perhaps the most direct benefit is learning from the other institutions by sharing information and experiences.

The Service Tradition

Service is an important part of the mission and tradition of all colleges, especially historically black colleges and universities, and I believe it is a tradition we should continue. Students learn a great deal from working in the community or working on various service-related activities, both from a perspective of personal growth, as well as academic interest. In fact, the experiential aspect of service can actually help students be more successful in their academic pursuits.

At Morehouse, we have a number of ways we do this. We have informal activities where students are encouraged to work in neighborhood organizations, but we also have a college-wide community service office that coordinates our community service and service learning programs. In addition, we belong to national organizations such as Campus Compact.

Bright Future for Morehouse

From my perspective, the future of Morehouse College is very bright and will continue to be so through the twenty-first century. As I have said, my vision is that Morehouse will be among the finest undergraduate, liberal arts colleges in the nation — period — and the college of choice of African American men.

We already are the college of choice; we have achieved that. To achieve our goal of being one of the finest liberal arts colleges, we have a five- to ten-year plan that includes measurements and assessments of how we compare to institutions against which we benchmark ourselves in everything from retention, to placement of students in graduate schools, to the quality of faculty. So, we have a fairly clear strategy and plan to move us to where we want to be — one of the nation's very best liberal arts colleges with a particular history in the black experience, like any other school has its own particular history and experience. That is our goal.

My vision for Morehouse's future is based in no small part on my experience of its past — of what I remember the school was and what it meant to me as a student. I was admitted to Morehouse on an early admission scholarship that was awarded as a result of a nationwide examination that was given to 10th graders. I came simply based on the fact that the school had recruited me out of 10th grade and I could attend on a scholarship. That was in the mid–1950s, and Morehouse was much smaller, maybe a fifth of the size it is now, with about 600 students. The College was in a segregated, black community on the southwest side of Atlanta. The campus was surrounded by a thriving economic community, with black-owned businesses, barbershops, drug stores, and theaters. It was very similar to my hometown, Hattiesburg, Mississippi, in the sense that the faculty lived in the neighborhood and were part of the community, so they had influence way beyond the classroom.

Like many of the historically black colleges then and now, although the student body was all or mostly African American, the faculty was very mixed, so our role models were not all black. One of the two professors who really inspired me was my physics teacher, Dr. Sabinus H. Christiansen, a white gentleman who came down from the North to teach, as many did. The other was Dr. Henry McBay, an African American, who taught me chemistry. Beyond our professors, we were also exposed to national and international speakers who would give lectures at campus-wide assemblies, or what we called Chapel. We heard politicians, heads of foundations, heads of state, even sports figures.

Of course, Dr. Mays was a source of inspiration for all of us, and probably the most memorable chapels were the ones he presented himself. I did not have a personal relationship with Dr. Mays, but he set the tone for the faculty's message to the students, which was: You can do whatever you are inspired to do if you work at it. We were also told that Morehouse would hold us to very high standards, even higher than those we would be held to in the non–African American world. We were told we had to be better than everybody else, and that, as Morehouse men, that is what we had to strive for.

These messages—about the value of community, setting and achieving high academic and personal standards, the importance of role models—were delivered to us in various ways throughout my entire time as a student at Morehouse, and they are the same messages we deliver to our students today. Benjamin Mays believed, and so do I, that historically black institutions can maintain their culture and heritage, predominant flavor and vision and also be excellent institutions.

I hope that historically black colleges and universities will be able to achieve this goal, that we would be able to say that there are historically black institutions—and that Morehouse is one of them — that can compete effectively with any other school in the nation of similar size and character, and that this question of the relevance of historically black institutions would be so ridiculous to ask it won't be posed. Through my efforts at Morehouse, I hope I will be seen as playing some role in helping to bring this about.

3

NORMAN C. FRANCIS

President, Xavier University of Louisiana

Dr. Norman C. Francis is the president of Xavier University of Louisiana. Francis holds the distinction of being the longest sitting university president in the United States. In 1968 when St. Katharine's Sisters of the Blessed Sacrament handed over governance of the only historically black Catholic university in the western hemisphere to Francis, he became the first lay person and the first African American to head the institution considered the crown jewel of the Sisters work in the field of education.

Francis has a relationship with Xavier that extends more than four decades. In 1952, he graduated from Xavier on scholarship, and he served as an administrator at Xavier for ten years before being named president. In 1955 Francis was the first African American to graduate from the Loyola University Law School.

Under the able leadership of Francis, Xavier University has grown from an "outstanding" institution that the "world didn't know" to an excellent institution that is consistently held up as a national model of success in higher education. Indicative of the major growth and expansion spearheaded by Francis, Xavier has more than doubled its enrollment, broadened its curriculum, expanded its campus and physical facilities, and strengthened its financial base.

All of this growth has been built on a foundation of academic excellence. Year after year Xavier University receives national recognition as a leader in minority education. Xavier ranks first nationally in the number *of African American students earning undergraduate degrees in the biological and life sciences and physics. Xavier has been especially successful in educating health professionals. The College of Pharmacy ranks first in the nation in the number of Doctor of Pharmacy degrees awarded to African Americans, and the school is credited with educating nearly 25 percent of the African American pharmacists practicing in the United States. In premedical education, Xavier places more African American students into medical school than any other college or university in the nation. And 92 percent of those who enter medical school complete their degree programs.*

In addition to his distinguished role in minority education, Francis is a noted leader in the wider world of American higher education. He has served as chair of the board of the Educational Testing Service, the Carnegie Foundation for the Advancement of Teaching, the Southern Education Foundation, the Southern Association of Colleges and Schools, and the American Association of Higher Education. Francis is the recipient of 28 honorary degrees — most recently from Harvard University and Dartmouth College — and 16 major awards.

I started in higher education administration in 1957. That now covers roughly 48 years in higher education. I became president of Xavier in July 1968, and had ten prior years of experience, serving in several administrative positions. My views are in the context of both black higher education and higher education, in general, because of my service in major higher education organizations. I served as chairman and a board member of the College Entrance Examination Board from 1972 to 1980 and with the Educational Testing Service in Princeton for almost 12 years. I served as chair of the Southern Association of Colleges and Schools, and chaired the Executive Council of the Commission on Higher Education, the body

Norman C. Francis (courtesy Xavier University; photograph by Irving Johnson III).

responsible for decisions for approval for accreditation. And then I chaired the entire board of the accreditation agency that covered elementary, secondary, and higher education.

Those experiences brought me into the heart of higher education. I worked with people who represented every southern college and university. I saw higher education in these respective roles as closely as one could ever see. My day-to-day world was the HBCU community, so I could juxtapose the challenges that I was facing as a historically black university president against those that were being faced in higher education in general. There obviously were differences. One of the major differences was related to resources, in terms of availability of resources for the historically black colleges and universities in those early days. However, that condition still continues today. Although there have indeed been some improvements, they have not been nearly sufficient for the HBCU contributions to this nation.

HBCUs at the Crossroads: Changes and Transformations of the 1960s

When I started in higher education administration there were professions that were closed to African Americans, closed by virtue of prejudices and discrimination, company policy, even national mores. By and large, prior to my tenure, there was a saying that African Americans populated the healing, the teaching, and preaching professions. We served in the medical, dental and other health professions, the teaching industry, and, of course, the ministry. And with few exceptions, those were the predominant roles. Obviously we did have social workers in the field, but not to the extent that we probably should have had or have now. So when I make the healing, teaching, preaching statement, I am talking about those were the important professions of college choice that African Americans viewed as paying jobs to raise a family.

There was a monumental shift in the 1960s when President John F. Kennedy issued his Executive Order 10925, which mandated that federal agencies should start recruiting African Americans in disciplines that the federal government used and needed. That included everything from business graduates to the social scientists. Any field or discipline that the federal government needed, his order was that the agencies should start hiring African Americans in those areas.

Every major cabinet member was now being mandated to be

affirmative and recruiters in the federal agencies started coming in greater numbers to black colleges. I remember it as clear as day how the IRS and other agencies started coming to hire and recruit young people at Xavier. To the recruiters' educational enlightenment, we had people graduating in business, in pharmacy, in arts and humanities, in the social sciences, and in natural sciences.

There were recruiting fairs developed. One of Xavier's strategies for increasing our enrollment in these disciplines was to publicize in the local black newspapers the pictures of Xavier students who graduated and received an offer from the federal government. We also sent this information out to their respective high schools. The strategy obviously was that we would be sending the message to our communities that these fields are now open, go to school, get educated in these fields, and you will at least have federal employment. At the same time, the President dictated that contractors dealing with the federal government had to do the same due diligence in looking for African Americans. So the first wave of recruiters, generally, were federal recruiters and they were followed by the government contractors, and the jobs started to open.

Major shifts then started taking place. One shift was that females who were formerly going automatically into teaching started going into these new careers, and I am talking, particularly, about African American females. The teaching side numbers started to drop. Some of the parsity that one reads about with regard to the representation of African Americans in the teaching field comes from a combination of things. I remember at one time black teachers represented maybe as many as 15 percent of the teaching force in America, and it has dropped to almost eight percent. The combination was you had black teachers retiring, and you had fewer teachers coming in. So you had the double losses from retirement and lack of new teachers, particularly African American females who were the predominant force in teaching were now going into other careers. The same phenomena applied to males, as well, but the numbers were certainly higher on the female side. Therefore the impact was a shift of economic opportunities for African Americans, and we saw a great challenge to the historically black college to increase its coverage of disciplines that were needed in the work force.

For many of us, and for Xavier I know this is true, we made sure that we participated in the collaborations that were encouraged by President Lyndon B. Johnson, Kennedy's successor. Johnson started a plan for progress where black colleges had initiatives called "cluster" programs where both government and business assisted us in understanding the requirements for some of the new opportunities for African Americans. Business departments started to flourish, as did the social sciences. Young people started going on to law school for private practice, and for careers in business, as well as in government. Corporate law practice was much behind government opportunities. It was a blooming of a new day, not only for African American students, but for black colleges as well in the late 1960s and into the 70s and 80s. It put major challenges on black colleges to keep up with their curricular changes and their recruitment of teachers who would come for the salaries that were available. At the same time the black college did not give up its basic mission to educate African Americans for these leadership opportunities. There was a heritage that was maintained, and there was nothing inconsistent about that. White students were certainly welcome, if they chose to come, but even if they did not come, the need for educating African Americans was as great, if not greater than at any other time in our history.

So the period from the 1960s to the 1980s witnessed this transition when opportunities were available to students and we were recruiting students for those opportunities. But let me point out a very significant component of the access part. The opportunity to receive federal financial aid resources was totally critical. Grants, work-study, and loans from the federal side were important factors for black students getting into school and being retained. Financial aid continues to be critical today for black students. I said it 30 years ago and I will say it now, if federal financial assistance as we know it and have known it were cut out, 70 percent of black colleges would fold and thereby could not serve the nation's "common good and general welfare." Financial aid for students to enter school, and to pay their bills are important for the nation and productive leaders represented by African Americans of the future.

Black colleges, understandably, had to increase their meager tuition to assure quality services because the comparative costs to go to a black college, especially a private black college, was substantially lower than for a majority of private colleges. To be competitive, therefore, the black colleges had to offer better salaries, add new curricular, facilities, and equipment to sustain our mission. However, when one raises tuition, without having available financial aid, students were adversely affected. I only make the point that financial aid is probably the highest and the number one priority for black colleges. It was then and is still now even when our tuition remains low. We have served the national interest for increasing what we call the economic development and leadership status of African

Americans for greater, percentage wise, than all other institutions in this country for the past 150 plus years. In the last century we responded to the curricular needs for jobs that were now open and financial aid was made available. I saw that transition, and I witnessed the growth of the enrollments in black colleges and I can say to you as of today, that potential for even further growth is on our doorsteps. We are seeing the number of black students choosing black colleges in outstanding numbers, with the continuing and equal need for financial aid.

HBCUs: Pioneers of Higher Education Access and Opportunity

America would not have had the professional cadre of African Americans that it has today and has enjoyed over these many years had it not been for black colleges. In the past 25 years black colleges have represented three percent of the total number of higher education institutions in this nation, that is three percent of the universe of colleges in the country, and yet in the early years we produced 50 to 55 percent of all blacks who received undergraduate degrees in America. We were carrying the major role of educating in the undergraduate service of African Americans for this country. In fact, the phrase that the nation is using, which I find is very appropriate, is also an accurate phrase to describe the historical role HBCUs played in higher education: Leave No Child Behind.

HBCUs were the carriers of that professional cadre of black people. Seventy-five percent of the African Americans who were officers in the military were graduates of black colleges; almost 60 percent of those who got PhDs were graduates of black colleges. Today, of course, the percent of our comparative numbers have dropped but they are still significant. We have three percent of the population but we are still producing roughly 30 percent of all blacks with undergraduate degrees in this country. Of the top 20 institutions producing African Americans who go on for PhDs, 12 of the top 20 institutions are black colleges. We are major producers. The latest 2004 numbers on the productivity of African Americans who receive undergraduate degrees in certain disciplines reveals the disproportionate contribution some of us are making against the general numbers. I will use Xavier as an example.

We have roughly 3,000 students at Xavier in the Arts and Sciences. Sixty-two percent major in the natural sciences. Forty-seven percent of all majors in our entire graduating class go on to graduate and professional schools.

Here is an interesting statistic. Of the top 100 colleges in the country, black or white, producing African Americans in the biological sciences, Xavier is number one. And in the physical sciences Xavier is number one. We are the number one producer of African Americans who are admitted to medical schools in the United States for the past 12 years. That number one statistic includes, as well, all colleges and universities in the country, including black colleges. We are number nine with African Americans who get degrees in psychology. We are the number one producer of African Americans who get degrees in physics. Those are startling numbers for a school of 3,000. I am only using my statistics to make the point that other historically black colleges, in other disciplines, whether in history, political science, mathematics, are in the top 100 of productivity of African Americans in universities. My point is to make the case that the presence of black colleges and universities in the United States today is as important as it was the day the first one was founded 150 years ago.

If one looks at any of the statistics where there is a need for diversity or presence of African Americans HBCUs are the major undergraduate producers. Witness the teaching profession in higher education. There are probably no more, on average, than five percent of all college and university faculty who are African Americans. And if you take out black colleges that number drops to three percent. Therefore, when you ask the question where are the African American faculty going to come from to populate college faculties of U.S. institutions, the answer is from universities that are producing PhDs for faculty teaching. Then you say, who are the producers at the undergraduate level of those getting the PhD degree? And then I come back to the point; 12 of the top 20 undergraduate producers are black colleges. The productivity is disproportionately coming from black colleges.

It is irresponsible to say that black colleges connote that whites are not wanted or are not welcome or an institution which is called a black college teaches only subjects that are black and it therefore, has no relationship to the world, in general. That is totally inaccurate in the sense that black colleges have always been colleges of higher education with curricular offerings across the board, teaching math, chemistry, biology, history, political science, business, etc. But what we do accomplish is to make certain to teach those subjects wherein blacks contributed to America and the world. The contributions of African Americans were presented to college students, where that was not the case necessarily in other institutions of higher education.

We showed that we cared because we built our curricular offerings as a pyramid, that is, we built a big base of academic support. We took students with potentially high achieving abilities that may not have been identified many times in their earlier educational experiences in high school. We brought those students to the full bloom of their capacity to the extent that once they graduated from us those universities seeking to diversify were looking to us to recruit our students for graduate studies. Many of those institutions would not have admitted these students as undergraduates.

What I faced in my earlier administrative years was: how do you justify a black college in an era where some were saying everything is fine and the playing field is equal? Nothing could be further from the truth! The playing field is not equal now, has not been over decades and continues to be unequal. Black colleges have made the major difference by educating young people who were the beneficiaries of poor earlier educational experiences and we brought into fruition their God given talents.

An HBCU for the Twenty-First Century

Being a historically black college in the twenty-first century means that we are obligated to offer the finest quality education, humanly possible, for entry into professions available for young people in this nation, without regard to race, creed, or color. Our institutional missions remain committed, especially supportive of African Americans, who need both an affirmative caring system and access to the quality education we offer. As long as the playing field is not equal, we are obligated to make sure that the access and opportunity for higher education is available for African Americans, and we are willing to and prepared to be judged by accountability measures of our students' competitiveness in the world of work and graduate and professional study.

We must continue to emphasize the heritage aspect of the mission. There is no reason not to, and particularly when we are open to anyone who wishes to come to receive the quality of education we offer. I will refer again to my personal experiences at Xavier.

When I became President in 1968 there where only two pharmacy schools in the state of Louisiana, and both were in New Orleans. One was at Xavier and one at Loyola University. When Loyola dropped its

College of Pharmacy, a state school in Monroe, in the upper part of the state, had just opened. It had not yet offered its first degree. You had now two pharmacy schools in Louisiana, one in the southern, and one in the northern part of the state. Xavier had the predominantly black college of pharmacy. The vast majority of white students went to Loyola. When Loyola closed those white students started looking to go to Monroe. Then within three years they started thinking, "Well wait a minute, Xavier has a college of pharmacy, its graduates are passing the licensure exam, and they are being hired." We started getting a trickle of white students. Today about 30 percent of our college of pharmacy enrollment is not black. Interestingly the other 70 percent of those students who are black make us still the number one producer of African Americans who get the Doctor of Pharmacy degree, the professional degree in pharmacy. My point is that people start to look past race when they see that what you have is as good as if not better than any other institution. We have proved that quality is universally recognized.

Xavier University: A National Leader in Higher Education Diversity

Roughly 95 percent of pharmacists in New Orleans— be they Asian, black, or white — are Xavier graduates, and the growing part of the population for Xavier in pharmacy is Asian. When one talks about diversity, we are more diverse than perhaps any other college or university in the country. Our professional staff, inclusive of administrators and faculty, is 50/50. You could not find a more diverse faculty in the United States. The absolute teaching faculty is probably 53 percent white and 47 percent black, but roughly 80 percent of our professional administrators are black.

Xavier is also a unique institution in that it is the only historically black catholic college in the United States. That particular aspect of our heritage undergirds our vision in the twenty-first century in the sense that our mission is to create "a more just and humane society." When in fact you offer a quality education, and do so with an ethical and religious commitment to humanity, you can serve people for who they are and not simply the color of their skin or their race or their creed. There is no inconsistency in being committed to what we call a black heritage and at the same time a Catholic religious foundation. For example, as is the case of many Catholic high schools and elementary schools in urban areas, the predominant religious faiths of students at Xavier is not Catholic. We have a diversity of young people, both in race and religion. The Judeo-Christian beliefs are part of the Catholic tradition, as well as parts of many other Protestant religious denominations: belief in God and the ultimate respect for humanity as the reflections of their Creator.

I think every institution has an obligation, an particularly in this current economic environment and society where race and color still matters, to reach out to recruit people of different backgrounds. Institutional curricular approaches should reflect appreciation of those cultures and racial backgrounds. Once you recruit students of diverse backgrounds there has to be a welcoming environment and a respectful environment so that those persons can fulfill their careers as an undergraduate or graduate student. Many colleges that are trying to diversify have struggled with that responsibility because inside the hearts of those institutions you have some faculty and students who believe that if you are of a different race, for example, that somehow you are not capable of doing the work at that institution and you are there only because of your race. This is another form of racism and ignorance. Some of these attitudes have benefited black colleges. We have some of the brightest students who could be anywhere they want to be but they are choosing black colleges.

There has to be an affirmative approach to diversifying campuses, and I am obviously a strong believer in affirmative action. I believe that people ought to be sought after just as we seek out people with talents of all kinds. I think race is still a factor and will continue to be for a while, and that is how we will have to diversify. And leadership is going to have to come from the total institution, as it must, also come from the board, the president, the faculty, and all professionals who are administrators in the institution.

Institutional Advancement: A Major Priority

We are doing better in fundraising but we are nowhere near where we ought to be. We are certainly doing much better than when I came into this business. The greatest challenge is having the personnel to do all the things that predominantly white schools have been able to do over the years in fundraising. The recent major grant from the Kresge Foundation to support increasing our fundraising capacity has been magnificent. We doubled our staff and are able now to make the cases for a new audience, major givers. It has always been difficult to get to those donors. That is a major challenge for presidents of historically black colleges, and certainly for us in identifying private donors.

Secondly, the challenge also is that we have to convince many corporations, some foundations, but not all, about our value to America. It is in everybody's best interest to produce young people who will become producers of economic wealth and productive citizens and taxpayers. A very key component of this fundraising side is that we in black colleges must be able, not only to show, but we must be able to produce, in a focused way, young people who are justifiably capable of doing anything that is needed of them in the workforce.

Each of us has strengths and we ought to be enhancing those strengths so that each of us, when put together, will show the productivity across the board. We cannot be everything to every student. We are known for our sciences. Roughly 65 percent of students at Xavier major in the natural sciences, and that is a high number. We have 1,100 biology majors. We have more black biology majors at Xavier than five of the major eastern institutions, put together, in this country. So we are known for the sciences. Do we do other things? Absolutely, but 65 percent of our young people major in the natural sciences. And it happens to be now that this area of the natural sciences is one of those key disciplines that America needs today. The economy is looking for computer scientists, for biologists, for chemists and so on.

Four years ago the University of Maryland got a lot of attention because it produced three black females who received PhDs in Mathematics. If you look at the history of producing a black female with a PhD in mathematics; some years none, some years one, maybe two, and then comes three out of one school. One of those three was a Xavierite. And behind her is another Xavierite, black female, who will have a PhD in Mathematics. Our focus in the sciences is a distinction and so we have a great case to make to America. Invest in the future by investing in historically black colleges.

Two years ago we were one of six schools to receive, out of a pool of 66 schools competing, funds from the Kresge Foundation to increase the number of professionals in our Institutional Advancement department. For the first 30 years of my administration I had a development director who was excellent. He was with us for 30 years. We had one public relations officer. We had three professionals in development at the most. The Kresge grant allowed us to more than double our staff so that now we have 14 professionals in development and public relations for the last four years.

We are now in a capital campaign, and about the business of raising

$100 million. We raised $25 million in the first phase and built the science annex building to accommodate growth. We are in the $75 million phase now and we are doing well.

Reaching Out to the Local Community

Service is a major component of the mission of Xavier University. We have an untold number of students who volunteer in services to this community. I recently left a community meeting and a lady who works in the toughest project in New Orleans asked to talk to me. She has been volunteering at a school for years; she is a grandmother who volunteers. She said: "Mr. President, I hope you will continue to send those 20 Xavier volunteers to our school. They are doing a marvelous job."

We have a coordinator for service in the community for our students. In addition, we have a partnership with Tulane called the National Urban Center were we work in housing projects for the tutoring of students, and for helping people get jobs. We also have a neighborhood community development corporation (CDC) called Xavier Triangle. It helps with building and renovating houses. We have a heavy service community contribution concept at Xavier.

The Future: HBCUs and America

I believe fundamentally, and it can be documented, that America continues to need minorities, and particularly African Americans in a number of key career areas. I would say across the board, but certainly in a number of key areas in America's best interest. Number two, race and color still matter in America, and because that is so America's historically black colleges and universities are going to continue to carry the disproportionate role of educating African Americans in this country. We recognize that many of the high schools and elementary schools from whence these youngsters are coming have not educated them to the degree of their talents. They need extra attention and assistance. We have served this mission for over 150 years. Ironically these efforts are as critical, in the twenty-first century, as it has ever been. The challenge continues to be for us to get America to invest in what we do so we can continue to offer the quality that is expected. We are not asking for any diminution of the requirements. We will meet the accountability standards. We have done so in the past and will continue to do so.

We must all be guided by the admonition regarding potential talent and fortitude to develop it: "not every flower blossoms on the first day of spring, some need more rain, more sunshine, and more loving care." The young people who now populate our justice system and legislative halls; who are in operating rooms; who are in military leadership roles; and who are working in social services areas; who teach and research, all serve the quality of life in America. There are many more who are hoping to do the same.

4

CAROLYNN REID-WALLACE

Former United States Assistant Secretary
for Post-Secondary Education

Former President, Fisk University

Dr. Carolynn Reid-Wallace has had a long and storied career in higher education as a teacher, scholar, academic administrator, and policy maker. From 1991 to 1993 Reid-Wallace served as the Assistant Secretary for Post-Secondary Education at the United States Department of Education. In that position, she was the nation's chief officer for higher education, post-secondary policy, and student aid. She served as the thirteenth president of her alma mater, Fisk University, in Nashville, Tennessee, from 2001 to 2003 and was the first female president in Fisk's more than 137-year history. Prior to her tenure at Fisk she provided leadership to a number of institutions including serving as senior vice president for education and programming at the Corporation for Public Broadcasting, vice chancellor for academic affairs of the City University of New York, director of Pre-collegiate Education and assistant director of the Division of Education Programs at the National Endowment for the Humanities, and dean of the college and vice president for academic affairs and acting chief executive officer at Bowie State University. As committed to teaching as she is to administration, Reid-Wallace has taught and mentored students at Bowie State University, Talladega College, Grinnell College, Howard University, and the University of New York. She received her master's degree in dramatic literature from Adelphi University and a doctoral degree in English and American literature from George Washington University.

Fisk University is a tradition-rich institution. It was founded in 1866, and in 1930 became the first black higher education institution to gain full accreditation by the Southern Association of Colleges and Schools. In 1952 it became the first historically black college to obtain a chapter of Phi Beta Kappa. Some of Fisk's notable graduates include W.E.B. Du Bois, Aaron Douglas, James Weldon Johnson, John Hope Franklin, and Nikki Giovanni. During her leadership of Fisk University Reid-Wallace declared as her central mission the goal of positioning the institution within the emerging global context for higher education. She revitalized Fisk's liberal arts curriculum, reinvigorated critical curricular complements such as the college's Race Relation's Institute, hired significant numbers of new faculties, attracted new donors, and engineered innovative partnerships with Vanderbilt and other major research universities. Additionally, she worked to diversify Fisk at all levels, with particular emphasis on building a more "internationalist" student body. She frequently spoke of recruiting Hispanic students, students from Asia, Africa, the Caribbean, and white American students. Fisk University, she often stated, must become "a laboratory of democracy."

Carolynn Reid-Wallace (courtesy Carolynn Reid-Wallace).

The question that this study proposes is a question that has occupied an extraordinary degree of our time at Fisk during my administration, which has been the last 12 months. I have insisted that we grapple with the question, "What does it mean to be a historically black institution in the new millennium?" And from my judgment it does not mean what it meant in the nineteenth and twentieth centuries. Being a historically black institution in the twenty-first century, I believe, means being a school that has a very clear understanding of its origins, why it was established in the very beginning, and having an understanding of its contributions and its measurable outcomes as a result of the need to have those institutions. That is the historical part of it. But in the twenty-first century, these schools cannot, nor should they, be what they were in the beginning: a haven for blacks who had absolutely no entrée into the larger society. Because the universe has changed black people now have an opportunity to matriculate at a variety of institutions across the country and even if they do not get in, legally, constitutionally it is not supposed to be because of color. Wherein the beginning, no matter how bright we were we simply could not defy the laws of the state and the laws of the nation, which basically said "separate but equal," which we all knew not to be true. Separate but equal meant you go to your black school and you leave our white school to us. That has changed and as a consequence, what it means to be a historically black institution in the twenty-first century is not unlike what it means to be a majority white institution in the twenty-first century.

It means that you have to have a competitive curriculum. It means that you have to have a very strong faculty. It means that you have to look for a rich diversity of students. Those students should come from many different parts of the world; and so you are looking for international students from Europe. You are looking for them from Africa, from the Caribbean, from Asia, and from South America. You are looking for white students, which was not a part of the nineteenth and twentieth centuries. In the twenty-first century, for historically black institutions such as Fisk, Howard, Hampton, Spelman, or any school to survive, they must diversify. They have got to emphasize quality, and they must provide programs of study of the highest quality, which prepare students for intellectual and social leadership in a highly technological society, a highly pluralistic society and a multicultural world. You also have to be prepared to maintain a strong record of excellence in teaching to be, in my judgment, a twenty-first century historically black institution.

You have to encourage the creation of new knowledge through research and scholarly activities of faculty and your advanced students. One has to offer a well-planned program in the liberal arts tradition, which develops among its students a broad understanding of the basic principles and values of the arts and humanities and the natural sciences and social sciences. In short, being a historically black institution in the twenty-first century, in the United States of America, means that you have an intellectually rigorous curricula and a powerfully strong faculty. It means that you are as conversant with the broadest range of academic courses as any other school, and that you have those courses on your books and you have the facilities to support them. It means that you have technology. It basically means that you as a black institution have the right institutional values, the right mission statement, and the right goals.

And I happen to think that Fisk's mission statement is one of the best I have seen. I will quote it: "It is the mission of Fisk University to provide a liberal arts education of the highest quality. The ultimate goal is to prepare students to be skilled, resourceful, and imaginative leaders who will address effectively the challenges of life in a technological society, a pluralistic nation, and a multicultural world." And Fisk has, in the last 12 months reconfirmed its institutional values; and those values are quality, compassion, innovation, diversity, community outreach and service.

Diversity, as normally accepted, recognizes that you have a wide range of types and kinds within a setting. The long-term goal of focusing on diversity is to offer an extraordinarily wide range of people who are different in many ways but similar in many other ways, an opportunity to experience a first-rate education. And one hopes that the accomplishment of that objective will allow this community of people to go out into the world and be better citizens; more thoughtful, more reflective, more competent in both their disciplines and in the civic responsibilities and duties that they assume.

We have several strategies for achieving diversity at Fisk. One of them is to develop a really powerful distance learning technology system that will allow the institution to offer credit, non-credit, and degree programs across the country as well as the world. We have put a great deal of money into staffing up, so that we have some of the countries best theoreticians and technologists to begin to help faculty members make the transfer from the traditional classroom lecture materials to putting that material in an online format. We have just begun the process, but it is very clearly, as our strategic plan indicates, designed to allow us to stretch our arms into South Africa, to stretch our arms into Europe, and into Africa, the Caribbean, Asia and other parts of the world, and also to diversify through this technology in the United States and indeed our own state.

Another strategy that we have used to achieve greater diversity is in our recruitment efforts. We have made a very conscious decision that we have to find a way to bring to Fisk a larger number of Hispanic students.

It happens that in this city alone, that particular community of people has grown exponentially in the last five years. And large numbers of Hispanic students, if they finish high school, end up working at Kroger as baggers or working at McDonalds. We are working with the Hispanic community. One of the strategies is to engage the community. To the Hispanic community we say: Fisk University is not as large as Vanderbilt University, nor do we want to be. We are a small, first-rate liberal arts institution, and we have many things in common with your community. We have a good number of Hispanic professors on our staff; we have a good number of Hispanic artifacts in our library and in our galleries. We would welcome having your students, the best of your students, to come to our school to get a first-rate education. And to show you the good will that is behind that intent, I have said to the Hispanic community that I will accept, for this semester, as many students who are interested in taking computer technology courses. I will accept them into a specially designed program. We will teach in Spanish and in English, and we will offer the course for free, by way of showing the good will of this institution. And my phone is ringing off the hook with inquiries.

During the last semester, we went across this country speaking about Fisk to Hispanic communities of students, and to educators who are Hispanic. And I am very happy to report that we have in our dormitories now a few Hispanic students who, based on our recruitment efforts, have come to Fisk. And I run into the kids on campus and they seem perfectly happy. Well obviously in time, we expect the numbers to increase.

But it is not simply a matter of ethnicity or race, or geography, when I think of diversity. I think of diversity in the context of age. I know that there are a great many black women who dropped out of school after their sophomore year in college. They got married, they had children, and they raised their children. The kids are now off in college or are married, and they are wondering, what do I do with my life? And we are saying, we are looking for older, mature students who can come here and study for a degree. And we are going after that cohort as well. These are just a few examples of the kinds of strategies that we are using in an effort to accomplish the goal that we have established.

My experience as the president of a post-secondary institution has reinforced my deep-seated conviction that one effects change, that one can impact the larger community in a democratic society through education. I have always believed that education has the power to free the mind; education enables us to move past the theory and the conjecture into a practical and real-life field of experience. And I think education, the institution itself, is one of the most civil, and one of the most extraordinarily enriching opportunities afforded a human being to come to grips with life in terms of its differences, its challenges, and its complexities. You can do it in education. To give you one example: You can read an anthropological text and understand something about people who live in a society that is different from your own. And in the higher education community, or for that matter the post-secondary community, if you are really lucky, if you are in a diverse community, if you are in a cosmopolitan community, or even a provincial community that has diversity as a part of its overall mission, you can go from the anthropological text to having a roommate who is from that place. And that breaks down some of those stereotypes. Some people think that those who have a religion that is different from theirs, or who come from a certain part of the world, or for that matter, country, who are from a certain economic class, might be different. Well, in the educational arena, what you come to understand, through both theory and practice, is the power of information to transform your thinking. If your thinking has been transformed, then hopefully your practices and your attitudes will be enriched, enlightened, and enlarged.

Expanding Fundraising Capacity, Strengthening Academic Standards, and Improving Management of Financial and Human Resources Are Critical

It is clear to me that historically black institutions, like small struggling white institutions, have to find a way to get on a sound financial basis. I mean we have got to figure out a way to raise more money. Because if you do not have the money, all of the rhetoric in the world will not get you where you need to be. So one of the major priorities is to strengthen the institution's fundraising capabilities, and that has to be done in ways that are yet imagined. In fact, we are working on a couple of things. This priority is so great, and so it will require people to break down paradigms and to reconceptualize fundraising. To develop a more effective fundraising strategy is one of the largest, most pressing, most important priorities, I believe, facing historically black institutions.

Another priority that is important is to strengthen the university's academic standards, including its library resources. Black colleges have really suffered the brain drain with integration. Large numbers of people who would have come to work at historically black colleges do not consider these institutions. They are wooed away before they finish their PhDs. And they are working for more money, under better conditions in some cases, not always in others, at majority institutions. But we have got to find a way to strengthen our academic standards, and that includes finding the best and brightest faculty. But it also means doing things like turning our libraries into electronic libraries because this is a new age. And, while the book, from my own personal opinion, is still an extraordinarily important and I would say comforting resource to have at one's disposal, the truth of the matter is many students do not come to libraries because they are working through distance learning and they need to have access technologically. So we need to strengthen the university's academic standards, including its faculty and its library holdings.

Then, I would say that there is something that is almost too obvious to mention. But I think it is important. We must find a way to improve our management of financial and human resources. You know when these accrediting associations and these federal auditors come in and look at your books, you can lose your accreditation if your fiscal management is not sound. You can be put on sanction if your human resources records are not as they should be. Now the part that sounds too obvious is this: It looks as if we are not efficient fiscal managers. The truth of the matter is we are in so many cases very efficient. The problem is we just do not have enough hands to do all of the things that are required.

Priorities in the abstract mean nothing. What we have got to reckon with and understand clearly is that priorities only mean something if historically black colleges and universities are able to have the resources to do the things that are necessary. And that is why I led off with developing a more effective fundraising strategy. If you do not have the money, you cannot run a good financial human resources service. If you do not have the money you cannot strengthen the university's academic standards. That is the catch 22. And this is why, I think, black colleges will have to pool their resources and come together. For instance, and I am just hypothesizing now, let us say that I lived in a town where there were at least three historically black colleges that were private institutions in at least a 15-mile radius. I do not say they would have to merge, but I think it would be counter-productive for me to run courses when the other school might have those courses and faculty. I could send my students there on a shuttle bus to take those courses and then I could take students from their institution to study in areas where they do not have the faculty. So, in short, I am saying that one of the great challenges that I think we are going to have to come to grips with is finding a way to collaborate and to partner with sister institutions so that we can achieve cost savings, and instructional efficiencies that otherwise would not be available to us.

Institutional Goals: Recruit and Retain High Quality Faculty, Strengthen Communication System and Increase Student Enrollment

At Fisk we understand first and foremost that we are a national liberal arts institution; we are not a research institution. That basically means that our emphases are placed across the disciplines. I mean we really do look at the humanities, and we look very, very carefully at the natural sciences, and the social sciences. We think that well-educated people really do have to have a broad understanding of the basic principles and values in those disciplines. And I happen to believe in the interdisciplinary approach. I do not think that well-educated people are really well-educated people if they do not know the connection between the natural sciences and the humanities, and technology. Or if they do not understand that a great artist such as Picasso, or for that matter Romare Bearden, understood mathematics and anatomy. So being able to create curricula that engage students in the overarching connection of intellectual knowledge is something that I am passionate about, and it is where I put my emphases. And it is where I have, as an academic president, urged my faculty to focus their attention.

One of the big issues facing most small institutions, including historically black colleges and universities, is this whole business of money. How do you get the resources to retain and/or attract high-quality faculty? What do you do when you can barely meet payroll every month? When you are out there trying to increase your fundraising, and you get money but it is restricted money that allows you to use it for one thing but not another. What I have tried to do over the last year, and I have been here exactly 13 months now, is to find that way as we have gone about the business of recruiting new faculty. I am looking for what I call the young and the hungry. These are the young people who are fresh out of their graduate programs with PhDs but with very little teaching experience. But they have a strong commitment to historically black schools. They simply must, in order to come here. They must have really good academic training; they must have that PhD. They must have an understanding of the interdisciplinary knowledge that is out there.

I try to woo them. I have been saying, "Look, I know you are not going to stay with me forever, but if I can get you to come here for three years, and if I can give you a free townhouse that is safe and clean and fairly new, if I can pay you a small amount of money (when I say small, I am talking 40 to 45 thousand dollars), if I can give you an opportunity to go to at least two national conferences in your discipline, if I can assure you that the class size will not exceed 16 students, and seminars will be smaller could I attract you, could I interest you in coming?" I have done that to attract faculty and administrators. I have also looked for high-earning people who are making $140,000. And I have said, "Look, commit yourself to me and this institution for a relatively short period of time, three to five years, and have an opportunity to help transform a truly great university of the nineteenth and twentieth centuries into a remarkably powerful and great university of the twenty-first century." Some of these people have "bought in" because they liked the vision, and because they had enough money coming in to work for 60 or 65 thousand and still feel as if they were making a contribution. This is not an issue facing Carolynn Reid-Wallace exclusively. It is facing presidents of small schools and historically black institutions generally. It is a "small school challenge" to develop strategies that will bring to the campus first-rate scholars. By way of summarizing, I look for the very young, uninitiated, inexperienced, but brilliant scholars. And I look for the really brilliant older scholars in their 50s and early 60s, and maybe early 70s who have retired from really wonderful schools, and who are looking for another challenge. That is one of the things that I think has worked well for us, and is clearly one of the issues facing historically black college presidents: finding a way to get the faculty in place.

I emphasize to the faculty that this is a shared governance arrangement. You have to have shared governance. That is a basic principle of the academy. In the very beginning there were reasons why presidents had to be in the image of the president that Ralph Ellison describes in *Invisible Man*: dictatorial and authoritarian. There may have been some exigencies that made that necessary. But the truth of the matter is this is the twenty-first century, and the president has to do what a president is hired to do and faculty have the chief responsibility for deciding the curricula, for determining who teaches in those programs. And I basically tell my faculty: "I am not going to do your job because I have too much to do myself." This university has an extraordinary faculty. I have had such a good collegial relationship with them because we have our shoulders to the wheel and we are all working together, not separately. And I also believe that they believe it when I say this is a shared governance arrangement. We can be no stronger than our individual and collective inputs.

The other priority is finding a way to tell the story about what we are doing. Communications is a very big problem at our schools. We are doing some remarkable things but nobody knows about them. And because of that, I have decided that one of our priorities is to improve the university's communications system. The September 2002 issue of *Ebony* features a long pictorial essay about Fisk. We have been trying to strengthen the communication system. It is a challenge facing, not just my school, but also many other schools like Fisk.

The other priority is to increase student enrollment. We have got to increase the enrollment, and we have got to diversify the enrollment. You have to look for older students to put in the mix with the typical 17-year-old high school graduate. We have made a commitment that will be fulfilled. We are not there yet, but our commitment is, and I have said it to the faculty, I have said it to the students, I have said it to the board of trustees, and I will say it to the world — we must reached the disenfranchised. I am tired of young black men going on crack and going into prison. We, at Fisk, have made a commitment to go out into this community and we are going to addict them. We are going to sell them drugs, but the drugs will be called humanities and science; the drugs will be called arts and social sciences and natural sciences. We are going to sell them the "drug of education." And we are going to reach them before the guys on the streets reach them. And we are going to work with them at our expense. This is our investment in the city and in this country and in the people who look just like you and me, but who need somebody to reach out and touch them. When I became president of this school, I noticed the fences that separated Fisk from the community. I made them pull every single fence down. I said this is an open university. We are no different from the people out there but for the grace of God. Our job is to permeate those neighborhoods, to bring those kids onto this campus, whether they are seven or eight years old, and to nurture them and work with them until they become 16, and then we are going to have scholarships to bring them here as opposed to paying our taxes to send them to prison. Guess what? We have some of those little tikes now who come over and they knock on my door on Saturday saying, "I want to get in the computer room, you said we could go!" In turn, I say, "Wait a minute, I will take you over." We set up some things in order to begin to make this our way of reaching out and lifting up, and by so doing, strengthening both our own history and our nation.

The Challenge of Fundraising

With regard to alumni support, Fisk is above the average nationally. Statistics related to inadequate alumni support do not apply to this university. In 12 months, and we are still counting, but in 12 months we raised $18.4 million. $18.4 million from: alumni, from government contracts, and grants. An anonymous donor gave us $4 million that brought in $4 million in matching money from the United States government. Then a man whom we just recruited to our board of trustees promised to give us $2.5 million, and he is not an alumnus of Fisk. According to all of the statistics that I have looked at inadequate alumni support is a problem for a great many institutions. But in my own case, that is not our problem. What I will say is that alumni giving nationally is not as strong as it ought to be. Wherein at my university it is just extraordinary, and it has always been one of Fisk's great selling points. Why? If you talk to any people from Fisk's yesteryear they will tell you that this place was not just a university. I mean we married men from Fisk or from across the street at Meharry. We made best friends and were the godmothers of our roommate's children. This place was like a little world and so when people open their check books and they write checks to Fisk, they are not just writing a check to a university, they are writing a check to a place that was as much a part of their stability as let us say, your home was to your upbringing, or your local church was to your success. And that is, in my own judgment, the reason why we do not fall into that "below average" support cohort that you read about in some of the studies.

One thing I certainly say to presidents struggling with below average alumni support is to communicate regularly with your alumni. Let them know what is going on at the school. You can do it via the web; you can do it by just doing a front and back page one-pager that you send out. I have myself, just done something that was really very reinvigorating. I got on the road, and I went to at least 20 states where we have alumni associations, and I met with these people and I told them first-hand what was happening and allowed them to ask questions of me. Because it was so costly to do it when I did that, I also used that occasion to recruit. After I met with the alumni, they would have a luncheon or a dinner and maybe the next day bring a hundred students and their parents, for me to meet. So we did the communicating with alumni, but we used the alumni to help us reach out into their communities to bring prospective students to the occasion.

My biggest challenge is raising unrestricted money. We raised $18.4 million, but most of that money has been earmarked. It is restricted. It is saved for student scholarships or it is for construction. I need unrestricted money, as do most historically black college presidents; most presidents anywhere, need unrestricted money. And that money could be used to give raises to outstanding faculty; it could be used to send some of our brilliant professors in French literature off to Paris for the summer. We did it on a small scale. We identified seven meritorious professors and we gave them cash awards and public recognition. Now I am sure there were more than seven, but those selected were the cream of the crop. I am the kind of president who would like, in addition to giving that little bit of money, which was only $2,000 per person, to have that professor and his family go off to Martha's Vineyard for one week at our expense with a box of books with the goal of relaxing on the beach, and reading and thinking. When you come back you are intellectually reinvigorated. If you had that unrestricted money, you could do those extra things to give people a sense of community and appreciation.

As far as federal support for higher education is concerned, I know exactly what college presidents can do to increase their access to federal funds. I was an Assistant Secretary for Post-Secondary Education in the United States Department of Education. The first thing presidents have to do is to get out from behind their desks and come to Washington, and they have to meet with high-ranking people as well as middle-management people in government. Presidents have got to send letters to their congressmen and their senators. We hired a lobbyist in Washington, DC, because you have to have a physical presence in Washington, somebody advocating on your behalf every day. We have to do the same thing that the president of Harvard or the president of Yale or Dartmouth, or any other institution does. You have to be there. You have to be present; you have to write things and send them to these offices. Let them know what your new curricula plans are, let them know what is happening in your art gallery. And you have to do it every week. As I have said to my staff, doing it once a semester will not suffice. Every week your responsibility is to produce a well-written document. It does not have to be long, but something that you feed to Washington, DC, because that is how you stay on the radar screen. And at a certain point, you get their support. That is how it works. I had a multibillion dollar budget when I was an assistant secretary. And you know who got a lot of that money? The people, including some historically black college presidents, who were always in my office, sending me material, because from time to time things come up and you remember, "Oh, Fisk is the institution that has this fabulous art gallery, with all of that rich art," let's send them half a million dollars. Remember, government people are trying to close their books at the end of the year, and they give support to the people they know will handle it responsibly.

Fisk University: A Tradition of Training Leaders

The contributions of historically black colleges are too many to enumerate. But one certainly is the fact that through the establishment of these institutions, so many of us had an opportunity to become educated. Without these institutions, up until the early seventies, large numbers of the educated population that we now know would not exist, because we would not have been allowed to go to other schools. I can use myself as a perfect example. I was born two blocks away from the second oldest college in the United States of America, a college that has graduated at least four, maybe five, United States Presidents. But because of segregation — and incidentally, when I graduated from high school I was the recipient of a Rockefeller scholarship, I had high board scores, and I had won almost every state contest given academically — I was not allowed to go to that institution. Fisk University, which is my alma mater, accepted me. This is a perfect example of the contributions of these schools. They have given to large numbers of people opportunities to study and to come to discover who they are. I had no idea, no clue that I could one day become the president of a university, that I could one day make my mark on society. I, like some people, had the good fortune to be brought up in a family where people said to me, "You matter. Your humanity matters, and it is not your failing that other people do not understand it. Your challenge is to help them understand it." So I had that understanding. As a result of a school like Fisk, I came to understand the power of the mind.

Fisk gave me a rigorous intellectual grounding. It forced me to read and think deeply about everything from Socrates and Plato to Matthew Arnold to Ralph Ellison to Richard Wright. It gave me this extraordinarily eclectic, rich, intellectually cohesive grounding. That is one excellent example of the strength and contribution of these schools. Another one is that these institutions for many, many years were places of employment; in fact they still are, for a significant number of people of color. Without them, some of us could not have made our livelihoods because once we had finished undergraduate and graduate school we returned to these institutions to work and to do our research, and to teach another generation of students to believe in themselves and to go forward. Just as important is the fact that these institutions, the historically black institutions, enabled you to understand your worth, your power, your potential, and your strength. They ennobled individuals to go forth and to be full citizens. That is in itself an extraordinary benefit that comes when schools are created as a result of a genuine response to a societal need.

5

MICHAEL L. LOMAX

President and CEO of the United Negro College Fund

Former President, Dillard University

Dr. Michael L. Lomax is the president and chief executive officer of the United Negro College Fund, the country's oldest historically black higher education consortium. Prior to his leadership of the Fund, Lomax served as president of Dillard University, New Orleans, Louisiana, from July 1, 1997 to July 1, 2004. During his leadership of Dillard, Lomax executed an ambitious strategic plan to reposition Dillard as one of the premiere liberal arts colleges in the South. The primary objective of his administration, he states, was to "reinvent" Dillard for the twenty-first century by merging the vast opportunities of the present with Dillard's tradition of excellence. Among his many achievements toward the accomplishment of this goal were the revitalization of the University's advancement program, a complete overhaul of the curriculum to bring it to a competitive liberal arts standard emphasizing globalization and internationalization, the expansion of the enrollment by over 40 percent with students representing every region of the United States, the Caribbean and Africa, and the recruitment of well-qualified faculty members and administrators to enhance an already strong teaching and administrative cohort. Additionally, Lomax forged partnerships with several major research universities and multinational corporations. In 2002, the U.S. News and World Report *ranked Dillard University among the top*

20 comprehensive colleges in the South. Lomax's expertise and success in higher education leadership and management earned him a seat on the White House Board of Advisors on Historically Black Colleges and Universities.

Before assuming the presidency of Dillard University, Lomax gained a wealth of administrative experience through service and leadership in the classroom and political arena. He has taught at Morehouse and Spelman Colleges, Emory University, the Georgia Institute of Technology, and the University of Georgia. As a leader in politics, he served 12 years as chairman of the Board of Commissioners of Fulton County in Atlanta, Georgia. Additionally, he holds leadership and membership positions in numerous civic, social, and service organizations. He is founding chair of Atlanta's National Black Arts Festival, a trustee of Emory University, and serves on the boards of the Studio Museum in Harlem, the Carter Center of Emory University, the United Way of America, and Teach for America. Lomax earned his bachelor's degree from Morehouse College, where he was elected to Phi Beta Kappa, and received his doctoral degree from Emory University.

Michael L. Lomax (courtesy United Negro College Fund).

My service as a president has reinforced for me the notion that education remains, certainly in the United States, the number one opportunity for advancing yourself individually and for groups to advance themselves collectively. This is a meritocracy, at least in its values. Certainly race and gender have been barriers for African Americans and for women. And having said that, education is just the *sine qua non* for advancing. And we see students every day who come from low- to moderate-income families, work hard, get a good education, and immediately improve their economic chances. Being a president has only reinforced for me the notion that education is the foundation for social advancement in this country and for changing the society in which we live in and for improving the lot of individuals in groups, and it is a very efficacious way of transforming the society in which we live. I am a stronger believer than ever before.

Black colleges and universities have provided access to education for African Americans. That has been the number one important role that we played, certainly since the nineteenth century when African Americans were excluded from every level of educational opportunity, until the twentieth century when, at least for the first half of it, historically black colleges remained the primary opportunity for post-secondary education for African Americans. Today a significant number of college educated African Americans are graduates of historically black colleges. So access has been the primary function they have served. In addition, these institutions have been the most successful educators of African Americans, and they have demonstrated that a supportive, nurturing environment is the kind of educational environment that African Americans require to be successful and to negotiate the post-secondary educational environment. So access and substance have been the two most important elements that these schools have provided over the last century and a half.

Dillard has a rich heritage, as do all of the historically black colleges. The ones that have survived are often over a century old. They have weathered a great many storms. Obviously they have survived in an environment of adversity and scarcity. They have been the primary producers of the leaders of the race, as well as the sort of nameless, faceless middle class that has provided all the professional services and backbone for the African American community. Dillard is no different. Having said that, rich heritage notwithstanding, Dillard, like other similar institutions has really had to figure out how to negotiate a changed environment in the post-integration era. We do not have a captive market. Students have access to other institutions—state institutions, private institutions. We do not have the resources to compete with many of those institutions. So, the question is: How do we survive in an era of new and different challenges? And I think that was the focus of my attention over the years that I was at Dillard: How to build on the rich heritage that we have, but to build on it in a new and changed and highly competitive higher education environment. How do you attract large numbers of students? How do you retain them? How do you attract quality faculty? How do you ensure that you have competitive facilities? How do you do this in a way that is not financially out of the reach of the students that you are attracting? It is a highly challenging environment. We have a strong tradition here. We have survived and prospered for 130 years. The real question is: Will we be able to fashion an environment that can be relevant to this new century and millennium?

Being a historically black college in the twenty-first century means that you have a certain heritage of embracing and nurturing and celebrating and perpetuating the history, the culture, and the social fabric of the African American community. It means that we continue to have doors wide open to a significant number of African American students, first-generation and an increasing number of legacy students who come because their parents or grandparents attended these institutions. So there is a heritage factor in this community. Dillard and other HBCU's view the educational enterprise as a highly individualized and nurturing experience. On the other hand, like every other institution, we must provide high-quality academic programs that prepare our students to compete regardless of race or gender in a highly competitive global environment. So on the one hand there is an element to our institutions that is historical and cultural. On the other, there is an element that is comparable to that found in other highly competitive institutions; the academic performance standards are the same as those of majority institutions.

Black colleges should keep a very strong sense of their social, cultural and historical traditions and heritage. Maintaining focus on a nurturing, individualized environment also is very important. Moreover, these schools have to produce the new leadership for a new millennium. In part they do that by re-emphasizing some of the values that have been important in the past, like service. There is an expectation that our graduates will be engaged in their communities, that they will be leaders. These are values that have been important elements of the heritage of these institutions, and ones that we do not want to lose sight of at all. On the other hand, we have got to prepare these students with all the skills and habits of mind and approaches to lifelong learning that will make them competitive in a tough marketplace of graduate and professional schools and professional employment. So there is a kind of historical quality to what the new role of the institutions must be. And there is also the necessity to ensure that academic programs emphasize contemporary expectations, including technological competence, analytical thinking, strong communications skills and knowledge in areas of mathematics and the sciences.

At Dillard we are trying to create an institution that respects its past. And so we are unabashedly embracing the fact that we are an African American institution. We want our students to come here to learn about the history, the culture, and the contribution of African Americans. There is a heritage emphasis in my vision for Dillard, which is central to what the institution has been and what it will be in the future.

On the other hand, we also believe that our students are going to be competitors in the global marketplace. They are not just going to leave here and go back home to be teachers, doctors or lawyers. They are going to really have an opportunity to go out into the world at large. So, we want our students to be able to communicate. We are emphasizing foreign language studies, and study abroad. We believe that while the bachelor's degree is the foundation for a productive life, we want more of our graduates to go immediately to graduate or professional school. Accordingly, we are emphasizing the development of those skills and capacities that will better prepare them for graduate and professional school, which means a very strong emphasis on communication and research skills. And so we are emphasizing the undergraduate thesis as a differentiator between Dillard and other institutions. Those are two of the key elements that we see as important to a Dillard education of the future. And again, emphasis on leadership, on service, on engagement in the community, so that we are not just preparing a cadre of highly qualified but self-absorbed graduates. They have a responsibility to engage in their communities to help transform the world in which we live.

I think that a lot of the schools have gotten away from the service tradition. The institutions have lost sight of the old notions of service and focused on the credentials for their students and preparing them for individual careers. At Dillard, we are re-examining the issues of ethics and leadership, and the relationship of the individual to the community, and determining how that reinforces those values as a part of the undergraduate experience here.

Creating a Diverse Educational Environment

I do not see a conflict between our emphasis on heritage and the national agenda of diversity and multiculturalism. We look at the world from an African American perspective, but we look at the world. Ninety-nine percent of the students that are here are of

African descent. But they learn about Europe, about Asia, about the Middle East, and about American history. Oftentimes they learn about those other places, and other cultures and other societies, from the perspective of the impact they have had upon people of African descent. It is just a lens through which they look at the world. But we teach our students to be respectful not only of themselves, but also of others in the world, not to marginalize anyone, and to understand that there are other peoples and other experiences that are just as rich, just as important, and just as valuable as the African American experience. I think we teach in a globally and culturally respectful environment.

Dillard, as with all historically black colleges, did not begin its history with the intent of excluding anyone. All of these colleges opened their doors with the intent of including everyone who came seeking education. Dillard's faculties and administrations are diverse and, increasingly, its student bodies are diverse. There are students studying at Dillard from Europe, Asia, Africa, the Caribbean, and South and Central America. The vast majority of those students are of African descent, but there are European and Asian students here as well. They come expecting a rich and unique educational experience, and Dillard hopes to make it that. What makes America and American higher education so interesting is that it is diverse. There is a broad menu of choices, from Hispanic-serving institutions, to schools with strong religious backgrounds, to schools like the historically black colleges with a specific racial heritage. That does not make them exclusive or that anyone is barred. It emphasizes, rather, just what our history is.

Dillard has some very exciting opportunities to ensure that it offers a diverse environment. One is that there are a number of exchange programs from European institutions. There are students there studying from Austria, Ireland, and France. Dillard recruits actively in the Caribbean and South and Central America as well as on the continent of Africa. Dillard thinks that diversity is not just the color of your skin but also national origin, religion, or ethnic identity. There are students of African descent whose primary language is French, or Spanish, or Portuguese. That means that Dillard is a diverse environment. The kids may by and large be of African descent, but they are very different nonetheless. Students are encouraged to explore the world through study abroad. And, of course, the college has a diverse faculty and administration.

The Curriculum: Preparing Students for the Global World of the Twenty-First Century

Dillard is going to teach the liberal arts academic disciplines and it is going to have a strong emphasis on science and technology just like everyone else. There is one sense in which there is really no difference between Dillard and other comprehensive colleges in the United States. What will make its curriculum distinctive is certainly an emphasis in the humanities and social sciences, on the specific cultural contributions, social and historical experiences of African Americans, and that will be reflected in courses that are a part of the curriculum. Again, Dillard knows that students are going to compete in a global environment and therefore it is emphasizing heavily the international dimensions of academic studies. For example in business, international business is a very popular major. And that is linked to the foreign language study and so at Dillard you could be learning Japanese and that can be the focus of your international business major, or you can be studying in Spanish or French or Portuguese. So, I do not know that in one sense there is a very big difference in the curriculum between historically black institutions and others, but there may be some cultural and historical emphasis that you will find in the social sciences and humanities.

I think Dillard is constantly looking at what students' expectations are and what preparation the students must have to be competitive once they leave the institution. There are certain areas that more focus should be placed on, such as undergraduate research. How do you infuse that research model into the entire academic enterprise? How do you increase the interest in studying foreign languages when so many students come without that as a high priority? How do you get the capacity to examine the use of technology and then embed it within your academic program? Those are all questions that Dillard is giving consideration to. How do you create an exciting, innovative, challenging curriculum which students will find attractive and challenging and which will prepare them for the world of graduate/professional school and higher quality employment once they graduate?

Again, we emphasize the notion that when your students graduate, they are not just going to be American students; they are going to be global. The workplace that they will have an opportunity to be employed in won't be just domestic, it can be international. In order to take full advantage of that, one venue has been created on the campus, the Global

Studies program, which is designed to pull all of the international threads together in one highly visible location. It coordinates all of the international study abroad programs; it reinforces foreign language training; and it advocates infusing international themes and dimensions into all academic programs.

Institutional Advancement

Fundraising is the area that absorbs most presidents' time. But having the support staff as well as the organizational structure in place that allows you to be an effective fundraiser is a big challenge. Dillard is part of the program that the Kresge Foundation has underwritten to build fundraising capacity at historically black colleges. This has enabled the hiring and training of acquisition of donor management technology, and the creation of a professional and competitive advancement operation. This has already begun to yield impressive financial results, thus addressing one of the most formidable challenges facing presidents of HBCUs, namely fundraising.

The fundraising challenge facing many of the historically black colleges is that they have not had as strong a base of donors—alumni, organizations, corporations, or wealthy individuals. Now, some of that is changing. Certainly, Dillard and other colleges are learning how to nurture and develop a tradition of giving among our alumni, and we are beginning to see strong results there. Because African Americans still are not as wealthy as white Americans, even though we are seeing increases in giving from alumni, the potential is not as significant as it might be for majority institutions. Furthermore, we still do not get the same level of support from foundations and corporations that the majority institutions get. There is some resistance in the corporate community to treating historically black institutions on par with majority institutions.

I do not know if we will ever adequately tap government resources. We have certainly increased significantly the amount of funding that we are awarded from all sectors. But there again, it takes time and resources to gain the resources. So Dillard has had to invest in advancement operations to hire the development officers, the grant writers, and the grant administrators. With all of that, the amount of money that is raised, has been significantly increased but you have to prune the pump with investments before you begin to see a return. Not many small colleges have the working capital needed to make the preliminary investments.

Alma Mater: The Legacy of Morehouse College

Growing up in Los Angeles, I did not know much about historically black colleges. There were no historically black colleges in California. My paternal grandmother graduated from Fisk, as did other members of her family. My father's college roommate became the president of Atlanta University (now Clark Atlanta University). So, I at least met a historically black college president early in life. My real introduction came in 1964 when I went to Morehouse College. And there I came under the influence of some of the most important leaders of black colleges in the history of the country. My college career was the time that I got to see what the black colleges were like and the influence that they could have shaping, not just me, but also all of my classmates.

It was fortuitous that I decided to attend Morehouse. I was going to be living in Alabama for my senior year of high school, and I did not want to attend a segregated school in rural Alabama. I applied to Fisk and to Morehouse in the hopes that they had a senior year program, which neither of them had, but they both had early admissions program and admitted me. So, instead of finishing high school, I wound up going to college a year early. It was not my plan; it just happened that way. I thought that I was going to go to an Ivy League college, but this was one of those circumstances that transformed me and changed the direction of my life.

The influence of Dr. Benjamin E. Mays, the iconic president, was pervasive at Morehouse. I was there during the last three years of his presidency and for the first year of Hugh Gloster's, his successor. Morehouse was a very small school, less than 1,000 students. It had a relatively small, but very well-prepared faculty. Classes were small and the environment was both nurturing and challenging. It did not have all of the technological infrastructure that we have today and, by the standards of the day, would have been viewed as under-resourced. But it had a competitively credentialed faculty who engaged students and the curriculum focused on developing a unique individual: "the Morehouse Man." Long before branding became fashionable, the College distilled from the tracts of its most famous alumni—Martin Luther King, Howard Thurman and others—those characteristics it felt were important to pass on to all who attended the institution.

The debate that I particularly recall in the late 1960s and early 1970s was whether historically black colleges should really become what was then termed "black universities." During that period of Black Nationalism, some advocated a role for the institutions that would limit them to Afrocentric curricula taught by faculties of color. That narrow debate did not reflect the tradition of the institutions or the direction that they would continue to pursue. While HBCUs did re-examine their curricula and did give them a more Afrocentric cultural and social focus, their primary institutional purpose did not change and remains the same, and that is to prepare graduates for full participation in American society.

HBCUs in the Twenty-First Century: Survival and Prosperity

When I ended my political career in 1993, I knew I wanted to return to higher education because I think it is the most productive way to make the kinds of societal contributions and changes that I think are important. I decided that I wanted to focus my attention around ensuring a bright and hopeful future for African Americans. I think one of the most important ways to do that is in the educational arena. For me, historically black colleges are the community in which to do this work.

At Dillard, everything that is being done is designed to strengthen the institution, to ensure not just its survival, but also its prosperity, to ensure that it is serving the maximum number of students it can serve effectively, and producing in them the strongest possible academic results. We would like to have about 2500 full-time undergraduates and about 500 students in evening and continuing education program. It would like to have an endowment well over $100 million. It would like to have a modern campus, and it would like to continue to attract the best and the brightest of high school graduates and serious adults who want to continue their educations. Those are the goals: to be ranked among the top colleges in the region and nation, not only in terms of the test scores of Dillard's students but also in terms of the numbers who go on to graduate and professional schools, and the numbers who contribute back to their institution. I worked to stabilize Dillard, to strengthen it, and give it a solid foundation so it can weather the storms of the twenty-first century.

I feel very connected to HBCU. My parents did not attend historically black colleges, but my grandparents did and I feel that so much of the success that my family has had over the last 100 years has been directly related to the educational opportunities with which they were blessed at the dawn of the twentieth century. I have seen in my own life that education and opportunity are linked. Just as there was a powerful mission for historically black colleges in the years following the Civil War, and at the dawn of the twentieth century, I think there is a powerful mission for these schools at the dawn of the twenty-first century. There are still too many Americans of color who have not been granted educational opportunity. Their lives have not been as enriched because of it. I believe these institutions, like Dillard, are powerfully important institutions in transforming the lives of individuals and ensuring the opportunities of my people. This work is important, it is vital, it is challenging, it is gratifying, and I feel blessed to be involved in it.

6

HENRY R. PONDER

Former President, Talladega College

*Former President and CEO of the National Association
for Equal Opportunity in Higher Education*

Former President, Fisk University

Former President, Benedict College

*Dr. Henry R. Ponder recently retired after more than five decades of
service in higher education leadership. Ponder entered higher education in
the mid–1950s, in the immediate aftermath of* Brown v. Board of Education, *and for most of his career was in the vanguard of efforts to lead the
nation's historically black colleges and universities through the changes and
transformations of the post–Civil Rights era. From 1996 to 2001 he served as
president and CEO of the National Association for Equal Opportunity in
Higher Education (NAFEO), a membership organization of 118 historically
and predominantly black colleges and universities. Prior to his leadership of
NAFEO he served as president of Fisk University in Nashville, Tennessee,
for 12 years, and president of Benedict College in Columbia, South Carolina,
for 11 years. Most recently he served as the eighteenth president of Talladega
College, in Talladega, Alabama. In 1986, Ponder was honored as one of the
"One Hundred Most Effective College Presidents in the United States." Additionally, he served as chairman of the Members of the United Negro College
Fund, on the Executive Council of The Commission on Colleges of the*

Southern Association of Colleges and Schools, and president of the Tennessee College Association.

In addition to his immense contributions to higher education, Ponder is a recognized social and civic leader. He has served on the board of numerous organizations, including the American Council on Education, the Nashville Chapter of the United Nations, and the Bishop Desmond Tutu Southern African Refugee Scholarship Fund. It is the mission of President Ponder to position Talladega College to be a leader in the global world of higher education in the twenty-first century. Since assuming the presidency of Talladega, Ponder has revitalized the college's advancement program, increased the visibility of the college, and enhanced the College's curriculum. Ponder received a bachelor's degree from Langston University and a master's degree from Oklahoma State University. He earned a doctoral degree from the Ohio State University.

I lived and worked through many of the great changes and transformations in American higher education in the twentieth century. I started out in higher education in the immediate aftermath of *Brown v. Board of Education*. When I entered the field America was still wrestling with the effects of the ruling. Many of the southern states were trying to come up with strategies to circumvent the desegregation mandate. States like Virginia, Mississippi, and Alabama were embracing the "states' right" ideology of resistance. I was working at one of the historically black colleges that was completely segregated at this time because we had not progressed very far from *Brown v. Board of Education*.

This was a time in our nation's history when if you were African American and living and working

Henry R. Ponder (courtesy Henry Ponder).

in one of the southern states and wanted to go to graduate or professional school at a majority institution of higher education, you could not go. That was against the law. But the states had a way around that. They would give you a stipend to go outside the state for graduate and professional study. They would give you a stipend to go to the northern states that would admit you to get your education. When you look at it in broad terms it was certainly an advantage to African Americans who wanted further study. Keep in mind that if African Americans could have gone to colleges and universities in the South they would have had to finance their total education because there would have been no money available to them. But if African Americans went up North the southern states would give them monthly stipends to help finance expenses of living and for education.

In a way that was good for African Americans who received such support, but it was certainly bad for the whole system of higher education. I do not want that point to be misinterpreted. It is kind of like saying that even from bad things there might be something good that comes out of it. I think this would be one of the good things that came out of that era. A number of African Americans did get their master's and doctoral degrees with this type of study, and they returned to their home states in the South and worked in higher education and other fields. This was the environment when I came into higher education.

The nation moved from that and at some point it was decided that it was okay for African Americans to go to predominantly white institutions. We were gradually admitted to graduate and professional programs in the South. Now I have seen the full spectrum of it in that if minorities apply to any school in this country if they meet the admission standards they will be accepted. Race is not a question in terms of your admittance. I am not talking about the Affirmative Action programs that are going on. That is a different ball game. But now if you are graduated from an undergraduate school in the South you can go to any graduate or professional school in the South, and race is not a question. So I have lived through a time when African Americans were trying to get admission to majority southern colleges and universities—I remember the struggles of Hamilton Holmes and others—to the time when now you just apply and you are accepted. Looking at the whole spectrum, today is much better than it was 30 or 40 years ago.

The changes have been good for higher education. The teachers at majority institutions are now becoming familiar with the fact that African Americans are just as smart, are just as dumb as all other college students. Before they either thought that they were all dumb, or that they were all smart. They did not see the whole spectrum of graduate students or undergraduate students at these places. So the changes have been good for higher education.

I have also seen during that time at some of these colleges and universities the black undergraduates are now saying that they want a black student union, or they want a black student dormitory and all these things. I have seen that. I won't put a value judgment on it. We have evolved from a time when we could not get in to now, when we are demanding that we have a special kind of treatment once we get there. I have seen all of that.

I have also seen where we have now become concerned about test scores on the SAT and ACT as a requirement for admission. Again, I am not putting any value judgment on it, but initially we did not worry about those things. If you graduated from a high school in the state that you were applying to, you were just sort of automatically admitted to the school that you could attend. If you were African American it had to be the black colleges. If you were white it had to be the white colleges. But no one ever talked about whether you made a high score on the SAT. As a matter of fact, in some cases they did not even care whether you had a SAT score or not. I have seen that. We have gone from that to now when everyone is concerned about an SAT score or ACT score. When I first entered the field all of the nation's colleges and universities, except the Ivy League and elite private schools primarily, did not require standardized test scores. All you had to do was apply. If you could show that you had graduated from a high school you would be admitted. Now we have gotten to the point where you must have a certain score on the SAT or the ACT in order to get admitted. Before, they were almost open admission colleges. Today, colleges and universities are very selective. They now try to screen people out rather than help people get in. I have seen that. Again, I am not putting any value judgment on it. I am just trying to give a flavor of what I have seen in higher education.

I was also at the black colleges at a time when corporate America suddenly discovered that African Americans could do well in corporate America. They were raiding the black colleges and universities to get some of the younger faculty members to come into the IBMs, the Pepsi-Colas, and the Coca-Colas of this world. Some of the black faculty went, and they did very well. Some of these are the people who are retiring now from those positions. I have seen that. I had some invitations to join corporate America myself, but I did not go because I had dedicated myself to the black colleges.

I also remember when the corporations began to actively recruit for the graduates of black colleges and universities. I remember the first wave of our students going into those jobs. I have seen that to now when it is no big deal when the graduates of historically black colleges and universities enter corporate America. We have run the whole gamut from the time when you were really special if you got a job with IBM to now when you are just another person who got hired. Race does not matter.

These changes have brought the whole system of higher education, with just a few exceptions, to believe that there is an educational advantage to having diversity in the student body. We have evolved from a time when you had to be white or you had to be black to go to a particular school to a time now when we all think that diversity is good. Diversity is not just race. We now understand that it is good to have some economically disadvantaged people in the classroom with the affluent people. It is good to have middle-class people in the classroom with the less than middle-class people. I think that we have now come to the realization that diversity is good.

I have seen the *Bakke* case. In that particular case the Court ruled that colleges and universities could use race in admissions. Now we are seeing the University of Michigan case where some are saying that schools should not have race as one of the criterion for admission. I have seen the whole gamut. I find myself in a very fortunate position, having lived and worked through all of the changes and transformations in higher education in the twentieth century. I can look back now and say that all of it had good points, and all of it perhaps had bad points. What we need to do in higher education is try to take advantage of where we are now and make sure that every youngster has the right to attempt to get a college education.

The changes and transformation in higher education that I lived and worked through did not disturb the mission of historically black colleges. The mission of the black college remains the same. As a matter of fact, one of the good things about historically black colleges and universities is that throughout this period of time they have not changed their basic mission. They have added components to that mission. They now talk about international education. They talk now about technology. But basically, somewhere in there you will see in all of the mission statements something about how we believe in providing an opportunity for youngsters to pursue higher education. That has been basically the idea all along.

What we did was to decide that there is now a more global market for our graduates. So now rather than just preparing our graduates for a segregated world where they will only be working with African Americans wherever they go, we now must prepare them so that they might work wherever they might go, be it in government, in corporate America, in finance, or so on. The teachers understood this mission in a hurry. They began to expand their horizons of thinking. They began to think more in terms of what the world stage was all about and we must now make sure that the graduates that we put out can meet that world stage competition. We boasted that our graduates could do well wherever they went. We were proud of that fact. And teachers took pride in it and worked hard to make sure that when a youngster graduated from one of the historically black colleges that youngster could go to Harvard and do as well as anybody who graduated from some place else. We took the challenge to make sure that our graduates could perform wherever they went.

Presidential Priorities: Institutional Advancement, Student and Faculty Recruitment and Retention

I have led three historically black colleges. Fundraising has been one of the primary concerns at all of the institutions that I have led. When I went to Benedict College we had to get into the fundraising business in a hurry. At Fisk everybody knew what was happening there when I went. The national news media talked about the fact that the college was in bad shape financially. We had to hit the ground running for that. The same thing was true at Talladega. We had to hit the ground running, trying to get money. The big thing at all three schools was getting the financial resources necessary to keep the institutions viable. That would have been number one. Tied in with the finances was the fact that we had to build an endowment, obtain money in order to give faculty higher salaries, acquire funding to take care of deferred maintenance, and so on.

After the financial issues, the second priority was students. We simply had to get more students into each of these institutions to make sure that the institutions remained viable. So again, the whole recruiting effort — how do you manage recruitment efforts, how do you position yourself — was critical. We started at a time when the primary way that we recruited students was just to print brochures and send them out, or take them out wherever we went. I have seen the nature of recruiting efforts go from letter writing to now, when you go out and you make sure that you go to college fairs. You have to have a traveling budget now for your recruiters that is almost as much as the basketball coach has. I have seen that. We went from advertising in the black newspapers for youngsters to now when we advertise in all of the newspapers. We went from advertising on black radio stations to advertising on all of the radio stations. And from radio we moved into television. So I have seen the whole gamut of the recruitment efforts.

The third priority was to continue to recruit the faculty that was necessary to keep up with the latest techniques involved in whatever disciplines you were offering in terms of majors at the college and university. I have seen over time that the way that you teach — not just the techniques but the course material covered — has changed in almost all of those areas. You had to constantly recruit faculty members who had had the latest training in graduates and professional schools to come in and keep the older faculty abreast of what was going on. Those were the three major things that were involved there.

The Legacy of the National Association for Equal Opportunity in Higher Education

From 1997 to 2001 I served as president and chief executive officer of the National Association for Equal Opportunity in Higher Education (NAFEO), a membership organization of 118 historically and predominantly black colleges and universities. NAFEO was established in October of 1969. At that time a meeting of black college presidents was convened in Mobile, Alabama. Richard Nixon was President of the United States at the time. The presidents of the black colleges were concerned that the historically black colleges and universities were getting literally next to nothing from the federal government through the agencies. We had a meeting to say we just had to do something to change this. Those presidents then decided that they were going to petition President Nixon for a larger part of what the government was giving out in higher education. Those were the events that led to the start of NAFEO. It was not to become a political organization. It was to become what might be termed a lobbying organization to get more consideration for historically black colleges and universities. We did get an audience with President Nixon and because of that audience some things came our way that would not have come our way otherwise. And we have succeeded in having audiences with other Presidents since then. So NAFEO has remained viable over time.

The role of NAFEO over time, and still is today, is to petition the government, through its agencies, through the President, through the Cabinet Secretaries, all of those, to say we need for you to consider the historically black colleges and universities when you are talking about the budget that you have for higher education. Through NAFEO and others, for instance, the United Negro College Fund, we were able to get the Title III legislation when it was renewed to include race specific language. That is why today we have Title III for African American colleges and universities. We have another title for Native American colleges and universities. And we have another one for Hispanic-serving institutions. We, the black college leadership, did it first, and we got the federal government to say we need to do something for black colleges. Without being pejorative, the other minority-serving institutions kind of looked and saw what we were able to accomplish and they decided to follow the same route and were able to get the same thing. We feel good that NAFEO, UNCF, and our other organizations pioneered race-specific language with the federal government.

I lived through a time when there were some people who were very concerned about using race in federal programs. There was a thinking that we had gone beyond that stage and so forth. But we fought for that. Dr. Kenneth Tollett, a Howard University professor, and I were two of the people who strongly felt that we needed race-specific language. Finally, that prevailed. Everybody is glad we did it. I have also worked with United Negro College Fund on initiatives to increase public support to historically black colleges and universities.

I have also worked on efforts to increase public support for higher education in general. In the early 1990s I served as president of the Tennessee College Association, an arm of the Southern Association of Colleges and Schools. At that time the colleges needed to get influential persons statewide not involved in higher education directly, for instance politicians who were state senators and state representatives and corporate leaders within the state, to serve on the association's committee. We needed them to bring to the committee the kinds of input that persons not involved with education could bring to accreditation evaluations. That was a big thing — trying to show those persons that their civic responsibility required them to serve.

HBCUs in the Twenty-First Century:
The Tradition of Excellence Continues

In the multiplex of 3,100 colleges and universities in America only 118 are historically or predominantly African American. But some how the black colleges and universities have still been able to educate the majority of African Americans who have bachelor's degrees. That is a tremendous accomplishment. In terms of total numbers, more African Americans attend the majority institutions than go to the historically black institutions. But the black colleges still graduate a disproportionate number of African Americans who get bachelor's degrees. That is worthy of note. The black colleges enroll less than 20 percent of the African American college student population but they produce 28 percent of all black college graduates. That is really important.

Our graduates are wooed by the most prestigious colleges and universities in this country. The Harvards, Yales, University of Michigans, and Stanfords of the world love to have our graduates in their graduate and professional school programs. That is a legacy that we are rightly proud of.

Here at Talladega one of the things that we have been able to do is to somehow ingrain in our students that they ought to be leaders after they leave here. We have been able to do that. When they leave here they take leadership roles across the spectrum. This has been one of our fortes. The other thing is that over time we have been able to say to our youngsters that a bachelor's degree from Talladega College just prepares you for education. You have to go to graduate and professional school. You cannot stop here. And over time at least 80 percent of our students have gone on to graduate and professional school. Research shows that a greater percentage of African American students enrolled at historically black colleges and universities express aspirations of wanting to go to graduate or professional school than do African American students enrolled at majority institutions. We do something to encourage our students.

Another thing that is important is that several of our colleges and universities decided that they were going to do some niche work, and they have done it very well. I will point to the example of Florida A&M University. Florida A&M has more African American Merit Scholars enrolled — they have been number one, two, or three every year for the last ten years — than all of the other colleges and universities in the country. Florida A&M beats the Harvards, the Yales, and all of those. That is the example of Florida A&M University.

Then there is the example of Xavier University of New Orleans. More of its graduates go on to medical and dental school than any other college or university in the country. We have been able to take our students and decide we want them to do something and we put some effort into making sure that they do it. That is tremendously important.

Talladega College: A Legacy of Achievement

Talladega College is a tradition rich institution. During my two years there I traveled and talked to alumni around the country, and I never heard an alumnus say an unkind thing about Talladega College. Never. It is the only college that I have been associated with where I can make that statement. The alumni are wild about Talladega College. The alumni have been supportive of everything that we have done. Therefore we are proud of them.

Our graduates serve in state legislatures from California to New Jersey. Thirteen of our graduates have served as college and university presidents. Research conducted by the United Negro College Fund a few years ago highlighted the fact that of all the member institutions in the Fund Talladega College had more of its graduates working in executive positions in corporate America than any other college or university. Again we send about 80 percent of our students to graduate and professional school every year. We have been considered a leader among all colleges and universities in the United States in the percentage of our graduates in the sciences that go on to graduate and professional school. Our graduates go on to earn doctorates in all disciplines. Keep in mind that we have never had more than 1,000 students in a year, even in our heyday. So we have never had a lot of students. But the caliber of the students that we have graduated have gone on to do all of these things. It is that legacy that keeps me motivated.

My dream is to have black education to the point where no one will ask, "Why do we need black colleges?" My dream is that we reach the point in the next few years where everybody understands "why we need black colleges," and therefore will not be asking. If we could reach that point, I think that we would have turned the corner. I hope everyone understands that right now, this spring, if every youngster who graduates from high school decided to show up on a college campus next fall, there would not be enough room for them in the colleges and universities we now have. Rather than wondering why we need these colleges we need to understand that we need *more* colleges. We should not be talking about getting rid of any. We need to be talking about adding to these institutions and making them better.

I would like to see a time when higher education will move back to the status that it once had. There was a time when parents said to their youngsters: "You must get an education because no one can take that from you. Anything else that you get, money or an automobile, someone can take it. But when you get knowledge no one can take that." There was an appreciation for knowledge that parents had even though they themselves did not have much formal education. I hope that somehow we can get back to the point where this whole society has an appreciation for what higher education means. That is what I hope for.

II. The Public Historically
Black Colleges

7

RONALD F. MASON, JR.

President, Jackson State University

Dr. Ronald F. Mason, Jr., joined the Jackson State University commu-nity, Jackson, Mississippi, as its president on February 1, 2000. In addition to his leadership of Jackson State, Mason serves on the White House Board of Advisors on Historically Black Colleges and Universities. Mason came to Jackson State University from Tulane University in New Orleans, Louisiana, where he worked in various capacities, including senior vice president and general counsel, vice president for finance and operations, and most recently founder and executive director of the Tulane-Xavier National Center for the Urban Community. Mason was educated at Columbia University, where he received his bachelor of arts and juris doc-torate degrees. He completed additional graduate work at the Harvard Institute of Educational Management.

Mason is a nationally recognized expert in higher education, commu-nity development, and legal issues. During his tenure as executive director of the Tulane-Xavier National Center for the Urban Community, he served as chief coordinator of the two universities' extensive involvement in pub-lic housing, economic development, and public education. The Center's programs to support self-sufficiency among residents of New Orleans' pub-lic housing communities and to implement welfare reform and welfare to work programs was funded through a $10 million grant obtained by Mason from the United States Department of Housing and Urban Development. In 1996 Secretary of Housing and Urban Development Henry Cisneros

119

appointed Mason executive monitor for the Housing Authority of New Orleans.

Mason's commitment to expansion and innovation in higher education has resulted in this being new and exciting times at Jackson State University. Mason has strengthened and enhanced existing programs in critical areas such as the sciences, mathematics, and teacher training. Additionally, he has made enhancements in the University's physical facilities. Mason has also maintained his commitment to service through programs and partnerships with the local community designed to improve public education and promote economic development.

The historically black colleges and universities educated those citizens that did not have access to equal opportunity in higher education in America. The institutions have been a safety net for the members of society that society wanted to ignore. Jackson State University is 125 years old. The university was established in 1877 by Baptist missionaries to train newly freed slaves to become teachers. We started out as a private institution but it was later designated as a state institution. We are the only university in the largest metropolitan area and capital city, in the state of Mississippi. We are also historically black.

Jackson State University educates more than half of the African American undergraduate scientists in the state of Mississippi. We have always been one of the largest employers of African Americans. In the days of segregation Jackson State University was the only employer for many African Americans. We were the heart of a thriving African American community in the city of Jackson. Many parts of the neighborhood have since deteriorated as part of the cycle of urban decay. Part of our job now is to restore the neighborhood. Most of the school teachers in

Ronald F. Mason, Jr. (courtesy Jay Johnson photography).

the Jackson public school system were educated at Jackson State University. Jackson State University is the African American community and the African American is Jackson State University.

The defining legacy of the university has been the ability of the institution to survive. John A. Peoples, the former president of Jackson State University, and who is probably the greatest president of Jackson State University, wrote a book called *To Survive and Thrive*. When you understand what African American higher education leaders of the segregation era faced — for instance, lack of resources and a hostile state — you can appreciate the fact that the school has survived for more than a century. Students who were first-generation college students, in many cases, packed their one change of clothes and the clothes on their backs and came to Jackson State without any money. Jackson State found a way to help these students be successful. Many of these students are elected officials today, lawyers, doctors, and so on. But most are just hard-working people who would not have had an opportunity for gainful employment but not for Jackson State. To be able to survive under those circumstances is really amazing. Dr. People's did the survive part. We see our job now as to do the thrive part.

Things have changed and they have not changed. There are some obvious examples of success in the African American community. If you look at the numbers the gap has continued to grow. There still are two Americas. Institutional racism in America is still alive and well. As long as that is the case we will always need institutions like a Jackson State to be a safe haven for students who are not prepared to deal with the harsh reality of the kind of society that we have here. It makes a big difference for a student to come to a Jackson State and have four years to be prepared to step out, and to be taught how to deal with that kind of a world, as opposed to going directly out of high school and have to confront it at 17 years old.

The way that I describe our role is that we are here to correct the problems caused by America's failings. If America was doing its job with all Americans and all students in this country, then you would not need institutions that are specifically here to solve the problems that are caused by America's failings. That is what historically black institutions do.

At Jackson State we aim to show that you can be best and black at the same time. Our competition is not necessarily historically black institutions in terms of our product, both academically and educationally. Our competitors are schools like the University of Mississippi, the University of Southern Mississippi, Mississippi State, and other research- intensive schools. We think we can compete with them at every level if one thing can happen: if we can raise money.

Jackson State University is historically black and we are proud to be historically black. Historically black institutions have never excluded anybody. We are historically black but we are also historically Jackson, historically Mississippi, and historically American. People tend to focus on only one part of our history, but we think we can focus on that part and also get people to focus more and more on the other parts of our history as well.

We have students from 40 different states, 30 different foreign countries, and we have faculty members from all over the world. We have programs in Eastern Europe, Africa, and Central America. Our job is to build the best university that we can build and to let who ever wants to come here come here. I am in favor of diversity mainly because I think it is good for the students. The world is becoming smaller and smaller and more and more mixed in many ways. The more we can duplicate that on our campus the better off our students will be when they leave the campus.

Training Future Leaders of America

There are more African American men in jail than there are in college. It is clear to me that but for institutions such as Jackson State University and other historically black institutions that figure would be much, much worse. There are very few African American PhDs, especially in areas of science and mathematics. Historically black institutions such as Jackson State University have contributed to the production of African American doctorates in these areas. We train our students to be change agents. They graduate from here and go out and make the world a better place.

Jackson State University is the fastest growing producer of African American PhDs in the country. We start early on emphasizing to students the importance of graduate and professional training. Part of our culture is to encourage students to get a doctorate. Traditionally most African American PhDs have been in education. The cultural overtones of the value of a doctorate pervade the institution here. We push our students in that direction, which is why most African American PhDs come from historically black colleges and universities. Whether they go to a majority school to get the doctorate, or whether they get it at black institutions, more or less they come through a historically black college. We try to identify the talent, expose them to the area of interest, partner them with faculty mentors, and then they go on to the next level.

We do a lot of undergraduate research programs, too. For instance, we send students out to Oakland, California, every summer to conduct research at Livermore Lab. They work with researchers on various projects. The students come back and report to their supervisors on what they have done out there. The other program that we have is the Science and Engineering Alliance with Southern University, Alabama A&M University, and Prairie View A&M University. The program is specifically designed to create African American PhDs in the sciences. We have had success with that as well.

Jackson State University: Mississippi's "Urban University"

Jackson State University is designated as Mississippi's "urban university." We have embraced the role and the term. The term "urban university" means three things. First, we are the only university in the largest metropolitan area, so we have to stand for educational excellence. Two, it recognizes the reality of where our students come from. Besides coming from Mississippi, they also come from Chicago and Detroit, Memphis and Indianapolis, Saint Louis and New Orleans, Atlanta and Dallas, and other large urban systems.

The third part of being an "urban university" means that we have a special relationship with our city and our community. We have done many things. For instance, we have entered into agreements with the city where they have internships for our students and we offer courses to its police force and their fire force. We have carved out five square miles around Jackson State that we call "e-city." Everything that we do with this initiative is focused on bringing back this area of town in a way that connects all of our intellectual and material resources to help make that happen.

The term "urban university" also means that we just reorganized our curriculum so that where possible we are going to tie classroom work with experiential learning based out in the community. We will be doing things in the community that tie directly to the learning experience in the classroom. We also are doing something really exciting with the public school system. We have partnered with them to form a quasi-independent K-12 academy, which is going to be Jackson State University's laboratory school. The school will generate a lot of research about urban education and how to fix the problems in the public school system.

The historically black college was born out of a need to serve. We rose up because we had to for the sake of the people that we were here to serve, which entailed more than just opening up a classroom. We had to worry about the clothes; we had to worry about feeding them; we had to worry about finding money to help them get through school. We had to work with the churches to solve the needs of the community. That is why we are the conscious of America. We have not forgotten that part of our mission.

The Tulane-Xavier National Center for the Urban Community: A Model of University and Community Engagement

When I was at Tulane University I served as founding executive director of the Tulane-Xavier National Center for the Urban Community. This was a program designed to coordinate Tulane and Xavier's involvement in urban communities in New Orleans, specifically in the area of public housing, economic development, and education. I started developing this community development program, which was a little idea. I approached Henry Cisneros, the former secretary of Housing and Urban Development, for grant support of my work. Cisneros said, "I got a better idea, why don't you fix public housing in New Orleans." The federal government gave Tulane $10 million to create university-based programs to work with the residents of public housing over five years. In exchange, Tulane gave 50 percent of me to public housing. My task was to fix the public housing authority in New Orleans, which was the worst in the country at the time. So I was doing two jobs for about four years. Out of that grew the National Center for the Urban Community.

We did some neat work. We brought service learning to Tulane. We had courses where students got credit for doing the service. We created Individual Development Accounts, which are all over the state now, where banks and businesses invested in accounts for poor people who were on a life development plan. At successful completion of the plan, the individuals were allowed to use the funds in the account to support a college education, or whatever they wanted to do. The program is statewide now, and it started with my center in New Orleans.

Marie V. McDemmond

President, Norfolk State University

Dr. Marie V. McDemmond is the president of Norfolk State University, the nation's fifth largest historically black university. Appointed in 1997, McDemmond is the University's first female president and the first woman to serve as chief executive officer of a four-year, state supported university in Virginia. McDemmond is also a member of the White House Board of Advisors on Historically Black Colleges and Universities.

McDemmond brings to Norfolk State University a wealth of experience in higher education business and financial management. At the time of her appointment by the Board of Visitors, she was serving as vice president for finance for Florida Atlantic University and its seven campuses. Before joining the administration of Florida Atlantic, she served as director of finance for the 15 community colleges in Massachusetts, assistant vice president for finance at Emory University, vice president for budget and finance at Atlanta University, and associate vice chancellor for finance at the University of Massachusetts at Amherst. McDemmond received her bachelor of arts degree from Xavier University of Louisiana, and her master's degree from the University of New Orleans. She did additional graduate work in public finance and management at the State University of New York at Albany and received her doctoral degree from the University of Massachusetts at Amherst.

As a result of the leadership of McDemmond Norfolk State University has entered a new era in science and technology. The university is strengthening existing programs and building new concentrations in a number of *science and technology fields. The centerpiece of the science and technology emphasis is the ongoing construction of the RISE Center (Research and Innovation to Support Empowerment), a complex of two buildings — a 150,000 square feet building and a 240,000 square feet building — that will include research space and data center space. The RISE Center will complement several existing "Centers of Excellence" at Norfolk State University, one of which is the Center for Materials Research, a hub for graduate work in the sciences. New degree offerings include master's programs in chemical physics, electronic engineering, and optical engineering.*

Additionally, McDemmond is making concerted efforts to empower the community. A key component of the RISE Center will be a center for entrepreneurship to help small and minority-owned businesses develop. In an effort to improve public education at the secondary level McDemmond has partnered with NASA to provide a pre-service teacher training program called the BEST Lab (Bringing Science and Education Together). The BEST Lab focuses on teaching education majors enrolled at historically black colleges and universities effective pedagogical methods for teaching math and science to elementary level students. The University also operates a Children's College, a year-round program that offers local public school students the opportunity to enhance their skills in reading, mathematics, and computer while enjoying the environment of a university campus. Additionally, McDemmond is working on plans to build a university laboratory school serving kindergarten through sixth grade that will take students and improve the way they are being taught math and science.

All of these initiatives are built around McDemmond's commitment to diversity. She has made special efforts to recruit Hispanic students, one of the

Maria V. McDemmond (courtesy Norfolk State University).

fastest growing population groups in the Hampton Roads area. Indeed, Norfolk State University is a proud member of the Hispanic Association of Colleges and Universities — the only historically black institution so affiliated. McDemmond has also made efforts to recruit Asian American students, Filipino American students, and international students, especially from Africa and the West Indies. Moreover, Norfolk State has established partnerships with several universities abroad, including one with a university in the Virgin Islands.

The most important priorities facing the presidents of historically black colleges and universities in the twenty-first century are related to available resources. Just like all college presidents, we have a tremendous need for resources to keep the physical facilities and the infrastructure, particularly technology infrastructure, hardware and software up to date. Uniquely to the historically black colleges, and maybe not if you look at what is going to happen in the next five to ten years in all of higher education, is to be able to secure quality faculty. As you know, the faculty is aging and all universities will have a very big push to be able to retain or hire new faculty to replace those that will be retiring. The final priority is to help people understand that historically black colleges and universities still have a role to play in this whole arena of higher education. It is still very hard for traditionally black colleges and universities to prove their worth in the circles of American higher education.

Norfolk State University has a unique history. It started as a part of Virginia Union University and then as the two-year division of Virginia State College, providing education for African Americans in the Tidewater Virginia area. We did not become a full university in our own right until the late '60s. And because of that history we have a very, very diverse population of alums who have connections both here and at Virginia State. But that alumni population is very, very supportive.

I inherited a lot of very excellent programs. For example, Norfolk State was one of the first historically black colleges to gain accreditation for its School of Business. When I arrived we had a fully accredited School of Education. And the same for the School of Social Work. We also had a tremendous wealth of alumni.

The number and quality of African American professionals produced by the historically black colleges and universities has been our number one contribution. And that we are continuing to do. My alma mater, Xavier University, for example, produces the top number of African Americans going on to medical school. That is not by accident. That is by a plan that they have developed and implemented.

How do we define our mission in the twenty-first century? In our mission statement at Norfolk State University we address the question of our role in today's rapidly changing society. We have focused on that as a primary objective: what it means to be a twenty-first century historically black college and educating for this rapidly changing global society. And we are focused on the very key points. First of all, it requires that you have the technology and computing power to give out the capabilities and the experiences, usually those entities—technology and science—that any student at any university would have.

I really worry about any school that cannot provide the kind of access to the technology of the future, or the current technology that will lead to the future. I think critically we have to be able to produce competitively qualified students, and that will require technology. It also requires students who can be very well written and who have good interpersonal skills and oral communication skills, and who will be able to address the many social changes that are going to come about. And as we work to do that we must carve out missions, as at any university today, but particularly traditionally black institutions, about what we are going to be strong in. We cannot be strong in everything.

I think historically black colleges should preserve their heritage and historic mission. Just like the women's colleges are preserving their heritage of women's education and the commitment to women that these women's colleges have, we must continue to do that as our commitment to our students. If we look at that commitment, it maybe taking a different form, but the heritage never changes. We will always be historically black institutions and there will always be the need for us, now and in the future, as there was in the past.

Maintaining the emphasis on heritage is just a better way to understand the country, the cultural-ethnic background of our people. For example, at Norfolk State we have a really very large push to diversify our student population. That means bringing in students—Hispanic students, Asian students, and Filipino students—which constitute a very high population of the Hampton Roads area. We have a Hispanic lab and we have a Hispanic recruiter. We go to the Hispanic areas. We are the only historically black college that belongs to the Hispanic Association of Colleges and Universities. We are making a concerted effort because we see that it is a growing population that has very similar socioeconomic backgrounds and concerns as our students here. And I see that as a way and another context by which our students and the majority students who come to our institution understand their culture; that they really have to live in another culture in some ways, and quote another culture, just like we did, as we attended their institutions. They are prone to be more adept to the culture of our institutions.

And we have foreign students, the majority from Africa or the West Indies. We have 30 percent of our student population from outside of Virginia, and about ten percent of those are international. And we have done some things in international education, working and helping out a new university in Ghana. We do some work in the Virgin Islands by offering the Master of Social Work (MSW) program down on St. Croix and St. Thomas. Our professors were actually down there to start the MSW program to the needs of the Virgin Island community. The end result of diversity is enabling people to get along better. To help people accept differences is the end result of diversity; accepting differences and not trying to acclimate everybody to one ethnic or cultural bias.

A Curriculum for the Twenty-First Century

With regard to the curriculum of traditionally black institutions in the twenty-first century I believe that if a historically black college is going to be a good teaching university and focus on liberal arts and undergraduate education it ought to do that without trying to do master's programs or research, or getting a research grant that does not reinforce the curriculum. I believe everything that we do on a campus must reinforce the curriculum from which the college or university has its mission to deliver. One notion of strategic planning is that you start off with what is called an environmental scan. And that environmental scan has to say, "Okay, Where am I seated? Where do I live? Where does this college or university live? And what do we need to provide because we live here?" And what I mean by that, particularly those of us that are state universities, is "what do we owe back to the benefactors of our university, those people who support us with their tax dollars?" They owe to be produced a student or citizen eventually, who has the capacity of producing additional tax dollars. So we want to make sure we produce marketable students.

We have focused on five schools. When I came here we had nine. Now, we have five schools: Education being along with Social Work, a long-standing strength, the Business School, which is fully accredited, our Liberal Arts, which is the core of all universities, and finally, our Science and Technology. As a school we have decided to place emphasis on science and technology. We decided that because of where we sit in Virginia and

Virginia's emphasis on the Internet, and northern Virginia now looking for a way to expand that region's impact on the rest of Virginia. Looking at Hampton Roads being a capital of the military — the largest naval base in the world is here. All of these things reinforce that our students must be technologically competent.

And so we are increasing our programs and strengths in the science and technology fields. For example, we have a master's in chemical physics now and world material science. And we have a center that we started, even before I came here, about seven years ago. That institute, the Center for Materials Research, has done extremely well in being able to garner research grants and to get assistantships for graduate students. So we have been able to produce students fulfilling their master's in that program.

We said we need to build on that. And some programs that go on with that are electronic engineering and optical engineering. Through the office of Civil Rights Settlement with the State of Virginia last year, we were able to outline and define two new degree programs, undergraduate and master's in electronic and optical engineering. We have an undergraduate degree program in computer science already, which is fully accredited, and we are now beginning to offer a master's in that field. These programs offer us a big focus on being able to push the Science and Technology School, to enlarge it, to be able to have more students attend it.

Another key program of our science and technology emphasis is the RISE Center. RISE stands for Research and Innovation to Support Empowerment. The Center is going to be built on land in an empowerment zone and an enterprise zone. We are a community that needs revitalization. So, we want to capitalize on the capabilities that those types of designations provide. The RISE is going to be two separate buildings joined together by an atrium. The first will be a multispace, 150,000 square feet building that will include research space, data center space, and a center for entrepreneurship so that we can help small and minority-owned businesses develop. And it will also have a workforce and daycare component. We want to be able to help this area of Hampton Roads increase the wage base of the people in the area, not just the minimum-wage jobs. We want to be able to do workforce training and development that will enable not only the students, but also the community residents, to go out and get higher paid jobs in the technology fields. That will be part of it.

The second building is going to be a public-private partnership. It will be 240,000 square feet. It will be leased out to businesses and corporations that want to train community members and students as workers. These will be companies that want to reside in the empowerment zone. Why is that? Because they get a tax break. They get tax breaks for having a business in the empowerment zone. And they also get tax breaks for providing or hiring people who live in the empowerment zone and training them in their businesses so that they become gainfully employed. So we are trying to capitalize on that. And we see the real possibilities in generating revenue from the rental space in the private-public partnership that will be built by a company with us out of Connecticut. We will use the revenue to further reinforce our curriculum here.

We have another initiative we are focusing on. It is connected to RISE, and it is called our University Lab School. About six years ago, we developed with NASA a partnership for pre-service teacher training. We have defined here at Norfolk State University "Centers of Excellence" and one is our BEST Lab. It is a lab whose initials stand for Bringing Education and Science Together. What we began to see was that the teachers who do not know math and science well, or teachers who are afraid of math and science themselves, do not teach math and science well. So what you have to do is to take the fear away from those teachers and give them better ways to teach math and science. So this BEST Lab developed a number of new mechanisms. And in working with math, NASA has a part of its education focus to increase the number of all people, but particularly people in the math and science fields where minorities are underrepresented, particularly African Americans. Therefore we have structured over the last five years, a large grant program with NASA called the Pre-Service Teacher Institute where, in the summer, we take students from a number of historically black colleges and universities and they come here to NASA Langley in Hampton, Virginia. And we train them in how to teach math and science better, in a nonthreatening way, particularly those who are going to be elementary and secondary teachers because that is where the kids get turned off, in the first, second, and third grades, on math and science.

The program has been so successful that it indeed has been expanded to two other NASA sites. The one in Alabama is NASA Johnson. And then the one in Mississippi is NASA Stennis. We have been able to help many more students who want to teach math and science better, but themselves who do not have the background. These are people who are education majors at historically black colleges and universities. So they come out with a better understanding on how to teach math and science.

Now to capitalize on that, I said well, why don't we just have our own elementary school here at Norfolk State? Many of the historically black colleges had university lab schools; they used to call them university laboratory schools. Many of the majority schools have them. When I was at Florida Atlantic University in Boca Raton, Florida, before I came to Norfolk State, my son attended the university lab school. And they had a major focus on computerized education because IBM had a plant directly across from the university. So, I want to structure the Norfolk State University lab school starting kindergarten through sixth grade to take students and teach them math and science better than they are currently being taught — so that they will have that positive self-concept about their ability to learn math and science. It is almost too late after third grade.

A prominent component of higher education in the twenty-first century is online or distances degree training. At the historically black colleges, I believe, we need to live within our financial means. And many of us do not have the capability to offer distance education. Last year, the Southern Association of Colleges and Schools, our accrediting body, held a conference. I was the chairperson of a workshop presented by a researcher from the University of Virginia, but who has been at George Mason and Virginia Tech. And what he proved in this workshop, it was about a four-year study he had done, is that distance education is more expensive to deliver than regular classroom education. So my problem is that many of us cannot afford to offer distance education. And there is a uniqueness to what historically black colleges and universities offer. And that uniqueness is that we do academic preparation in a very nurturing environment. Often that nurturing environment is missed through the computer. I believe that we need to do what we do best. I am not a big proponent. We do have some small distance-learning programs. But we are not into it in a big way.

Governance and Management

We are much more participatory in our governments and management now at Norfolk State than I think many historically black colleges and universities have been. We have a faculty governance and faculty senate kind of committee and we have a chapter of the American Association of University Professors. We do not do a lot of committees here. We do have the normal standing committees that universities have. But we have faculty working groups, particularly task based groups that work to identify problems as well as to resolve those problems. The faculty working group concept has allowed many of the faculty to have input. They volunteer to serve on the different committees. They have input into the decision-making process.

We also completely decentralized the university budget process. Many universities, black and white, keep the budgeting and allocation of resources very closed and close to heart. What we have done at Norfolk State is that the university-wide budget process involves a faculty representative from every school and allows them to work with the administration and the faculty senate to really structure the financial allocations.

We have funded a great deal of faculty development. We have an office that allowed faculty, up until this year because of the budget cuts, to go off and get their training up to date. We do a lot of training on campus through our Office of Information Technology. I think what you have to do is make the opportunities available both financially, so faculty can go off and be developed. And we have used some of our Title III money, for example, to assist some of our faculty in completing their terminal degree. And you have got to encourage faculty to take advantage of on-campus training programs such as how to use computers or how to use the new student advising system.

Fundraising and Development

One of the biggest challenges confronting the presidents of historically black colleges and universities in the area of fundraising and development is staffing — to be able to provide the staffing to raise money. First of all, it costs money to raise money. A lot of people do not understand that. A lot of historically black colleges and universities have really just looked at soft money as a way to raise money, and soft money being grants and contracts, or going to foundations and corporations. Nationally, 70 percent of all money raised for higher education comes from individuals. And unfortunately, we have not nurtured or cultivated our alumni enough; those are generally your big donors, your alumni, at most institutions. Many of our alumni, though, are not as wealthy as the alumni of majority institutions. We have to take that into consideration. That is a big issue. Having the staff and having the people or the areas to cultivate so they will see the advantage of giving a large or major gift to your university, a historically black college or university.

We have been very active on our Annual Fund. For example, when

I came here we raised about $600,000 to $700,000 a year. This year we raised over three million dollars. And we have been very active with developing contributions from churches and contributions from alums that we have not been in touch with for a long time. Also, with our faculty, they are out there. Some of them build a competition every year to see who raises the most money or contributes the most money to the university. So we use that strategy and constantly telling people that we need money. We raise money mainly for only one purpose and that is student scholarships. That is where our need is. We have around 88 percent of students on some form of financial aid. We need to provide our students with the resources to go to school.

There are many things historically black colleges and universities can do to increase alumni participation. I think first, by involving the alumni, having alumni chapters spread throughout the state where there is a large population of alumni. I think that is one big thing. Secondly, the schools must have a very active national alumni board, where they are invited to campus, where they still have a hook into the campus with either homecoming football games or other activities. The president has to visit alumni chapters. I spend a great deal of my time going to alumni banquets or fundraising events in California, Washington, DC, Baltimore, or wherever.

With regard to increasing federal support to historically black colleges, there are specific funds that we get as Title III money. But in addition to that, I think we can make sure we have a product that the government would want to buy into, be it some type of research, or a training grant for our students and faculty so that we can do the best training job that we can because some of the historically black colleges are not able to do high-level research that some of the majority institutions are receiving a great deal of money for.

An important federal initiative on traditionally black colleges is the White House Board of Advisors on Historically Black Colleges and Universities. The Board was started under President Jimmy Carter. It started out as an executive order. And every President since Carter has issued an executive order on Historically Black Colleges and Universities. Now each order is slightly different, but they all specify several major things. One relates to the question of how historically black colleges can get more money from the government. The order says that the government should "earmark funds for historically black colleges and universities to obtain"— some kind of earmarked funds that would enable the college to enhance itself, that enhancement aspect of our historically black colleges. Now every President, as I stated, has issued a revised order and has appointed the presidents of historically black colleges and some corporate leaders to be on the Board. I am a member of the current White House Board of Advisors on Historically Black Colleges and Universities.

The Historically Black College Week is a major event that is held annually in Washington, DC. The White House Initiative Office is the one that sponsors the program. And we have a lot of sessions with agency heads and people representing the agencies to talk about what historically black colleges do and how we can do it better with additional resources from them.

Is there a specific agenda that I have? Yes. And that is to be able to provide a higher profile for historically black colleges in Washington. To make people understand that our students are a valuable commodity for the country and prove that we produce a number of the leaders that will be leading our country in future years.

The Importance of Institutional Partnerships and Cooperatives

I think there should be partnerships between historically black colleges and majority institutions or between traditionally black colleges and other minority-serving institutions. No college or university today can afford to offer all of its own majors without cooperation. We have several partnerships here at Norfolk State. For example, we have cross registration with Old Dominion University, the majority state-supported institution here. If we are not offering a course here, our students can take it at Old Dominion, and vice versa. In addition to that, we have structured a task force with Tidewater Community College. I think historically black colleges have not cooperated or worked well enough with the community colleges. We have some of the similar populations of students and we have always been afraid that they are going to take our students. But we have begun raising admission standards at Norfolk State University too because the state does not allow us to offer any remedial education anymore in state universities. So, I did not want our students to come here and fail. I think it is worse for a student to fail, for his or her self-concept, than maybe to have never come here at all. So we wanted to make sure that our students were successful, that we did everything possible to guarantee their success. So, students with under a 2.0 average from their high schools and SATs under 825 were advised to go to the community college, to this Task Force Program. Now at the community college they were able to take the remediation that they need, particularly in math, science, or English. They can also take credit courses, which when they are ready to come back to Norfolk State they can transfer. We assign mentors to them, our educational office professionals or classified staff in the offices, who are people that they need to know in the departments and everywhere. Those mentors call them and see how they are doing and try to stay in touch. We invite them to the football games. And those students can come back to Norfolk State when their grade point average is above 2.5 and they have completed the remediation they needed. And they come back without even having to reapply. And they do not have to finish the associate degree at the community college.

Students: Career and Professional Choices

In terms of the career and professional choices of our students generally, we are seeing that many more of them are going into the sciences, into technology, particularly into computer science. We are seeing not as many wanting to be in education or business as before. There is still a large percentage of them that want to be in social work and the social sciences. Generally we see the students picking up on the technology and, in some ways, the hard sciences trend that we see the country going with.

The presidents of historically black colleges and universities can also play an important role in increasing the number of African American students who go on to graduate and professional programs. First of all, the presidents must let freshmen know that graduate school is an option, that graduate school does not need to be expensive, and that if you do well you can get a scholarship that will provide full funding for your graduate program. Depending on your major there may also be a teaching assistantship. It should be seen as an option in the very beginning of the freshman year for students rather than waiting till their junior year, and then maybe not having the grades to go on to graduate school. So make that an option in the very beginning. Have students understand what graduate education entails. Our students participate in a number of programs during the summer that relates to special grants from the GEM program (National Consortium for Graduate Degrees for Minorities in Engineering and Science) to increase opportunities for underrepresented minority students to obtain graduate degrees in engineering and the natural and physical sciences. We also have the AMPS program (Alliances for Minority Participation) here, which works with many of the students in the sciences so that they participate in summer internships. With such research scholarships they can be involved in research even before they will go on to graduate school. These programs give students a realistic idea of what graduate school entails.

A Commitment to Service

At Norfolk State University we are also continuing the tradition of community service. Service to our community is paramount. We were just in a study about a year ago with the University of Michigan. We were the only historically black college in the study. The study evaluated the commitment to service sophomore students had. And in regard to commitment to service we came out very, very high. And what we say to students, I say it in graduation speeches, convocation speeches, everything, is that you have an obligation, because you have made it this far, to go back and educate those in your community, those from where you have come, be it family, neighbors, or whatever. Education is the great equalizer. So we stress service. We are trying to put together right now a service-learning component — much more than we have had here. We have service built in the courses, but we clearly want to have more.

Alma Mater: Xavier University of Louisiana and Its Historic Commitment to Academic Excellence

There was never any question that I was going to college. It just seemed the natural progression for me. That was because my hometown of New Orleans was home to two black colleges, Xavier and Dillard. So there were these options for us to go on even though schools were not integrated when I grew up in New Orleans.

The Sisters of the Blessed Sacrament that founded Xavier really did inspire me. It is not so much that they were nuns or anything because I went through Catholic high school and elementary school. I went through 15 years of Catholic education under the Sisters of the Blessed Sacrament. What I mean is that you were told that you could do anything. You were not given any doubt that you could not succeed. No matter how poor you were or whatever. Xavier contained that philosophy from the Sisters of the Blessed Sacrament and it was expected for you to do well.

Academically, Xavier was very strong when I was there, as it is now. Xavier Prep, where I had gone, was the university preparatory school. We took Latin in my freshman and sophomore years. We took physics. We took those kinds of courses that were really truly college preparatory courses. Xavier socially was really very rigid. We had to wear stockings every day on campus. There were single-sex dorms. No coed dorms. So it was a very close-knit, but very conservative social environment as well.

My Vision for the Future of Norfolk State University and Black Higher Education

I picked out Norfolk State about five years before I even knew the president was retiring. I went through cycles in my professional career where I wanted to be a president, and where I did not want to be a president. I wanted to be a president because I thought I had learned a great deal and that I could help better institutions in higher education, especially historically black colleges, and also because I felt a commitment to historically black colleges. And I saw a need that historically black colleges had to improve and to advance faster than they were if they were going to survive. Finally I wanted to go back to a historically black college to be a president because the monetary skills I have picked up, in particular, are critical.

Norfolk State is in a region of the country that I like very much. Virginia is beautiful. It is right on the water. The other part of it is that Norfolk State has some excellent academic programs that I talked about before. So that attracted me to Norfolk State University, and my commitment is only to Norfolk State. I will not be president anywhere else. I have been nominated and have not accepted nominations. I am going to retire in a few years. I made a commitment to stay ten years because I think some presidents tend to stay too long.

Where will Norfolk State be five years from now? Clearly we will have the RISE Center fully functioning. We will have much stronger programs in science and technology. And we will have a student body just about where we are right now, seven to eight thousand students, focused on undergraduate programs namely, but 20 percent of them in master's programs and a few doctoral programs sprinkled here and there. We currently have two doctoral programs. One is a joint program with other schools, and then one in social work.

Where would I like to see historically black colleges and black higher education generally five to ten years from now? I would like to see us better respected among higher education circles. Secondly, I would like to see us with stronger management and stronger academic programs. I think that is true of any university, though. And historically black colleges have improved and have stronger academic programs. So I do not want to sound like I am saying we do not have them now. But we all have to improve and I want to see us being able to do that. I think also being on better financial footage.

I do not believe black colleges are overall noted for the treasures that they are. If we did not exist then we would have limited opportunities for the students we educate to become productive citizens. And that would not provide a good population, a good workforce for the United States as it has been with historically black colleges and universities. I think also that in the twenty-first century I would like to make sure that we are progressing at the level where we produce the most competitively qualified students. If we are not doing that then we have to reshape and revisit some of our institutions.

9

Carlton E. Brown

President, Savannah State University

Dr. Carlton E. Brown assumed the presidency of Savannah State University, Savannah, Georgia, in July 1997. Prior to his leadership of Savannah State University, Brown served as vice president for planning and dean of the Graduate College at Hampton University, Hampton, Virginia. From 1987 to 1996 he served as dean of the School of Liberal Arts and Education at Hampton.

In addition to his administrative background, Brown brings extensive teaching experience to his present position. He served on the faculty of the School of Education of Old Dominion University from 1979 to 1987, and worked as a high school teacher and counselor from 1971 to 1974. His research and scholarship focused on issues related to multicultural education, teacher education reform, and urban school renewal. Putting theory into practice, while serving as a high school teacher and counselor, Brown established and managed programs designed to improve the secondary school experience of minority students. And while on the faculty of Old Dominion University, he directed a major collaborative research project on minority student involvement in disciplinary incidents in Norfolk area schools. Additionally, Brown also served as an associate of the Center for Urban Education.

Since his appointment to Savannah State University in 1997, Brown has worked with the Board of Regents to implement a strategic plan to position the university for growth and expansion in the twenty-first century. He *has launched an aggressive technology enhancement initiative, including new state-of-the-art student housing, new ultra-modern laboratories and classrooms, and a well-wired campus. Savannah State university is one of only two campuses in the University System of Georgia that is completely wireless. At the same time, he has championed increased academic, cultural, and service opportunities for students and faculties by restructuring the university's curriculum to include greater emphasis on globalization and internationalization, forming partnerships and exchange programs with universities in China and Ghana, establishing an institute to coordinate university research, and creating a small business entrepreneurial center to foster economic development in the local community.*

Brown has also made clear his commitment to diversity. Savannah State University enrolls a significant number of other-race students, and the university's radio station was the first Savannah area station to offer Hispanic programming. A native of Macon, Georgia, Brown earned his bachelor's and doctoral degrees from the University of Massachusetts at Amherst.

For most of the history of historically black colleges and universities, they were literally the only preparation points for African Americans to enter key professions. There would not be an established middle class as a part of the African American community without the presence of these institutions. What we have found here at Savannah State University is that there are some historic strengths that have been developed that one would not normally have expected. Just the simple fact of leading people out of the countryside and the cotton fields and creating the dream of a higher education is substantial by itself. But when we dig a little bit deeper than that we find a significant legacy in the sciences and in technology.

That legacy in the sciences and in technology has served as a base for the development of some of

Carlton E. Brown (courtesy Carlton E. Brown).

our most successful programs. For example, it has served as a base for the development of our very historic naval ROTC program. Roughly 50 percent of the African American physicians in Savannah completed their undergraduate training at Savannah State University. And Savannah State University was also the focal point for the Civil Rights Movement in southeast Georgia. The university produced every one of the community's legendary heroes, including all the folks who ran the NAACP and who led the marches and who participated in the marches. So an enormous scientific legacy and a very strong civil rights legacy is at the heart of Savannah State University. And of course throughout its history the University has been a primary preparation point for teachers.

All college presidents, whether they are leaders of historically black colleges and universities, or any other institution, must develop a vision in the context of the society itself. But certainly that becomes a critical factor for the presidents of the institutions of traditionally African American higher education because without the context of vision for the institution, which also constitutes a continual redefinement of role as the society advances or issues related to race ebb and flow, each of those movements changes the position of the historically black colleges and universities in the society itself. So contextual vision is the number one priority.

Developing a niche is an important aspect of contextual vision. I tell my folks all the time if all we do and say in our undergraduate programs is what bigger institutions did then we have failed. We have to do what is expected of an undergraduate program, but we have to add some elements to that that makes it unique and makes it particularly responsive to our student clientele, and that positions our students differently in the job and graduate studies market upon completion. And obviously, we must obtain the resources to make all of that happen. Those three things — vision, niche, and resource allocation — are the top three priorities.

Institutional Identity: Heritage Is Important

When we say historically black college we are talking about one of the places that has as a primary focus the preservation of a history and a legacy, not just as an institution, but for the African American culture and experience. The black college should be an environment that maintains and enhances a set of traditions that are particularly important to African Americans. A most obvious example of a difference in culture and nature has to do with how we go about the business of celebration.

This is a place that preserves that particular pattern and defines community in a particular way. It is a place that provides a contextual education that is different from what you would find at the University of Georgia or even a similar resource and size state institution even in the same city that is not historically black. The vision has to be about how the education is provided, how the community is developed, how the institution advances itself, how the college community connects to its environment, and how it allows, or perpetuates, or facilitates the growth of the individual who chooses to reside on campus. All of that of course creates a set of expectations from faculty and staff, as well as from alumni for how they interact with the campus.

Our particular vision is to make this institution, as the legacy institution of southeast Georgia, the choice not only for any student from southeast Georgia, but a choice for having an understanding of context that we are not going to change who we are to diversify to any greater extent that the University of Georgia changes who it is in order to diversity. We will remain culturally and contextually African American as we grow and expand. We are a forum for the address of African American issues and concerns focusing on how they impact our students directly and as they impact our local and larger community. We are a place where those issues can play themselves out, not only in open forum, but also in curricula and programming. We believe maintaining a true community in the sense of how we communicate on campus, how we organize ourselves, how we address our concerns and issues in largely a very supportive, family-oriented atmosphere.

University Outreach and Engagement

From students, faculty, and administrators, who are interacting inside and outside the classroom, our emphasis on community service helps to create greater external interaction from the classroom. We connect to the city in ways that are uniquely ours. For instance, we operate a Small Business Development and Entrepreneurship Center in the city for the purpose of developing minority businesses. The objective of the Small Business Development and Entrepreneurship Center is to make a permanent change in the structure of the minority business community in this area. The middle class and the business community have remained essentially unchanged for about 50 years. The same small businesses still predominate; they are still the same range of mom and pop shops that come and go and no new impact on the business environment.

What we seek to do is to very aggressively develop new businesses that are at the center of the economy and that capitalize on the skills that exist in the community. For example, historic preservation is a big industry in Savannah, and many of the historic artisans have been African American. What we are seeking to do is to form a company and build it to the point where it contracts and subcontracts work like any other company and put in all the expertise that we can. We are very deliberately developing specific businesses that we think can live and grow at the center of the local economy. That is one avenue that we are working with.

Another one is people who have their own business ideas and who just need some help in putting it together and figuring out how to make it work. We service those folks, too. We provide course work to teach people how to put together an accounting system, how to build business plans, how to do marketing, how to carry out long-term business plans, how to obtain facility leases, how to go about equipment and material purchasing how to do employee configurations, how to reinvest profits back in the business, and so on. We also assist them with grant writing and loan applications. We are connected to two of the federal government small business loan centers.

We have grown about five small businesses and most of them remain successful. We have one clothing specialty store that is doing fairly well. We have an entrepreneurial business and technology software development that I think is going to do very well. It just landed its first two government contracts of $1 million each. We are considering it a fairly successful venture at this point.

We run the city's Black Heritage Festival every year. We interact with neighborhood associations, and in fact helped to build a new neighborhood center. Those are the things we do that make a difference — there are many more of course — that both define our niche and our method of operating. We put our students in the middle of all of those activities.

We do other service-related work. Our Social Work program works with a number of community agencies. What we try to do, in addition to what you normally do with social work and areas like that, is internships in standard organizations. We also try to tie our classes to specific issues and concerns in the community because we want our students to learn how to make change. We designed a new program for children in a very depressed neighborhood in another section of the city. There was some housing that we knew would be eliminated in the next few years. But in the meantime, children's lives were at stake and so we helped the neighborhood build a reading center and provided some services for students there.

We also involve our students directly through classroom work. In our College of Business we believe in practical application. For example our students in marketing will survey a community and determine some needs that are not addressed. We have the Ralph Mark Gilbert Civil Rights Museum here in Savannah. Our marketing students developed a website for the Museum. The students continue to provide ongoing assistance to the site, making sure it is operative and continual.

Twenty of our students intern in the Small Business Development Center every year. They are directly involved in the development of new businesses. So in addition to preparing them for more traditional roles in big corporations, they also learn how to do this kind of work. Everybody who is successful in the big business world at some point entertains the idea of starting their own business. Our students will actually know how to do that. Most do not. Our students will come away with critical skills.

Education is a mechanism of advancement. But what we try to focus on is the idea that advancement cannot be simply for the individual. It has to be the individual and responsibility to a larger community. If it is just the individual then the impact is severely limited, and you do not get to cause real change in the society. What we try to do is to help our students understand that in addition to taking care of themselves and their families they have obligations to the larger community.

I have had the kinds of experiences that I really want my students to have, which is involvement in actual change and then seeing the impact on individuals and on communities. Once you know what is possible if you make certain changes then you cannot help but continue to try to engineer change and improvement and demonstrate to people that there are things that are possible that they had not even been able to dream about.

Savannah State University: A Model of Diversity in Higher Education

Diversity is a critical aspect of my vision for Savannah State University. We have launched a new approach to increase the number of Hispanics and Asians on our campus. We believe that we will do well with that. In addition to providing a new set of services to those students, we are also continuing to be who we are. We do not find any contradictions at all. We will always be predominantly African American, and will always be historically black, and all the things that that means.

We employ a variety of strategies to attract Hispanic and Asian students. We are going directly to the organizations in the community that support local Asian and Hispanic populations. Our campus radio station was the first in the region many years ago to offer Hispanic programming. We have connections that we can exercise, and we are just getting more aggressive about our recruitment. We also boast the most diverse faculty in the University System of Georgia.

Our Center for International Education infuses internationalization and globalization components into both the curriculum and the campus environment. The center in its interactions with other departments addresses the questions that are designed to create a curriculum with more diverse perspectives, connects our students and our institution with other parts of the world, and assures us that those viewpoints are a part of the education that our students receive. We have students on our campus from 47 other countries. These include Asian, African, European, and Caribbean countries.

We also have a very active study abroad program. Every summer we send groups of faculty and students to China, and also to Ghana and West Africa. We hope to develop these programs into exchanges where students and faculty from those areas can come here. We have worked with two universities in China to the point where we are receiving our second exchange faculty member from there. We have several Ghanaian students on our campus, as well as a number of students from the Caribbean. People often make the assumption that historically black colleges and universities are all black. That is just not the case. Our institutions are very diverse.

Coming of Age in the Segregated South: Remembering the Important Role HBCUs Played in Black Community Life

I grew up in Macon, Georgia. I have vivid memories of the important role black colleges and universities played in African American community life during my youth. Every spring as we neared graduation there were certain people who would bring some of the students who were graduating from high school and just walk them around the neighborhood. These young people would talk about where they were going to college, and it was usually Morehouse, Spelman, Clark Atlanta, and places like that. We knew that was a big deal. And all though you knew these young people they looked special on those days. They looked extra powerful, and so all you really knew was that was who you wanted to be.

Most of my teachers in Macon were the graduates of historically black institutions. The most notable for me was my fourth grade teacher, a woman named Bertha Hughes, and who graduated from Spelman. One of my big memories of her is she used to teach us African American poetry — all about Langston Hughes and W.E.B. Du Bois and Countee Cullen, and so on. You gained some real sense of who you were coming out of Macon. Those were good memories — being able to grow up and know what Langston Hughes had said, and having in your head Hughes' poem "The Negro Speaks of Rivers."

Unfortunately, these qualities are missing from the public schools of today. I think we misread and misunderstood what desegregation was supposed to do. It should never take away anything that inspires young people to greatness. In the name of sameness we took away all of those things that inspired African Americans and left intact all the things in the school systems that inspire whites. Whites come up through the school systems and they know who they are, what they are about, and where they are going. African Americans robbed themselves of all of that.

Thoughts on the Future of HBCUs

The future should see historically black colleges and universities very strong. There will probably be fewer institutions, but those that remain should be strong and large, and at the center of the higher education enterprise. They will be acknowledged as major contributors to the economic and political development of the nation. And, they will be having a major impact on the outcomes of K-12 schooling because without that impact my clientele simply won't appear. Finally, they will be major addressers of social and political concerns in the country at large, but certainly in our localities and neighborhoods.

Localities in which historically black colleges and universities reside need to take a very hard close look at what that collaboration can really bring to the table for the communities. The communities themselves are not as advanced as could be simply because of their failure to take into full account the capabilities of historically black colleges and universities. We need to move to occupy a much more central role.

10

CALVIN W. LOWE

President, Bowie State University

Dr. Calvin W. Lowe has served as the ninth president of Bowie State University, Bowie, Maryland, since 2000. Lowe has been described as a "born leader" and an "individual who sees the endless possibilities that comprise higher education." Five years into his administration the extraordinary depth of his leadership skills and talents have been visibly manifested. The lodestar of the Lowe administration has been the enhancement of the university's curriculum in areas vital to preparing students to function competently in the highly technical and global world of the twenty-first century. The university has witnessed substantial growth and expansion in the areas of computer science, mathematics, information technology, and education. In addition to curricular improvements in mathematics and science, the university has improved the practical access of students to high technology by equipping all dormitories with computer labs and providing laptop computers to freshmen. The University also sponsors several initiatives designed to increase the number of students who seek advanced study in science, engineering, and mathematics. The most prominent of these initiatives is the Model Institutions for Excellence.

The labors of the Lowe administration have yielded bountiful fruits. Bowie currently ranks first nationally in graduating African American students with master's degrees in computer science and information sciences. These curricular advancements have paralleled a significant increase in student enrollment and retention. Lowe has also made service a key component of his administration. Bowie State University has formed several partnerships with Prince George's County to improve the academic performance of local public schools. Various programs associated with the partnership include a SAT Preparatory Saturday Academy, a program to improve student achievement in reading, and an effort to recruit future public school teachers. Lowe continuously speaks of his desire to recapture Bowie State University's prominence as a teacher training institution.

Lowe came to Bowie State from Hampton University, where he was vice president for research and dean of the graduate school. At Hampton, Lowe led several initiatives that culminated in the formation of the university's first doctoral program, which was in physics. He is also credited with securing a $10 million grant from NASA to establish the Hampton University Research Center for Optical Physics. Lowe has continued to engage in scientific research while serving in administrative posts and has authored numerous studies focusing on the optical properties of various compounds. He has received honors from several organizations for his research, including NASA and the United States Department of Defense. Lowe began his academic career as a member of the faculty of the University of Kentucky in Lexington. He has also served on the faculty and administration of Alabama A&M University. Lowe earned a bachelor's degree in physics from North Carolina A&T State University and a master's and doctoral degree in physics from the Massachusetts Institute of Technology (MIT).

Many people define a historically black college by the complexion of the students. That is in my estimation an entirely wrong way to define it. A historically black college is really defined by our sensibilities about how we teach. We embrace the basic concept that everyone who comes to the institution can learn and is worthy of our time as teachers to ensure that they learn. We attempt to compensate

Calvin W. Lowe (**courtesy Calvin W. Lowe**).

for learning deficiencies or disadvantages that students have. We try to provide an education that is broad — that is more than just "can you program a C++," "can you design web pages," "can you read," or "can you write," — but that provides some sensibility to what it takes to live. As a matter of fact, our tag line here at Bowie is "prepare for life." It has to do with preparing students to live in the world and to work in the world and do the real things that it takes to be a part of the future.

As we go forward our mission has to remain to prepare ALL students — not just African American students but any student who comes — for living in the future. We have to speak to our teaching paradigm that is more collaborative learning than competitive learning. We have to keep that going. There is going to be a need for that in the future because as other minorities — Hispanics and so forth — start to enter the educational market as first-generation college students HBCUs are the institutions that are best equipped to provide the kind of education these students will need just as with African Americans.

We are going to continue to be a school of opportunity. We are going to still have a fairly high percentage of first-generation college students. And we are going to do the things that those students need, such as educating people about how financial aid really works, how the college really works and so on. I do not see us moving away from that kind of paradigm of teaching in my lifetime.

Institutions are going to become more diverse as the population changes — that is just going to happen. You cannot stop it; you cannot slow it down; it is just going to happen. The question we will have to ask ourselves is: What are the things in our institution that goes beyond a value to black folks, or a value to white folks, or a value to green folks? What are the things that have that intrinsic value? Our teaching paradigm is something I believe that has intrinsic value, and we are going to have to work on how to use that paradigm to educate people — not just black people, not just Hispanics — but people. We know how to do this because we have been doing it for a long time. We know that when you are a first-generation college student there are things that you do not know about how to go to college — the things that when you wind up in a big majority high-powered institution can cause you to have a higher probability of not finishing because of something other than not being smart enough.

The only time that we will get into conflict with regard to establishing the mission of the institution is if we define the heritage preservation process or method as restricting or keeping our enrollment at 99.9

percent African American. As long as we do not define that as the level we intend to preserve the university system has no problem with it; neither does the federal government or anybody else. But if we use that as the criteria to define what "preserving our heritage" means, then everybody would have a problem, including me.

To me, preserving the heritage means that you preserve the way that you do things, preserve the paradigm of collaborative learning. You preserve the idea that you have as part of your mission an obligation to go out and help those students who would not ordinarily get a chance at performing at this level or learning at this level.

And so we want to make sure that our students understand how to interact with the real world, all the social parts and character parts and so forth. At the historically black colleges we know that when you cultivate the ground and fertilize the soil the produce is going to be bigger, prettier, brighter, and shinier than when you do not. That is the difference in paradigms that I am talking about. At the traditionally black colleges we spend more time cultivating and pruning and fertilizing the students so that when they arrive into those environments that are a little more hostile, they are better prepared to cope.

Recapturing Bowie State University's Legacy of Teacher Training

Bowie State traditionally was a teacher education college. One of my so-called grand challenges to the institution is to recapture our prominence as a teacher of teachers. There is a tremendous need for teachers and it is going to continue for some time. There is a need in terms of numbers, and there is also a need in terms of quality. We are going to have to bring our secondary schools— our elementary schools, middle schools, and high schools— up. They are going to have to do a better job of educating our students, especially minorities, than they are currently doing. Even in the best of situations they are not doing all that great a job. So we are going to have to make that better. Part of making that better involves making better teachers— more knowledgeable teachers in terms of subject matter and in terms of the psychological part of teaching.

We hired a new dean of education who came to us from Capital University whose research is on the education of black males. So we are putting more emphasis on the quality of what we are doing to train teachers, more emphasis on recruiting students into the program, and more emphasis on making sure that they pass the Praxis Examination.

At Bowie, in order to graduate with an education degree you have to pass the Praxis II Exam. Therefore, all the teachers that we graduate are certified. Last year we had a 98 percent pass rate on the Praxis Exam.

Vision and Planning: Core Values Define the Institution

As the president of a college or university the main challenge is to keep your eye on the ball in terms of what is the core value of the institution. It is my opinion that our teaching paradigm — this ideal of collaborative learning — is a core value of historically black colleges. It is a core value of Bowie State University. And as we go forward we have to make sure that that core value goes forward, too.

I keep pictures of my predecessors on the wall of my study to remind me I am not the first to arrive and I will not be the last one here. I stand on their shoulders and I have to provide shoulders for others to stand on. But also, just looking at them and the way they are dressed and their appearances from the periods that they were president reminds me of what is the core mission of this institution. We need that history all about campus, all around everything we do. We need to talk about our history, about how to use it as a guide, not an anchor.

Connecting Vision and Resources: The Special Challenge Facing Public Higher Education Institutions

The challenge is always resources. If you compare Bowie State University financially to the place I came from most recently — Hampton University — which is a completely private institution, we have about the same number of students, roughly 5,000. Our state appropriation at Bowie is about $25 million a year. Hampton's endowment probably produces about that amount of money. Their annual operating budget is about $100 million. Now, the tuition at Hampton is probably three times the tuition at Bowie, so they have more funds per student to operate with than we have. Our challenge is to find out how to close that gap without increasing tuition to the point of what you would pay at a private institution. That is really the challenge of almost every state institution. The difficult part is that foundations still think of state-supported schools as not needing money.

That is not the case, especially for historically black colleges, because states are not providing the kinds of resources that are necessary. I do not think it is easy for any institution, including ones such as College

Park, Howard, or Princeton. Any time that you are trying to make progress you are going to always be resources limited. Two words that are most amusing when placed next to each other are "limited" and "resources" because I have never been in any situation where the resources were unlimited. The only time that you do not feel that effect of having limited resources is when you are either sitting still — which means the institution is not making any progress — or you are slowly going backwards. Trying to make progress is the hard direction.

Enhancing University Management

In terms of making the university work better, I often compare the university's administration to an elevator. When you step in an elevator and you press the button to the top floor, what do you think about on your way up? You think about what you are going to do when the doors open. And unless you are going to the hundredth floor or something, you probably are not thinking about "Hmmm, I wonder if this thing is wired up right?" "I wonder if the doors are going to open?" "I wonder if the button that says five really stops on five?" You are not distracted by any of that. You are only thinking about what is going to happen when the door opens and you step out. I think when you come to the university, depending upon who you are, because we are here for different reasons — students are here to learn, faculty are here to teach and do research, and administration is here to administer — we all have different jobs. And anything that takes us away from that primary goal creates a distraction.

But when the university operates like the elevator, and you are a student on that elevator, you are just thinking about what you are going to do when you arrive at the end of the four years and you step out. Where do you go from there? You should not have to worry about the financial aid process, the registration process and so on. Those things should be painless. They should be as painless as pushing the button in the elevator. You just do it, and then that is over with and you get on with your main purpose for being there. That is where we have to get to now. We have to make that happen. It is difficult and it takes time and I hope that when it comes time for me to leave Bowie State that I can look back and say: "We made that happen."

I think for any leader of a university or organization the best you can hope for is that you have a good take on the big picture and that you are able to move toward that goal. It is like playing football. Your two yards may not be the ones that take you across the goal. Really what you want to do is to move your organization forward. You have to be realistic. When you leave the institution, no matter whether you have been a good president or a bad president, or whether you are going on your terms or somebody else's terms, the next person who comes in is going to be brought in to fix the things that you did not fix. So you have to be realistic about that. You should just try to see the big picture for the institution, and try to move the institution a littler closer toward that big picture.

Alma Mater: North Carolina A&T State University — A Stepping-Stone to Success

I grew up in North Carolina. For the first five grades I attended segregated schools. The schools had black principals, mostly black teachers, and all black students. I completed undergraduate work at North Carolina A&T State University in Greensboro. When I applied to A&T State University I also applied to the University of North Carolina at Chapel Hill. I looked at the difference in cost of going and financial aid and so forth and I wound up going to A&T because of cost, because of financial aid, and also because a lot of the people I went to high school with went to A&T.

I believe that A&T was the best place to go to accomplish the things I wanted to accomplish. In retrospect, I am very glad I did not go to Chapel Hill. I think that I would not have survived there. It would have been sufficiently inhospitable to make it difficult for this guy from a rural part of North Carolina with a tiny school system to survive at a place like that where the focus was on competitive learning. Many of my friends from high school went to A&T or North Carolina Central, and there were one or two who went to the University of North Carolina Chapel Hill and North Carolina State University. Of the ones who went to Chapel Hill or North Carolina State very few survived. But almost all of us who went to black colleges not only survived but *thrived*.

The environment of the historically black colleges made the difference. We were learners and we worked hard at making the next step. I think none of us — the kind of peer group I was a part of — thought of A&T as our final stop. We all realized that we were just passing through and we had four years to do all the things we wanted to get done. We were looking forward to the next step. It was clear to all of us that A&T was a stepping stone to something.

The environment of North Carolina A&T was very nurturing, but not to the point of being crippling. One of the things you have to be careful of in these schools is that you do not go overboard with the nurturing part because as a student the learning part is your responsibility. The teaching part is the institution's responsibility. And no matter how much the institution nurtures you, it cannot learn it for you.

Black Colleges at the Crossroads: Changes and Transformations of the Late 1960s and Early 1970s

I do not recall many debates in the late 1960s and early 1970s about the future existence of the black colleges. In fact, in the 1970s, the answer to that question would have been the same as the answer we talked about earlier. Okay, so shut the schools down — now what? Where are you going to put the students? Certainly the thought that there would not be an A&T or North Carolina Central was not something we talked about, or thought about.

I think the only dilemma was really one of trying to decide how much pain you wanted to endure for the cause. I do not think many people thought for instance about what would happen to the black secondary schools as African Americans integrated. We have witnessed the demise of the black high schools. At the end of legally imposed segregation black students were bussed to white schools and the black high schools became either secondary schools, or middle schools, or just went out of business totally. I do not think there was much thought about that. I think now the alumni of those schools — the last classes who graduated from those black high schools are in their 60s — are beginning to think about how much has been lost. That is one of those things that drive the black college existence debate.

Perspectives on the Future of Bowie State University: Using Our History and Traditions as a Guide, Not an Anchor

Bowie State University has many things going for it. It has a great location. It has a tradition in teacher preparation, which is something very important for the future of the country. In terms of location, there are many things around here. There are numerous federal laboratories and Washington, DC, has a wealth of resources. Bowie could really grow and become a good model of the historically black college of the twenty-first century. We could have a nice diversity of students here. We can have Hispanic students, Asian students, African American students, students from all sorts of backgrounds. We also have the information technology component that is going to make the natural science department interesting. We can have a very interdisciplinary approach to teaching science and training scientists.

The emphasis on historically black colleges has to be on the "H"—the historical. The mix of our clientele will change with the demographics. I think we will still be a majority minority institution, but we won't be the 90 plus percentage that we are currently. The future of historically black colleges, in general, is bright — with the proviso that we look to our history as a guide, and our traditions as a guide, not as an anchor. We cannot remain in the past. We have to go forward.

Appendix: Profiles of Historically Black Institutions

Alabama

Alabama Agricultural and Mechanical University. Huntsville. Founded 1875. Public, no religious affiliation. Enrollment: 4,332.

In 1873 Alabama A&M University (originally known as the "Colored Normal School at Huntsville") was established by decree of the state legislature. The school opened on May 1, 1875, and former slave and black educator William Hooper Councill served as the first school president. The principal mission of the school was to train Africa American teachers. In 1885 the school name was changed to State Normal and Industrial School of Huntsville and six years later, in 1891, the school became a designated land-grant college.

In 1927 Auburn native Joseph Fanning Drake became the fourth school president. Serving for 35 years—from 1927 to 1962 — Drake's tenure was one characterized by massive expansion and development of both the university's physical plant and academic programs. Indeed, Drake is widely recognized as the builder of the modern Alabama A&M University.

Alabama A&M continues to occupy a unique place in American higher education. It is one of only three historically black colleges offering a bachelor's degree in city planning and one of a few traditionally black higher education institutions with a bachelor's program in telecommunications.

Alabama State University. Montgomery. Founded 1867. Public, no religious affiliation. Enrollment: 6,038.

In 1867, blacks in Alabama, motivated by a desire to uplift their race through education founded the Lincoln Normal School in Marion. In 1868, the northern American Missionary Association (AMA), a leader in the development of black education in the South, took control of the fledging institution.

In addition to the contributions of local African Americans and the American Missionary Association, Peyton Finley, an African American who served on the Alabama Board of Education during Reconstruction, played a prominent role in the early development of Lincoln Normal School. In 1871 Peyton petitioned the state legislature to establish an institution for the higher education of black citizens. In 1873, after an initial rejection, the state granted Finley's petition and reorganized Lincoln Normal School as a state-supported educational institution for African Americans under the name the State Normal School and University at Marion. In 1886, the school moved to the state capital of Montgomery and greatly expanded it programs and offerings, evolving into State Teachers College in 1929, Alabama State College for Negroes in 1948 and Alabama State College in 1954.

Located in a city known as the "cradle of the Confederacy," Alabama State College played a pivotal role in the emerging Civil Rights Movement of the 1950s. Many Alabama State College faculty members worshipped at Montgomery's Dexter Avenue Baptist Church, where they heard a young minister from Atlanta by the name of Dr. Martin L. King, Jr. (then unknown outside of his immediate congregation), preach inspiring messages of racial uplift, interracial brotherhood, and social justice. Activist Alabama State College faculty, such as Dr. Jo Ann Gibson Robinson, a professor of English, played key roles in the Montgomery Improvement Association, the group that organized the 1955 Montgomery Bus Boycott that brought Dr. Martin L. King, Jr., to national prominence. Ralph David Abernathy, a 1950 graduate of Alabama State College, became known nationally because of his close association with Dr. King and his co-leadership of the influential Southern Christian Leadership Conference.

Concordia College. Selma. Founded 1922. Religious affiliation: Lutheran. Enrollment: 1,556.

Located in Selma, Alabama, Concordia is the nation's only historically black Lutheran Church-related college. As a four-year, coeducational institution fully owned and operated by the Lutheran Church-Missouri Synod "the Christian faith as taught from the Holy Scriptures is the foundation and guide for all programs, activities, and relationships at Concordia."

The origins of Concordia College date back to 1919 when the Lutheran Synodical Conference of North America sent missionaries into southern Alabama to assist in efforts to improve the spiritual and educational conditions of African Americans. Within three years, more than 20 congregations were established.

In 1922 the Synodical Conference established the Alabama Lutheran Academy in Selma for the special purpose of training professional church workers. The Rev. R.O. Lynn was the first president. Other the years, other capable and brilliant men such as Dr. Edward Wescott, the Rev. W.H. Ellwanger, Dr. Varnes J. Stringer, and Dr. Paul G. Elbrecht led the institution, and through their dedicated service made growth and modernization possible.

In July 1981 the name of the institution was changed from Alabama Lutheran Academy to Concordia College. In 1994 the school received full accreditation as a four-year institution.

Miles College. Birmingham. Founded 1905. Religious affiliation: Christian Methodist Episcopal. Enrollment: 1,660.

Miles College reflects the vision of African American churchmen and women who endeavored to uplift their race through education. Established in 1905 by the Colored Methodist Episcopal Church (now the Christian Methodist Episcopal Church), Miles has a long and proud history of training educational, religious, political, and community leaders for the African American community.

Miles College was chartered as Miles Memorial College in honor of Bishop William Henry Miles, a leader in the Methodist Episcopal Church. The school awarded its first baccalaureate degree in 1911.

For the first half of the twentieth century Miles College was the only metro Birmingham four-year college open to African American students, thus educating in the undergraduate service the bulk of black educational and political leaders in the area. Miles original mission of fusing religious ethics with the liberal arts tradition continues today. The school's curriculum emphasizes morality and ethics and adherence to Christian values.

Oakwood College. Huntsville. Founded 1896. Religious affiliation: Seventh Day Adventist. Enrollment: 1,805.

Oakwood College was founded in 1896. It is located in Huntsville,

Alabama, in the northwest region of the state, and is affiliated with the Seventh Day Adventist Church.

Oakwood College offers a liberal arts curriculum in a Christ-centered environment. As an institution of the Seventh Day Adventist Church the promotion and perpetuation of Christian values is an integral aspect of the school's outlook.

Diversity is an essential element of Oakwood College. The student body is comprised of students drawn from many foreign countries and over 40 states. The school fosters students' appreciation for cultural differences and actively promotes the development of self-esteem and respect for others.

Selma University. Selma. Founded 1878. Religious affiliation: Baptist. Enrollment: 287.

Selma University is a four-year, private, coed, liberal arts institution owned and operated by the Alabama State Missionary Baptist Convention. The school was founded in 1878 as the Alabama Baptist Normal and Theological School with the principal mission of training African Americans for the teaching and ministry professions. The institution was officially named Selma University in 1908.

Selma University is located in the "Black Belt" region of Alabama, an area well known for its central role in the Civil Rights Movement. The campus is located 45 miles west of Montgomery, the state capital, and the site of the famous 1955 bus boycott that marked the first display of African American massive demonstration and made Martin L. King, Jr., a nationally prominent figure. And the Brown Chapel Church in Selma served as the point of origination for the famous 1965 civil rights march on the Pettus Bridge led by King. Selma University continues to tower as a beacon of higher education access and opportunity for African Americans in the state of Alabama.

Stillman College. Tuscaloosa. Founded 1876. Religious affiliation: Presbyterian. Enrollment: 1,458.

Stillman College began in 1874 as a Presbyterian Church affiliated training school for African American ministers. The school was named in honor of Rev. Charles Allen Stillman, one of its founders.

Since its founding Stillman has evolved to offer education and training in a variety of fields, including junior and senior high school, junior college, and four-year college. In addition, between 1930 and 1946 Stillman operated a hospital and nurses training school.

Stillman experienced it most aggressive period of growth during the administration of Dr. Samuel Burney Hay, who served from 1948 to 1965. Under Hay the school grew into a full four-year college and significantly expanded its academic programs to meet the demands of the time. Much of the modern campus, including a library, a gymnasium, an administration-classroom building, two residence halls, and a chapel were constructed under Hay. The Southern Association of Schools and Colleges accredited Stillman in 1953.

Talladega College. Talladega. Founded 1867. Religious affiliation: Presbyterian. Enrollment: 1,458.

On November 20, 1865, two former slaves, William Savery and Thomas Tarrant, both of Talladega, Alabama, met in convention with a group of newly freed blacks in Mobile, Alabama. The conventioneers adopted the following statement of commitment: "We regard the education of our children and youth as vital to the preservation of our liberties, and true religion as the foundation of all real virtue, and shall use our utmost endeavors to promote these blessings in our common country." Out of this commitment to providing an education for former slaves and their progeny came the seeds of what today is known as Talladega College. Opened in 1867, Talladega College is the first institution in the state of Alabama established for the express purpose of educating African Americans.

From its humble beginnings, Talladega College has evolved into one of the best liberal arts schools in the country, and a leader in higher education at large. Talladega's record of achievement shines even brighter when one considers it in proportion to the school's resources and size. For a school with a student body that has rarely exceeded 1,000 students, Talladega has merited national distinction in many areas. It produces more of the country's African American Fortune 500 executives than any other historically black college and it is a leader in the production of students who go on to pursue graduate and professional degrees. Additionally, Talladega has a rich tradition of producing outstanding scientists. In 1996 Peterson's Guide to Colleges and Universities named Talladega as one of the 190 best colleges for science and mathematics in the country. From corporate America to the political arena to higher education leadership, Talladega graduates are well-represented among the nation's movers and shakers.

Tuskegee Institute. Tuskegee. Founded 1881. Private, no religious affiliation. Enrollment: 2,636.

Tuskegee Institute was founded in 1881 in Tuskegee, Alabama, by Booker T. Washington. The school was originally chartered as The Normal School for Colored Teachers.

By the early twentieth century, under the able leadership of Booker T. Washington, Tuskegee had become the pride and joy of black America. At a time when most private black colleges were run with white assistance, Washington maintained Tuskegee as an all-black owned and operated institution. Washington, a highly skilled organizer and fundraiser positioned Tuskegee as one of the best black colleges in the land. In 1915, the year of Washington's death, Tuskegee could boast of 1,500 students, a $2 million endowment, 40 programs of study, 100 fully-equipped buildings, and about 200 faculty. Washington's success at Tuskegee countered then widely held notions about the inability of African Americans to run complex institutions.

Beyond his leadership of Tuskegee, Washington garnered national recognition as a black leader. His 1895 "Atlanta Compromise" speech, in which he urged African Americans to forgo agitation for civil rights and instead seek first to build an economic foundation, catapulted him into the role of race spokesman. Washington went on to serve as advisor, counselor and confidant to United States Presidents and many of the leading businessmen, industrialists, and philanthropists of the era. Indeed Washington's influence on national issues of race in the early twentieth century was so profound that historians call the time period 1895–1915 "The Age of Booker T. Washington."

Washington was succeeded by Robert R. Moton who served from 1915 to 1935. Moton's successor Frederick D. Patterson continued the tradition of Tuskegee presidents shaping and influencing race relations and higher education on a national scale. During World War II, Patterson brought the Tuskegee Airmen flight-training program to the institute. And in 1944 Patterson founded the United Negro College Fund.

Today, Tuskegee University enjoys national prominence for its outstanding programs in business, the sciences, and engineering.

The Booker T. Washington Monument, called "Lifting the Veil," (dedicated in 1922) stands at the center of the Tuskegee University campus. The inscription at its base reads, "He lifted the veil of ignorance from his people and pointed the way to progress through education and industry." At Tuskegee, the tradition of enlightenment remains as strong as ever.

Arkansas

Arkansas Baptist College. Little Rock. Founded 1884. Religious affiliation: Baptist. Enrollment: 389.

In 1884 the Colored Baptists of the State of Arkansas founded a school called The Baptist Institute. The school was started to train blacks for the ministry and to provide liberal arts education for young African American men and women. The school grew rapidly and in 1885 the name of the institute was changed to Arkansas Baptist College.

The first president of Arkansas Baptist College was Dr. Joseph A. Booker. He led the school from 1887 until his death in 1926. Following Booker's death, equally high caliber men, including Rev. S.P. Nelson, Rev. R.C. Woods, and Rev. S.R. Tillinghast served as president.

As a church-related institution, Arkansas Baptist provides a liberal arts program in a Christian-centered environment. Arkansas Baptist College is fully accredited by the North Central Association of Colleges and Schools.

Philander Smith College. Little Rock. Founded 1877. Religious affiliation: United Methodist. Enrollment: 1,110.

Established in 1877 by the Methodist Episcopal Church, Philander Smith College is the oldest private historically black college in the state of Arkansas. The committed church men and women who established the school were guided by five aims: "to help persons face the vexing experiences of conflict and social change; to develop leadership for the African American community; to educate and help disadvantaged persons; to enhance the dignity of persons; and to facilitate the execution of justice and to advance human welfare."

Keeping with the vision handed down by its forefathers, Philander Smith is rapidly becoming one of the top liberal arts colleges in the South. The college currently has a 90 percent acceptance rate of students who apply to medical school and it offers the only minor degree program in Black Family Studies in the United States. The school's growth has been further advanced by the recent completion of a three-year, $30 million capital campaign.

Shorter College. Little Rock. Founded 1886. Religious affiliation: African Methodist Episcopal (AME). Enrollment: 320.

The forerunner of Shorter College was founded in 1886 under the name Bethel University. The establishment of the institution was spearheaded by the African Methodist Episcopal Church (AME), a leader in the development of black education in the South in the late nineteenth century. In 1903 the school was renamed Shorter College. It became a two-year college in 1955.

Shorter College is an open-admission school and prides itself on being a leader in the quest to expand higher education access and opportunity for self-development to all Americans. The school maintains a cooperative center with Arkansas Baptist and Philander Smith Colleges, the two other historically black colleges located in the city of Little Rock. Shorter is fully accredited by the North Central Association of Colleges and Schools.

University of Arkansas at Pine Bluff. Pine Bluff. Founded 1873. Public, no religious affiliation. Enrollment: 2,863.

The University of Arkansas at Pine Bluff is a state-supported land-grant institution. Established in 1873, it was originally known as the Branch Normal College.

From its status as a junior college the school expanded into a four-year degree-granting institution in 1929. In the 1930s an extensive building program began that laid the foundation for the modern campus facility. This period witnessed the construction of eight residences for instructors, a gymnasium, two dormitories, and a library. A subsequent building program in the late 1940s doubled the college's facilities. The University of Arkansas at Pine Bluff has grown and prospered over the years because of strong, visionary, and determined leadership provided by men such as Joseph C. Corbin, Jefferson Ish, Robert Malone, Joseph Brown Watson, and Lawrence A. Davis, Sr.

Delaware

Delaware State University. Dover. Founded 1890. Public, no religious affiliation. Enrollment: 3,610.

In May 1891 the Delaware General Assembly established the State College for Colored Students under the provisions of the Morrill Land-Grant Act. The purpose of the Morrill Act was to provide publicly supported higher education opportunities for African Americans in states maintaining separate educational facilities for blacks and whites. Hence the first and only public historically black college in the state of Delaware was born.

In its early years of operation, the school served the twin purpose of providing college preparatory education and teacher training. In 1923, a Junior College Division was added. The four-year curricula — with concentrations in the arts and sciences, elementary education, home economics, agriculture, and industrial arts — was established in 1932.

Today, Delaware State University is a fully accredited, comprehensive university with a diverse population of undergraduate and advanced degree students. In recent years the University has placed great emphasis on globalization and internationalization, forming and maintaining partnerships with institutions in countries such as Egypt, Nigeria, Serbia, Mexico, China, and many others.

District of Columbia

Howard University. District of Columbia. Founded 1867. Private, no religious affiliation. Enrollment: 9,300.

Howard University was founded in 1867. The school was named for General Oliver O. Howard, Civil War hero and, at the time, Commissioner of the Freedmen's Bureau.

In 1879, Congress authorized a special appropriation for the University. In 1928 Congress amended the charter to award the appropriation on an annual basis.

It was under the legendary Mordecai W. Johnson, who served as the thirteenth and first African American president of Howard University from 1926 to 1960, that the school became one of America's leading University generally and the premiere African American university. A visionary leader, Johnson secured the annual federal appropriation for Howard. He tripled the faculty, increased salaries, and toughened admission requirements. Johnson also devoted substantial resources to obtaining full accreditation of Howard's graduate and professional programs.

Johnson hired for the Howard faculty a cadre of outstanding African American scholars and intellectuals. From E. Franklin Frazier in sociology to Rayford W. Logan in history to Ralph Bunche in political science and Charles Drew in medicine many of the black intellectual giants of the early twentieth century practiced their craft at Howard. The work of these Howard-based scholars influenced generations of public policy and positioned Howard in the vanguard of knowledge production. Thurgood Marshall and many of the other African American attorneys who argued the 1954 *Brown v. Board of Education* case before the Supreme Court were trained at the Howard University law school.

University of the District of Columbia. District of Columbia. Founded 1851. Public, no religious affiliation. Enrollment: 5,175.

The origins for what is now the University of the District of Columbia go back to 1851 when Myrtilla Miner established the Colored Girls School in Washington, DC, for the education of African American girls. The name of the school was later changed to Miner Normal School and in 1879 it became a constituent institution of the public school system. In 1873, approximately 22 years after the founding of Miner Normal, the Wilson Normal School was established in the District for the education and training of white girls. By 1929 both schools had evolved to become four-year teacher training colleges. Then in 1955, one year after the historic *Brown v. Education* ruling that overturned racial segregation in public schools, Miner Normal and Wilson Normal united to form the District of Columbia Teachers College. In 1977, after a number of mergers and consolidations with other District-based higher education institutions, the University of the District of Columbia began. Lisle Carleton Carter was selected as the University's first president.

From 1977 to the present, the University has grown into a comprehensive college, offering programs of study in more than 75 fields through the college of arts and sciences, school of business and public administration and school of engineering and applied sciences. Additionally, the University offers a law program through its David A. Clarke School of Law. The University stands as the gateway to higher education access for the citizens of the District of Columbia.

Florida

Bethune-Cookman College. Daytona Beach. Founded 1904. Religious affiliation: United Methodist. Enrollment: 2,794.

In 1904 a determined young black woman from Mayesville, South Carolina, by the name of Mary McLeod Bethune founded the Daytona Educational and Industrial Training School for Negro Girls. Because Bethune had more vision than money, the school would become known as "the college built by prayer." Describing the school's founding, Bethune stated: "I had no furniture. I begged for dry goods boxes and made benches and stools; begged a basin and other things I needed and in 1904 five little girls here started school."

In 1923 Daytona Educational merged with Cookman Institute of Jacksonville, Florida, and became a coeducational high school. By 1931 it attained junior college status and became known as Bethune-Cookman College. Ten years later, in 1941, it evolved into a four degree-granting college.

Bethune's influence and stature in America went far beyond her immediate role as president of Bethune-Cookman College. Bethune was an advisor to United States Presidents, social activist, organizer of women, diplomat, and head of a federal agency. Bethune founded the

National Council of Negro Women in 1935, the premiere social and political organization for women of color. From 1936 to 1944, during the administration of President Franklin D. Roosevelt, she served as Director of Negro Affairs in the National Youth Administration. In this capacity she became the first African American to lead a federal agency. Bethune served as key advisor to President Roosevelt on issues related to African Americans, and she became a close friend and confidant of First Lady Eleanor Roosevelt. The power and influence Bethune wielded in the Roosevelt administration earned her the nickname "Chair of the Black Cabinet."

Bethune served as consultant to the United State Secretary of War for selection of the first female officer candidates and was appointed consultant on interracial affairs and understanding at the charter conference of the United Nations. She was elected Vice-President of the National Association for the Advancement of Colored People. And she was a delegate and advisor to numerous national conferences on education, child welfare, and home ownership. Mary McLeod Bethune was easily the most powerful and influential black person in America between the death of Booker T. Washington in 1915 and the emergence of Martin Luther King, Jr., in 1955.

The spirit of Mary McLeod Bethune continues to resonate throughout Bethune-Cookman College. The men and women who have led the school since her death — James E. Colston, Richard V. Moore, Sr., Oswald P. Bronson, Sr., and Trudie Kibbe Reed — are continuing the great legacy of faith, service, and scholarship begun by Bethune.

Edward Waters College. Jacksonville. Founded 1866. Religious affiliation: African Methodist Episcopal. Enrollment: 1,301.

Edward Waters College stands as a testimony of the work of the African Methodist Church in promoting black education in the South in the years after the Civil War. The Reverend Charles H. Pearce, Elder of the AME Church founded the school in 1866. Pearce had been sent to Florida by Bishop Daniel Alexander Payne to establish the African Methodist Episcopal Church. Arriving in Florida, Pearce found a largely uneducated black ministry and mass illiteracy among the new freedmen. Pearce immediately recognized the need for a school to educate and train blacks. Accordingly, Pearce raised funds and started a school in 1866. The school became what is now known as Edward Waters College.

Edward Waters College holds distinction as the first institution established for the education of African Americans in the state of Florida.

The college became a member of the United Negro College Fund (UNCF) in 1985.

Florida Agricultural and Mechanical University. Tallahassee. Founded 1887. Public, no religious affiliation. Enrollment: 13,100.

Florida Agricultural and Mechanical University is located in the state capital of Tallahassee. The school was started in 1887 as the State Normal College for Colored Students. Three years later the school became a land-grant institution, the only African American serving institution in the state so designated. In 1909 the name was changed to Florida Agricultural and Mechanical College for Negroes (FAMC). In its early years, the school was led by Thomas DeSaille Tucker, a prominent attorney from Pensacola.

Over the years Florida Agricultural and Mechanical University has grown into a national model of excellence in higher education. The university strongly embraces research and knowledge production as critical to learning and enlightenment. Many of its programs, such as Engineering and Pharmacy, have received national recognition for academic excellence. Additionally, the university consistently ranks among the top colleges in the country enrolling National Achievement finalists. Florida A&M University remains true to its motto: "Excellence with caring."

Florida Memorial College. Miami. Founded 1879. Religious affiliation: Baptist. Enrollment: 2,242.

Florida Memorial College was founded in 1879 in Live Oak, Florida, under the supervision of the Baptist Church. The campus moved to Jacksonville in 1892. It was on the Jacksonville campus that faculty member J. Rosamond Johnson and his brother James Weldon Johnson co-wrote *"Lift Ev'ry Voice and Sing,"* which is now known as the Negro National Anthem. In 1968 the College was relocated to Miami.

Florida Memorial College has grown to include a diverse population of students from all over Florida, the nation and the Caribbean. Its campus is considered one of the most beautiful in the state of Florida.

Georgia

Albany State University. Albany. Founded 1903. Public, no religious affiliation. Enrollment: 2,459.

In 1903 a coalition of private and religious organization established the Albany Bible and Manual Training Institute to train African Americans in the southwest region of Georgia. In 1917, the school transitioned into a public, two-year institution under the name Georgia Normal and Agricultural College. The college operated this way for 26 years and in 1943 became a four-year degree baccalaureate institution and was named Albany State College.

Albany State experienced its most marked period of growth in the years between 1943 and 1996. Five presidents led the school during this period, Dr. Aaron Brown (1943–1954); Dr. William H. Dennis (1954–1965); Dr. Thomas Miller Jenkins (1965–1969); Dr. Charles L. Hayes (1969–1980); Dr. Billy C. Black (1980–1996); and Dr. Portia Holmes Shields (1996–2005).

Albany State University offers a broad-based curriculum with majors such as biology, criminal justice, computer science, education management and nursing among the most popular. Additionally, the university offers advanced degrees in criminal justice, public administration, business administration, nursing and education. The university partners with the Georgia Institute of Technology to offer a dual degree program in engineering.

Clark Atlanta University. Atlanta. Founded 1988 merger between Atlanta University and Clark College. Religious affiliation: Independent. Enrollment: 4,915.

Clark Atlanta University was created in 1988 as a result of the merger of Atlanta University and Clark College. The Methodist Episcopal Church started Clark College in 1869, four years after the Civil War. The mission of the school, as it was conceived in the minds of its founders, was to train leaders for the black community, especially ministers and teachers.

In 1865, four years before the Methodists created Clark College, the northern white American Missionary Association had initiated Atlanta University. Like Clark, the mission of Atlanta University was to train a generation of African Americans who would lead the race in its quest for progress and advancement. With strong support from a coalition of African Americans and northern white supporters, Atlanta University grew rapidly and by the early twentieth century it had become an outstanding institution of higher learning, a "Black Ivy."

Throughout the period of Jim Crow segregation Atlanta University was home to a cohort of stellar African American scholars. From 1897 to 1910, Atlanta University was home to W.E.B. Du Bois, the preeminent black thinker, intellectual, and social activist of the early twentieth century. While on the faculty at Atlanta Du Bois researched and published groundbreaking works on black morality, urbanization, blacks in business, college educated blacks, the black church, and black crime. Indeed, Du Bois' work, collectively called the "Atlanta Studies," provided the first glimpse into the segregated black political economy. It was also at Atlanta that an ideological rift developed between W.E.B. Du Bois and Tuskegee Institute founder Booker T. Washington, prompting Du Bois to publish treatise after treatise critiquing and criticizing Washington's conservative racial views. In addition to Du Bois, other outstanding black scholars such as E. Franklin Frazier in sociology and Forrester B. Washington in sociology served on the Atlanta University faculty.

The merger of Clark College and Atlanta University in 1988 has given birth to an excellent, trend-setting institution poised to take its place among the best universities of the twenty-first century. As the university proudly declares: "We're still writing our history here at Clark Atlanta University."

Fort Valley State University. Fort Valley. Founded 1895. Public, no religious affiliation. Enrollment: 3,025.

In 1895 the Fort Valley High and Industrial School was established in Fort Valley, Georgia. Shortly after, in 1902, the State Teachers and Agricultural College of Forsyth was founded. In 1939 these two schools were consolidated and became Fort Valley State College. The name of the school was changed to Fort Valley State University in 1996.

In 1939, Horace Mann Bond, one of the most influential black intellectuals and educators of the mid-twentieth century, was appointed the first president of Fort Valley State College. A giant in the field of educational research, Bond produced seminal works on the interrelationship of race and black education in the South.

Today, the university offers more than fifty major areas of study and maintains exceptionally strong programs in education, business administration and agriculture. The university is also home to a highly lauded African World Studies Institute, which serves as a forum uniting students and faculty from around the world.

Morehouse College. Atlanta. Founded 1867. Religious affiliation: Independent. Enrollment: 3,100.

In 1867, Rev. William Jefferson White, a minister and cabinetmaker, established the Augusta Institute in the basement of Springfield Baptist

Church in Augusta, Georgia. In 1879 Augusta Institute moved to Atlanta and changed its name to Atlanta Baptist Seminary. As the name implied, its primary purpose was to train African Americans for the ministry and church leadership. In 1913, Atlanta Baptist Seminary became Morehouse College, changing its name to honor Henry L. Morehouse, the corresponding secretary of the Atlanta Baptist Home Mission Society.

Morehouse entered a new era of growth, development, and expansion in 1906 when John Hope became president of the college. A graduate of Brown University, Hope was the first African American to lead the institution. During his tenure Hope worked to foster at Morehouse an intellectual climate and atmosphere on par with the best white liberal arts colleges in the land. Hope expanded the Morehouse curriculum and attracted a cadre of top-notch faculty and administrators. It was Hope who conceived the idea of the "Morehouse Man," the well-educated, well-spoken, socially conscious male student who while representing the best of the black race would serve as a catalyst for change in American society. A close friend of W.E.B. Du Bois, Hope joined Du Bois in his critique of Booker T. Washington's program of vocational and agricultural training for African Americans.

It was under the leadership of the legendary Benjamin E. Mays, who led Morehouse from 1940 to 1967, that Morehouse moved to the lofty heights envisioned by Hope. Mays increased the student body, attracted outstanding teachers and scholars, built much of the modern campus infrastructure, and doubled the school's endowment. Mays also completed the groundwork necessary for Morehouse to obtain a chapter of Phi Beta Kappa in 1968, one of the first historically black colleges to do so.

Most importantly, Mays continued the Morehouse tradition of preparing African Americans for leadership in all areas of American life. Mays was mentor to an entire generation of young men who went out and changed the world including, Dr. Martin L. King, Jr., the leading figure of the civil rights movement; Maynard Jackson, the first African American to serve as mayor of Atlanta; Dr. Charles V. Willie, one of the first black scholars to teach at an Ivy League institution; Lerone Bennett, senior editor of *Ebony* magazine; and Dr. Louis Sullivan, former Secretary of Health and Human Services.

Morris Brown College. Atlanta. Founded 1881. Religious affiliation: African Methodist Episcopal. Enrollment: 2,400.

Morris Brown College owes its existence to the self-help legacy of the African Methodist Episcopal Church. The black Methodists started Morris Brown in 1885 making it the first educational institution in the state of Georgia fully established, owned, and operated by African Americans. The college was named to honor the memory of the second consecrated Bishop of the AME Church.

Throughout its existence Morris Brown has remained committed to providing educational opportunities in a Christian-centered environment. The school seeks to train students for ethical leadership in America.

Paine College. Augusta. Founded 1882. Religious affiliation: Methodist. Enrollment: 838.

Paine College began in 1882, 17 years after the Civil War. The school was established as a joint initiative between African American Methodists and white Methodists. Seeking to train African American ministers and teachers, the Colored Methodist Episcopal Church (CME) appealed to its white Methodist counterpart for assistance. The white Methodists responded favorably and sent out white Methodists who worked with the black Methodists to build Paine. Methodist leaders such as Bishop Lucius Holsey of the Colored (now Christian) Methodist Episcopal Church and Atticus Haygood, a Bishop in the Methodist Episcopal Church South (now United Methodist) were among those who worked to establish the school. The interracial collaboration behind Paine's founding was representative of the founding of many private higher education institutions for African Americans after the Civil War.

Paine awarded its first bachelor's degree in 1885. Today, the school is a member of the United Negro College Fund. It remains committed to its Christian heritage and as such seeks to provide a quality liberal arts education with an emphasis on ethical and spiritual values. Moreover, the school strives to place the black experience at the center of the curriculum.

Savannah State University. Savannah. Founded 1890. Public, no religious affiliation. Enrollment: 2,546.

Savannah State University is the oldest public historically black college in the state of Georgia. The school was originally founded in 1890 as the Georgia State Industrial College for Colored Youth in Athens. The school was transferred to Savannah a few months after its founding and offered its first baccalaureate degree in 1928. In 1932 the name of the school was changed to Georgia State College, and in 1996 was renamed Savannah State University in 1996.

Savannah State University is a trend-setting institution with the University System of Georgia. Savannah State is currently the most diverse campus in the Georgia System. The University's radio station was the first Savannah area station to offer Hispanic programming. Finally, the University maintains a strong international outlook, drawing students from over 40 countries and maintaining partnerships with universities in China and Ghana.

Spelman College. Atlanta. Founded 1881. Private, no religious affiliation. Enrollment: 2,063.

Spelman is the nation's oldest historically black college for women. The school was founded in 1881 as Atlanta Baptist Female Academy by Harriet Giles and Sophia Packard, school teachers and Baptist missionaries from New England. The academy first offered post-secondary education in 1897. The school was renamed Spelman College in 1924 in honor of Laura Spelman, John D. Rockefeller's mother-in-law.

Spelman made great educational strides during the presidencies of Lucy Hale Tapley (1910–1927) and Florence Matilda Read (1927–1953). Two males, Albert Edward Manley (1953–76) and Donald Mitchell Stewart (1976–86) led Spelman from 1953 to 1986.

From 1987 to 1997 the college experienced unprecedented growth under the leadership of Johnetta Betsch Cole, the first African American woman president of Spelman. Cole elevated Spelman to the national ranks of leading liberal arts colleges by strengthening the school's academic infrastructure and building a solid economic foundation through the successful completion of a $113.8 million capital campaign, which included a gift of $20 million from comedian William "Bill" Cosby and his wife, Camille Hanks Cosby.

From 1997 to 2001 Audrey Forbes Manley, former Acting Surgeon General of the United States, and a 1955 graduate of Spelman served as the institution's first alumna president. In April 2002 Beverly Daniel Tatum, dean of the college and acting president of Mount Holyoke College was named ninth president of Spelman. Tatum brought to the Spelman family 22 years of experience in higher education leadership. Tatum has initiated a strategic plan for Spelman that includes five goals—academic excellence, leadership development, improving the infrastructure, improving the visibility of accomplishments of the campus community, and exemplary customer service. Tatum's vision is for Spelman to be "Nothing Less Than the Best."

Spelman College has produced six generations of women who are prominent among the nation's academic, community, and professional leaders. Notable among the alumnae are Marian Wright Edelman, founder and president of the Children's Defense Fund; Ruth A. Davis, director general of the U.S. Foreign Service; Aurelia Brazeal, U.S. ambassador to Ethiopia; physicians Virginia Davis Floyd and Deborah Prothrow-Stith; writers Pearl Cleage and Tina McElroy Ansa; actress LaTanya Richardson; artist Varnette Honeywood; opera singer Mattiwilda Dobbs; singer Bernice Johnson Reagon, founder of the Grammy Award–winning female acappella group Sweet Honey in the Rock; and Uche Egemonye, executive director of the Disability Law Policy Center of Georgia.

Kentucky

Kentucky State University. Frankfort. Founded 1886. Public, no religious affiliation. Enrollment: 2,204.

Located in the city of Frankfort, Kentucky State University is a four-year, state-supported, coed liberal arts institution. The school's origins date back to 1886 when its was founded as the State Normal School for Colored Persons. In its early years the school's principal reason for being was to train black teachers for black schools in the state. In 1890, the institution transitioned into a land-grant college and significantly expanded its curriculum.

Over the years, the school's name changed several times to adequately reflect its growing and expanding curriculum and programs of study. In 1902, it became Kentucky Normal and Industrial Institute for Colored Persons. In 1938 the name was changed to Kentucky State College for Negroes. Fourteen years later, in 1952 the school became Kentucky State College. In 1973 Kentucky State College gained university status and subsequently the name was changed to Kentucky State University.

Louisiana

Dillard University. New Orleans. Founded 1869. Religious affiliation: United Methodist Church. Enrollment: 1,792.

Dillard University is a four-year, private, liberal arts, United Methodist Church-related, co-educational school. Dillard was created in 1930 by the merger of two institutions, Straight University, founded in 1869 by the Congregational Church, and Union Normal School, established in 1869 by the Methodist Episcopal Church.

From 1874 to 1886 Straight operated a law school. Union, which was renamed New Orleans University in the late nineteenth century, maintained a medical school, including a school of pharmacy and a school of nursing. Out of the seeds of these two pioneer institutions bloomed what is now known as Dillard University.

The Dillard presidency has been held by eminent African American higher education leaders such as Albert Dent (1940 to 1969) and Samuel DuBois Cook (1975 to 1997).

Dillard experienced its most marked period of growth and expansion under the leadership of Michael L. Lomax, who served as president from 1997 to 2004. Lomax's tenure was marked by intense fundraising campaigns and campus construction. Academic restructuring obtained for the school national rankings on *U.S. News & World Report's* list of the best comprehensive undergraduate colleges in the South. Additionally, Lomax increased student enrollment by 49 percent, private funding by 300 percent, and alumni giving by more than 2,000 percent.

Grambling State University. Grambling. Founded 1901. Public, no religious affiliation. Enrollment: 4,649.

What is now Grambling State University first opened its doors in 1901 as the Colored Industrial and Agricultural School. The school was started to educate African Americans in north central Louisiana. Its founder and first president was Charles P. Adams.

In 1905 the school relocated to the town of Grambling and was restructured after the Tuskegee model of education. The name of the school was changed to the North Louisiana Agricultural and Industrial School. As the school continued to grow it also adopted several more names, including the North Louisiana Agricultural and Industrial Institute, the Louisiana Negro Normal and Industrial Institute in 1918, and finally Grambling State University in 1974.

From 1936 to 1977, Ralph Waldo Emerson Jones served as the second president of Grambling. From 1977 until 2001, Grambling State University grew and prospered under the leadership of five presidents: Dr. Joseph Benjamin Johnson, 1977–1991; Dr. Harold W. Lundy, 1991–1994; Dr. Raymond A. Hicks, 1994–1997; Dr. Leonard L. Haynes III, 1997–1998; and Dr. Steve A. Favors, 1998–2001.

Southern University and A&M College. Baton Rouge. Founded 1880. Public, no religious affiliation. Enrollment: 9,000.

In 1879, in the nascent years of the Reconstruction movement in the southern United States, African American delegates to the Louisiana State Constitutional Convention called for the establishment of a state-supported institution of higher learning for African Americans. As a result of the agitation of those African American delegates Southern University and A&M College began in 1880.

Southern was originally located in New Orleans. In 1914 it moved north of Baton Rouge and was incorporated into the land-grant system.

Today, Southern University maintains satellite campuses in New Orleans and Shreveport. The University occupies a unique place in the state system of higher education, including being the first university to offer an undergraduate degree program in urban forestry, and maintaining the only doctoral programs in biomedical science, material science, math and science education, nursing, public policy, and urban forestry, as well as master's programs in urban forestry and physics in the entire state. Additionally, the university is home to a nationally ranked law school.

Xavier University of Louisiana. New Orleans. Founded 1917. Religious affiliation: Catholic. Enrollment: 3,725.

Xavier University is the only historically black college in the United States affiliated with the Catholic Church. Xavier was founded in 1915 by Blessed Katharine Drexel of Philadelphia and her Sisters of the Blessed Sacrament, a religious community dedicated to the education of African Americans and Native Americans. Over the years, the school grew from a preparatory academy into a full-fledge four-year degree-granting institution. The College of Pharmacy was added in 1927. Six years later, in 1933, the Graduate School was added.

Today, Xavier University is a national leader in minority higher education. Xavier ranks first in the nation in the number of African American students earning undergraduate degrees in biology, physics, and the physical sciences. It also ranks first in enrolling and graduating African Americans in pharmacy. Nearly 25 percent of the more than 6,000 African American pharmacists practicing in the United States were trained at Xavier University. Xavier is most renowned for its exceptional record of placing more African American students in medical schools than any other college or university in the land. Xavier graduates currently have a 70 percent acceptance rate for medical and dental school admission. This figure is almost twice the national average. And 93 percent of those who enter medical and dental schools complete their degree programs.

Maryland

Bowie State University. Bowie. Founded 1865. Public, no religious affiliation. Enrollment: 3,154.

Founded in 1865, Bowie State University is one of the oldest historically black colleges and universities in the United States. The Baltimore Association for the Moral and Educational Improvement of Colored People organized the forerunner of Bowie State University in 1865. In 1883 the school was restructured to operate as a school to train African American teachers. In 1908, the school came under the control of the Maryland State Board of Education, which relocated the campus to Prince George's County. In 1914 the name was changed to the Maryland Normal and Industrial School at Bowie.

In the 1930s Bowie became a teacher-training centered institution. In 1935 a baccalaureate program in elementary education was added and the school was renamed Maryland State Teachers College at Bowie. The school operated this way until 1951, when it implemented a program to train junior high school teachers. In 1961 the program was expanded to train high school teachers.

In 1963, after adopting a broad-based liberal arts program, the school's name was changed to Bowie State College. The College was upgraded to university status in 1988, and appropriately its name changed to Bowie State University.

Bowie State offers comprehensive graduate level programs. It grants the master of education degree, as well as a number of graduate degrees in technology and information science.

Coppin State University. Baltimore. Founded 1900. Public, no religious affiliation. Enrollment: 4,235.

Coppin State College is a four-year, urban liberal arts college. It offers undergraduate and graduate education in the arts and sciences and in professional and pre-professional areas, including nursing and teacher education.

Coppin began in 1900 when the Baltimore City Public School Board of Commissioners established a one-year training class for African American teachers. The school operated out of Douglas High School in Baltimore until 1909, when it became an independent institution.

Over the years, the school has evolved under a number of names ranging from Coppin State Teachers College to Coppin State College and finally Coppin State University. In 1988 it became a constituent institution of the University System of Maryland.

The college is named for Fanny Jackson Coppin. Coppin, who was born a slave in Washington, DC, gained her freedom, graduated from Oberlin College in Ohio and worked as a missionary of education among African Americans.

Morgan State University. Baltimore. Founded 1867. Public, no religious affiliation. Enrollment: 6,179.

In 1867 the Baltimore Conference of the Methodist Episcopal Church established the Centenary Biblical Institute for the purpose of training young men for the ministry. Out of the Biblical Institute grew the institution that is now known as Morgan State University.

Emblematic of the history of many black institutions, the historical development of Morgan State University is one defined by change, evolution, and transformation. Moving beyond its original mission of educating men, Morgan eventually opened its doors to women, who came in for the purpose of being educated as teachers. In 1890 the school was renamed Morgan College. And in 1939, when the state of Maryland purchased it, it transitioned into a public institution. The school was elevated to university status in 1975.

Today, Morgan State University is a national leader in black higher education. It graduates more African American students than any other institution in the state of Maryland and ranks among the nation's top colleges producing black students who go on to earn doctoral degrees.

University of Maryland-Eastern Shore. Princess Anne. Founded 1886. Public, no religious affiliation. Enrollment: 3,300.

Founded in 1886, the University of Maryland Eastern Shore is a land-grant institution. It began as the Delaware Conference Academy and operated as Maryland State College from 1948 until 1970.

In 1988, the University of Maryland Eastern Shore became a member of the University System of Maryland. Maryland Eastern Shore is fully accredited by the Middle States Association of Colleges and Schools.

Mississippi

Alcorn State University. Lorman. Founded 1871. Public, no religious affiliation. Enrollment: 2,555.

Alcorn State University is located in southwest Mississippi. The school was established in 1871 on land originally occupied by a Presbyterian-operated school for whites. The state of Mississippi purchased the land and designated the school for the purpose of educating African American citizens of the state. The name of the school was changed to Alcorn University in honor of James L. Alcorn, then governor of the state of Mississippi. Hiram Revels, an African American representing Mississippi in the United States Senate, became the first president of Alcorn.

As one of the nation's leading historically black colleges, Alcorn alumni are successful in various fields and pursuits such as medicine, law, education and business. Of the 15 presidents who have served Alcorn, Dr. Walter Washington, who held office from 1969 to 1994, was the longest serving. Alcorn continues the tradition of excellence.

Jackson State University. Jackson. Founded 1877. Public, no religious affiliation. Enrollment: 8,783.

In 1877 the American Baptist Home Mission Society initiated Natchez Seminary in Natchez, Mississippi, for the purpose of educating and training African American church leaders of Mississippi. In 1882, the school relocated to Jackson. Following the expansion of the curriculum the school was renamed Jackson College.

In 1940 Jackson College transitioned from private to state control, and operated primarily as a teacher training institution. The curriculum was broadened in the 1950s with the addition of a baccalaureate program in the arts and sciences and a graduate program. Jackson State achieved university status in 1974 and five years later, in 1979, the school was named the Urban University of the State of Mississippi.

Jackson State University continues to play a critical role in higher education in the state, the nation, and the world. It is the only university in Mississippi and the only historically black college offering doctoral degrees in both environmental science and early childhood education. It is one of only two historically black colleges offering a program in marine science and maintains the only undergraduate program in professional meteorology in Mississippi. The university is also home to the Margaret Walker Alexander National Research Center for the Study of the Twentieth Century African American experience.

Mary Holmes College. West Point. Founded 1892. Religious affiliation: Presbyterian USA. Enrollment: 340.

Mary Holmes College stands as a living example of the legacy of northern white church groups in the building of black education in the

South after the Civil War. The college was founded in 1892 as Mary Holmes Seminary by the Board of Missions for Freedmen of the Presbyterian Church. The idea for the school was conceived in the mind of the Reverend Mead Holmes, who named the school in honor of his wife, who had devoted her life to missionary work among the freedmen.

Mary Holmes was originally established for the exclusive education of African American women but in 1932 became coeducational. That year also witnessed the school add a college department. Throughout the first half of the twentieth century Mary Holmes College was renowned for its strong teacher education program. It produced a cadre of graduates who were highly sought after to teach in black schools in the South.

Mississippi Valley State University. Itta Bena. Founded 1946. Public, no religious affiliation. Enrollment: 2,283.

The Mississippi Legislature chartered Mississippi Valley State University in 1946. Because it started as a school principally to train teachers for rural communities and to offer vocational training, over the years Mississippi Valley served as the primary point of preparation for many African Americans who had no prior access to higher education.

The name of the institution was changed to Mississippi Valley State College in 1964 and then to Mississippi Valley State University in 1974. Notable alumni include National Football League wide receiver and future Hall of Famer Jerry Rice.

Rust College. Holly Springs. Founded 1866. Religious affiliation: United Methodist. Enrollment: 852.

Rust College holds the distinction of being one of the five remaining historically black colleges in America founded before 1867. The school originated in 1866 when missionaries of the Freedman's Aid Society of the Methodist Episcopal Church started a school in the facility of a local Methodist Episcopal Church. Like many black schools of the era, in its early years the school served students of all ages and levels, from adults to children. The school was named in tribute to the legacy of Richard S. Rust, Secretary of the Freedman's Aid Society.

Rust College maintains its historic ties to the United Methodist Church and prides itself on being the oldest of the eleven historically black colleges and universities related to the United Methodist Church. It further enjoys status as the second oldest private college in the state of Mississippi and the oldest historically black college in the state.

Tougaloo College. Tougaloo. Founded 1869. Religious affiliation: United Church of Christ. Enrollment: 890.

Tougaloo College in Tougaloo, Mississippi, is one of many private historically black colleges established by the northern American Missionary Association after the Civil War. The origins of the school date back to 1869, when the American Missionary Association established a school near Jackson, Mississippi, for the training of young people. In 1871, the school was charted as Tougaloo University.

Starting as a teacher training institution, the school offered its first courses for college credit in 1897, and awarded its first bachelor of arts degree in 1901. In 1954, after a merger with Southern Christian College in Edwards, Mississippi, the school was renamed Tougaloo Southern Christian College. In 1962 the name was changed again to Tougaloo College.

For most of the first century of its existence, the Tougaloo presidency was held by a succession of white males. This changed in 1964 when George Owens, a graduate of the college, became the first African American president. Owens ushered in a major period of growth and development for the college characterized by enhancement of the faculty, implementation of a new curriculum, and establishment of partnerships with major research universities.

Tougaloo has received national recognition for the high quality of its academic program. Moreover, Tougaloo ranks among the top institutions in the nation that produce African American students who go on to pursue graduate study in engineering, medicine, law, and other programs.

Missouri

Lincoln University-Missouri. Jefferson City. Founded 1866. Public, no religious affiliation. Enrollment: 3,311.

Lincoln University-Missouri was founded in 1866 at the behest of soldiers and officers of the 62nd United States Colored Infantry who desired to see the creation of an educational institution in Jefferson City for the benefit of the newly freed African Americans. The men of the 62nd contributed $5,000 and in January 1866, Lincoln Institute was established. Richard Baxter Foster, a former officer of the 62nd Infantry, was named first principal of Lincoln Institute.

In 1870 the state of Missouri authorized an annual appropriation for the Lincoln teacher-training program. By 1877, the curriculum was expanded to include college-level work and the period also witnessed further enhancement of Lincoln's teacher education program. Lincoln

Institute was formally incorporated into the state system of higher education in 1879, and in 1890, under the second Morrill Act, Lincoln became a land grant institution.

In 1954, following the historic Supreme Court ruling in *Brown v. Board of Education,* which overturned racial segregation in public education, Lincoln opened its doors to all applicants meeting its admission criteria irrespective of race. Thus today, Lincoln University serves a racially diverse student body.

North Carolina

Barber-Scotia College. Concord. Founded 1867. Religious affiliation: United Presbyterian USA. Enrollment: 543.

Barber-Scotia College began in 1867 as Scotia Seminary. Presbyterian missionaries from the northern United States established the school to train black women in the fields of education and social work. In 1932, following a merger with Barber Memorial College of Anniston, Alabama, the name of the school was changed to Barber-Scotia College. From its inception, the school continued on an upward path of progress, granting its first bachelor's degree in 1945, and in 1946, receiving four-year status. In 1954, the school transitioned into a coeducational college, opening its doors to men.

Prominent among Barber-Scotia alumni is Mary McLeod Bethune, an 1894 graduate of the college, and the founder of Bethune-Cookman College. Bethune Hall, one of Barber-Scotia's 25 buildings, was erected in honor of Bethune.

Bennett College. Greensboro. Founded 1873. Religious affiliation: United Methodist. Enrollment: 530.

Located in Greensboro, North Carolina, Bennett College was founded in 1873 as a co-educational, affiliate institution of the United Methodist Church. The school was named in memoriam of New York businessman Lyman Bennett, who donated funds for the fledging institution to acquire land and a school building. In 1926 Bennett was reorganized for the exclusive education of African American women.

Over the years capable, able, and visionary administrators have served Bennett. Notable among past presidents of Bennett are David Dallas Jones and Willa Player. Jones, a native of Greensboro, led Bennett for 30 years, from 1926 to 1956. Jones contributed to the growth and development of the college through physical development and beautification of the campus, as well as through quality teaching and acquisition of philanthropic support.

Following the death of Jones in 1956, Willa B. Player became president of Bennett. As president, Player substantially increased enrollment, strengthened the faculty, increased the endowment and modernized the physical plant. The highlight of Player's many achievements as president was the role she played in guiding Bennett toward membership in the Southern Association of Colleges and Schools, one of the first 15 black four-year colleges admitted to membership.

Elizabeth City State University. Elizabeth City. Founded 1891. Public, no religious affiliation. Enrollment: 2,100.

In 1891, Hugh Cale, an African American representative in the North Carolina General Assembly, introduced a bill to establish a state-supported teacher training institution for African Americans in his hometown of Pasquotank County. The bill was ratified and in 1892 the Elizabeth City State Colored Normal School began operation.

Peter Wedderick Moore served as the first president of Elizabeth City State. Under his administration, which lasted from 1891 to 1928, curricula and resources were greatly expanded. John Henry Bias served as second president from 1928 until his death in July 1939.

Elizabeth City State transitioned from a two-year school to a four-year teachers college in 1937. The first bachelor of science degree (in elementary education) was awarded in May of 1939.

From its origins as a predominantly African American–serving institution, Elizabeth City State University has evolved to serve a racially diverse student population. Currently, the school offers 26 degree programs, with particular strengths in education, business, science and history. The University also operates a high quality Department of Military Science.

Fayetteville State University. Fayetteville. Founded 1877. Public, no religious affiliation. Enrollment: 5,188.

In 1867 seven African American citizens of Fayetteville — David A. Bryant, Nelson Carter, Andrew J. Chesnutt, George Grainger, Matthew Leary. Thomas Lomax, and Robert Simmons— purchased a lot and started a school for the education of African Americans. The men name the institution the Howard School, and appointed Robert Harris the first principal.

In 1877, the Howard School became a public institution when the state legislature selected it to serve as the state-supported teacher training institution for black North Carolinians. After incorporation into the state system, the name of the school was changed to the State Colored Normal School, making it the first and oldest state-supported institution of higher education for African Americans in North Carolina.

Today, Fayetteville State University is a comprehensive university offering both master's and doctoral level programs. Moreover, the school carries the major responsibility of providing educational services for United States military personnel stationed in the area through its Ft. Bragg — Pope AFB Education Center. The school boasts of a new $6.3 million ultra-modern School of Business and Economics Building and a new $10.9 million Health and Physical Education Building.

Johnson C. Smith University. Charlotte. Founded 1867. Religious affiliation: United Presbyterian USA. Enrollment: 1,535.

In 1867, recognizing the need for the establishment of a school for the education of African Americans in the Charlotte area, the Rev. S.C. Alexander and the Rev. W.L. Miller, established the forerunner of Johnson C. Smith University. The two ministers served as the first teachers.

Several years after its establishment, Ms. Mary D. Biddle, a churchwoman from Philadelphia, Pennsylvania, after reading about the young school, donated $1,400. In recognition of Mrs. Biddle's generosity, the school was renamed Biddle Memorial Institute in honor of Biddle's late husband. The school later became Biddle University, then Johnson C. Smith University.

Livingstone College. Salisbury. Founded 1879. Religious affiliation: A.M.E. Zion. Enrollment: 1,000.

The African Methodist Episcopal Zion (A.M.E. Zion) started Zion Wesley College in 1879 as an institution to train African American clergy. The school was established under the leadership of Bishop James Walker Hood.

In 1882, Joseph C. Price, a protégé of Bishop Hood, was appointed president of Livingstone College. Price began his relationship with Livingstone as an agent of the school. During a visit to London for an Ecumenical Conference, Price raised $10,000 for Zion Wesley. Price was elevated to the Zion presidency based on his extraordinary fundraising efforts on behalf of the school.

Several years after its founding, Zion Wesley relocated to the neighboring community of Salisbury. In 1887 the name Zion Wesley College was changed to Livingstone College as a tribute to David Livingstone, the British Christian missionary, philanthropist and African explorer.

North Carolina Agricultural and Technical State University. Greensboro. Founded 1891. Public, no religious affiliation. Enrollment: 10,100.

North Carolina A&T State University was founded in 1891 as a land-grant institution. It originally operated under the name A&M College for the Colored Race. The first baccalaureate degrees were awarded in 1896 and it was renamed Agricultural and Technical College of North Carolina in 1915. The school became a member of the North Carolina University System in 1972.

North Carolina A&T has received national recognition and distinction for the high quality of its programs in the sciences and engineering. Indeed, A&T has trained the lion's share of the nation's engineers and scientists of colors. With stellar, ultra-modern research laboratories and institutes, the university has been in the vanguard of knowledge production. A&T's tradition of quality education is manifested in the lives and works of prominent graduates such as the late astronaut Ronald McNair; civil rights activist Jesse Jackson, Sr.; Congressman Jesse Jackson, Jr.; and Bowie State University President Calvin W. Lowe.

Among the school's main attractions are the H. Clinton Taylor Art Gallery, the African Heritage center, two outstanding museums, and a state-of-the-art computer center.

North Carolina Central University. Durham. Founded 1910. Public, no religious affiliation. Enrollment: 6,200.

North Carolina Central University was chartered in 1909 as the National Religious Training School and Chautauqua. James E. Shepard, the founder, led the school for the first 38 years of its existence.

The school's early years were defined by struggle for economic survival. One of the school's benefactors in this period was Margaret Slocum Sage, wife of Russell sage, the prominent financier and philanthropist. Because of the school's fiscal problems, the institution was reorganized in 1915 as the National Training School.

In 1923, the General Assembly of North Carolina purchased the school and made it a publicly supported institution under the name Durham State Normal School. The mission of the school was redefined to emphasize liberal arts education and teacher training.

Beginning in 1927, after receiving generous support from the Governor of North Carolina and a substantial gift from B.N. Duke, of the Duke tobacco empire, the school underwent a period of massive growth and development. In 1947 the school became North Carolina College at Durham.

Throughout its history, North Central has been an integral element of the life of black Durham. The school served as the intellectual center of an enterprising black community once dubbed the "capital of black America" because of its wealth of black owned and operated businesses.

Prominent graduates of North Carolina Central University include Sherwin K. Bryant, a professor of history at Northwestern University and Valinda Littlefield, a professor of history at the University of South Carolina.

Saint Augustine's College. Raleigh. Founded 1867. Religious affiliation: Episcopal. Enrollment: 1,598.

Saint Augustine's College was founded in 1867 as Saint Augustine's Normal School and Collegiate Institute by the Episcopal Church. In 1919, after operating since its inception primarily as a secondary preparatory school, Saint Augustine offered its first post-secondary level instruction. The school rose to four-year status in 1927 and in 1928 was renamed Saint Augustine College. The school maintains its core strength in areas such as liberal arts and teacher education.

Saint Augustine's is located in Raleigh, the capital of North Carolina. The school draws on the research infrastructure of nearby major academic institutions, including Research Triangle Park. Saint Augustine's is a member institution of the United Negro College Fund.

Shaw University. Raleigh. Founded 1865. Religious affiliation: Baptist. Enrollment: 2,615.

Shaw University was founded in 1865 as the Raleigh Institute by Henry Martin Tupper, a former Union army private and chaplain. Tupper, who served as the first president, established the school as a theological class. In its early years the school received financial support from the American Baptist Home Mission Society and The Freedmen's Bureau.

In 1871, the school became Shaw Collegiate Institute. The name was changed to honor Elijah Shaw who made a sizeable donation toward the construction of a new campus. In 1875 the school was chartered under the name of Shaw University. For most of its early years, Shaw operated several professional departments, including a school of pharmacy and a law school. The law school, which closed in 1914, was the only law school for African Americans from Washington to Texas.

Shaw University remains committed to its tradition of excellence in the liberal arts. As a culturally diverse institution, it strives to prepare students for leadership in the twenty-first century.

Winston-Salem State University. Winston-Salem. Founded 1892. Public, no religious affiliation. Enrollment: 4,000.

Winston-Salem State University's trajectory of growth started in 1892 with the establishment of the Slater Industrial Academy. The school's early focus was on the training of elementary school teachers. Reflecting this emphasis, in 1925 the school was reorganized and renamed the Winston-Salem Teachers College.

The Nursing School was established in 1953. A full four years course of study, the program places emphasis on both academic and professional education.

In 1969 the school attained university status. Today, it is one of the 16 member institutions of the University System of North Carolina.

Ohio

Central State University. Wilberforce. Founded 1887. Public, no religious affiliation. Enrollment: 1,800.

What is now known as Central State University began in 1887 as a normal and industrial department within Wilberforce University. The mission of the department was to provide both teacher education and vocational training for African American students. In 1941 the department split from Wilberforce University and became the College of Education and Industrial Arts at Wilberforce. In 1951 the school was renamed Central State College.

Charles H. Wesley served as the first president of Central State. Other men who led the institution include Lewis A. Jackson, Harry E. Groves, Herman R. Branson, Lewis A. Jackson, Lionel H. Newsom, Arthur E. Thomas, Herman B. Smith, George Ayer, and John W. Garland.

Central State University remains committed to its mission of providing an excellent education to all qualified students. Under the leadership of the current president John W. Garland, the University is experiencing all-around growth.

Wilberforce University. Wilberforce. Founded 1856. Religious affiliation: African Methodist Episcopal. Enrollment: 775.

Affiliated with the African Methodist Episcopal Church, Wilberforce University in Wilberforce, Ohio, is one of the oldest higher education institutions in the nation established by African Americans. The school came into existence in 1856, a tumultuous period in American history characterized by intense sectional fall-out over the question of the expansion of slavery. The school was named to honor William Wilberforce, one of the era's leading abolitionists.

Wilberforce University played a critical role in the antislavery movement. When the Ohio Underground Railroad was in operation as a means of escape for blacks who sought their freedom in the North and Canada, one of the destination points of this railroad was Wilberforce University. Escaped blacks to Wilberforce found an intellectually vibrant, activist community.

Wilberforce University has many distinctions to its credit. It was the first black school named as a center for military training and its campus is home to a Carnegie Library — a gift from the philanthropist Andrew Carnegie. Today, the campus is the location for the National Museum of Afro-American History and Culture Center.

Oklahoma

Langston University. Langston. Founded 1897. Public, no religious affiliation. Enrollment: 2,915.

In July 1892 the black citizens of Langston, Oklahoma, appeared before the Oklahoma School Commission to appeal for the establishment of a school for African Americans. Believing strongly that education was the key to true freedom, the African American petitioners were motivated to appeal for the school because African Americans were not allowed to attend any of the schools in Oklahoma. With the support of Governor William Gary Renfrow, a bill was passed establishing the university, which came into being as a land-grant institution under the name the Colored Agricultural and Normal University.

African Americans themselves provided much of the financial support for the fledging school. The local blacks organized picnics, auctions, and bake sales to raise money to purchase the land on which the school was built. The school's first session began in September 1898 and Dr. Inman E. Page, the son of a former slave, was appointed first president.

Page is credited with expanding the campus acreage, increasing both student and faculty numbers, and constructing new buildings.

Pennsylvania

Cheyney University of Pennsylvania. Cheyney. Founded 1837. Public, no religious affiliation. Enrollment: 1,059.

Cheyney University holds the distinction of being the oldest historically black higher education institution in America. The school was established in 1837 through a bequest from Richard Humphreys, a Quaker philanthropist. After witnessing first-hand the struggles of blacks in America, Humphreys, who was born in the West Indies, committed himself to providing higher education access for black youth. Humphreys bequeathed $10,000 to a group of his fellow Quakers and instructed them to establish a school for the education and training of African Americans.

The school operated under the control of the Quaker board for a number of years, and was later purchased by the Commonwealth of Pennsylvania and became part of the state system of higher education. Over the years, the school existed under several names, including The Institute for Colored Youth; Cheyney Training School for Teachers; State Normal School at Cheyney; Cheyney State Teachers College; Cheyney State College; and finally Cheyney University of Pennsylvania.

Cheyney University has continued to operate in accordance with the vision of Richard Humphreys. Its graduates are to be found among the nation's teachers, journalists, physicians, businessmen and entrepreneurs, scientists, attorneys, and government officials. Cheyney University is home to students from a diversity of races, cultures, nationalities, and ethnicities.

Lincoln University. Lincoln. Founded 1854. Public, no religious affiliation. Enrollment: 1,397.

Lincoln University is one of the oldest historically black colleges in the country. The school was founded in 1854 as Ashmun Institute and renamed Lincoln University in 1866 in honor of President Abraham Lincoln. The school, which began as an institution to train African American males, admitted its first women students in 1954. From its founding to 1945, when the prominent African American educator Horace Mann Bond became president, Lincoln was led by white males.

Lincoln University is an institution with a long, rich, tradition of academic excellence. Throughout the early twentieth century, Lincoln was called a "Black Ivy," one of the best black schools in the land. The school has trained at the undergraduate level 20 percent of the nation's African American physicians and 10 percent of America's African American attorneys. Moreover, graduates of Lincoln have led more than 36 colleges and universities. A cadre of Lincoln graduates, including Langston Hughes, Thurgood Marshall, and James L. Usry went on to leave their marks on the world at large. Lincoln also has a special legacy of training African students. Nnamdi Azikiwe, the first Prime Minister of independent Nigeria, and Kwame Nkrumah, the first Prime Minister of independent Ghana, were both graduates of Lincoln.

South Carolina

Allen University. Columbia. Founded 1870. Religious affiliation: African Methodist Episcopal. Enrollment: 425.

Located in Columbia, South Carolina, Allen University was founded in 1870 by the African Methodist Episcopal Church. The school was named to honor Richard Allen, the founder and first bishop of the AME Church. With its historic connection to the AME Church, Allen has trained large numbers of AME ministers and church leaders.

Today, Allen University continues its legacy of providing education and training in a caring, nurturing, Christian-centered environment.

Benedict College. Columbia. Founded 1870. Religious affiliation: Independent. Enrollment: 2,405.

Located in Columbia, South Carolina, Benedict College was founded in 1870 as Benedict Institute. Its founding institution was the American Baptist Home Mission Society. The school was named after Mrs. Bathsheba A. Benedict of Rhode Island in honor of the financial support she provided for the establishment of the school. Ms. Benedict contributed generously towards the purchase of an 80-acre plantation site on which the college was built.

The Benedict Institute embraced as its principal objective the rendering of educational programs and services to improve the social and economic conditions of black southerners. Beginning as an institution to train teachers and ministers, its early curriculum emphasized basic educational instructional. In the 1890s, an era that witnessed the dominance of Booker T. Washington and the vocational model of education,

Benedict added an industrial department offering carpentry, shoemaking, printing and painting.

Like many of the institutions operated by northern white church organizations for African Americans, for the first 60 years of its existence, the presidents of Benedict were white Baptist ministers from the northern United States. In 1930, leadership of the school transitioned from white to black control when the first African American was appointed president.

Prominent Benedict College alumni include Dr. Luns C. Richardson, President of Morris College in Sumter, South Carolina, and currently the longest serving college president in the state.

Claflin College. Orangeburg. Founded 1869. Religious affiliation: United Methodist. Enrollment: 1,161.

The origins of Claflin College go back to 1866 and the establishment of the Baker Biblical Institute in Charleston, South Carolina. In 1871, Claflin University, which had been founded in 1869 by the South Carolina Mission Conference, merged with Baker Biblical and became Claflin College. The new school was relocated to Orangeburg, South Carolina, whereupon the campus of the Orangeburg Female Academy was purchased for the school. The college department of Claflin graduated its first students in 1882.

Claflin provides to its students liberal arts education within a Christian environment. The curriculum emphasizes Christian values, service, and respect and appreciation for cultural diversity.

The campus is located on 29 beautiful acres. Its campus buildings represents a combination of historic and modern architecture. Claflin is a member of the United Negro College Fund. Among Claflin's distinguished alumni is Rev. Dr. Clyde Anderson, Executive of the United Methodist Church Global Ministries.

Morris College. Sumter. Founded 1908. Religious affiliation: Baptist. Enrollment: 1,006.

In 1908, the Black Baptist Educational and Missionary Convention of South Carolina established Morris College in Sumter, South Carolina. The school was established for the express purpose of training African American men for the ministry. Named in tribute to the Rev. Frank Morris, a pioneer leader of the Rocky River Association, Morris College came into existence as an example of African Americans proactively working to create educational opportunities for members of their race.

Because of its affiliation with the Baptist Church the school from its inception offered a theological program. Programs providing elementary, high school and college level education and training complemented the theological program. In 1915 Morris granted its first bachelor of arts degree.

Morris College grew and expanded substantially in the 1960s under the leadership of Dr. Odell Reuben. In 1974 Dr. Luns C. Richardson became president and initiated a period of sustained and aggressive growth and development. In 1978 Richardson led the school to full accreditation by the Southern Association of Colleges and Schools and in 1982 Morris became a member of the United Negro College Fund, the nation's largest and oldest fundraising consortium.

Under Richardson's leadership Morris College's physical plant has grown and expanded more than had been established during the entire first 70 years of the College's existence. Among the new facilities are a Learning Resources Center, a Fine Arts Center, a Human Development Center, a Chapel and Religious Center, the College's first full-scale Student Center, and three new residence halls.

Morris College is home to a high-quality teacher-training program. Over the years the college has trained the lion's share of teachers for Sumter County and environs. Because of their sustained record of success on completing the state's certification requirements Morris teacher education graduates are highly sought after. Throughout the state system of public education Morris College graduates are well represented among the ranks of classroom teachers, principals, and district administrators.

South Carolina State University. Orangeburg. Founded 1896. Public, no religious affiliation. Enrollment: 4,032.

Founded in 1896, South Carolina State University is the only public historically black college in South Carolina. In its early years the school operated as a land-grant institution providing agricultural and mechanical training. Through its extension program that trained farm and home demonstration agents, South Carolina State played a critical sole in efforts to improve life for black families in rural communities.

South Carolina State University maintains a high caliber teacher education program and as such has been a major producer of teachers for the public schools. In the mid–1940s the University also operated a law school. In the 1950s, like their counterparts at other colleges throughout the nation, South Carolina State students actively participated in sit-ins and civil rights demonstrations to desegregated public facilities and achieve full equality for African Americans. In February 1968, three South Carolina State students— Samuel Hammond, Henry Smith, and Delano Middleton — were slain and 27 wounded on the campus by state highway patrolmen in the Orangeburg Massacre.

Voorhees College. Denmark. Founded 1897. Religious affiliation: Episcopal. Enrollment: 932.

Voorhees College, originally known as Denmark Industrial School, was founded in 1897 by Elizabeth Evelyn Wright. A graduate of Tuskegee Institute, Wright established Voorhees on the principles of industrial and vocational education.

In 1929, when post-secondary education began the name changed to Voorhees Normal and Industrial School. The present name, Voorhees College, was adopted in 1962 when the school transitioned into a four-year college.

Tennessee

Fisk University. Nashville. Founded 1867. Religious affiliation: Independent. Enrollment: 840.

Fisk University was initiated in 1867 in the immediate aftermath of the Civil War by John Ogden, Reverend Erastus Milo Cravath, and Reverend Edward P. Smith, who envisioned an institution that would stand as a model of the highest standards of American education. The American Missionary Association, one of the northern leaders in black education in the South, supported the work of the founders. Over the years Fisk University has lived up to the grand vision embraced by its founders and garnered for itself distinction as one of America's outstanding universities.

In 1952 Fisk became the first black college to obtain a chapter of Phi Beta Kappa. In 1930 Fisk became the first black college to gain full accreditation by the Southern Association of Colleges and Schools.

The famed Fisk Jubilee Singers introduced the world to the Negro spiritual. The Fisk alumni include a cadre of distinguished educators, scholars, artists and intellectuals such as W.E.B. Du Bois, John Hope Franklin, David Levering Lewis and Nikki Giovanni. United States Representatives John Lewis (GA) and Alcee Hastings (FL) are Fisk graduates as is the former United States Secretary of Energy Hazel O'Leary. And over the years the Fisk faculty has featured distinguished African

American scholars such as Charles S. Johnson, Arna Bontemps, James Weldon Johnson and Aaron Douglas.

Lane College. Jackson. Founded 1882. Religious affiliation: Methodist Episcopal. Enrollment: 1,045.

In 1882 the Colored Methodist Episcopal Church established the C.M.E. High School in Jackson, Tennessee. The movement to establish the school was spearheaded by the Reverend J.K. Daniels. When the school opened its doors, Daniels' daughter served as its first teacher.

Lane's post-secondary department was implemented in 1896. At that time, the school name changed to Lane College.

LeMoyne-Owen College. Memphis. Founded 1862. Religious affiliation: United Church of Christ. Enrollment: 720.

In 1863 the LeMoyne Normal and Commercial School was established in Tennessee. The school was named to honor Dr. Francis Julian LeMoyne, a leading member of the American Missionary Association, who had made critical financial support to the school.

In 1954 the Tennessee Baptist Missionary and Educational Convention established Owen College in Memphis. Lemoyne Normal and Owen College merged in 1968, becoming LeMoyne-Owen College.

Meharry Medical College. Nashville. Founded 1876. Religious affiliation: Independent. Enrollment: 880.

Meharry Medical College was founded in 1876 by the Freedmen's Aid Society of the Methodist Episcopal Church. Named in tribute to Samuel Meharry, who had provided generous financial support to the school in its early years, the objective of the school was to train health care professionals to service the newly freed black community.

In the years since its establishment, Meharry has expanded in terms of its program offerings and specializations. The College presently includes the Schools of Medicine, Dentistry, Graduate Studies and Research, and Allied Health Professions. Meharry also sponsors the Lloyd C. Elam Community Mental Health Center and the Institute on Health Care for the Poor and Underserved, one of the first of its kind in the nation.

As the nation's largest private, historically black medical institute, the school has played an important role in educating African American health professionals. Nearly 15 percent of all African American physicians and dentists practicing in the United States are graduates of Meharry Medical

College. The majority of Meharry's graduates are to be found practicing in medically underserved rural and inner city communities.

Tennessee State University. Nashville. Founded 1912. Public, no religious affiliation. Enrollment: 7,451.

Tennessee Sate University was started in 1912 as the Agricultural and Industrial State Normal School. It became a full four-year university in 1958.

Texas

Huston-Tillotson College. Austin. Founded 1876. Religious affiliation: United Church of College. Enrollment: 650.

Huston-Tillotson College was formed in 1952 by the merger of Samuel Huston College and Tillotson College. The school welcomes all students without regard to race.

Huston-Tillotson has grown and evolved under the leadership of trendsetting presidents such as Matthew S. Davage, J.J Seabrook, John Q. Taylor King and Joseph T. McMillan, Jr. The current president is Larry L. Earvin.

Jarvis Christian College. Hawkins. Founded 1912. Religious affiliation: Disciples of Christ. Enrollment: 500.

The Negro Disciples of Christ spearheaded the founding of Jarvis Christian College. Jarvis started as a high school level institution and later evolved into a junior college. Four-year college courses were introduced in 1937, and shortly after the school awarded its first bachelor's degrees.

Paul Quinn College. Waco. Founded 1872. Religious affiliation: African Methodist Episcopal.

Ministers of the African Methodist Episcopal Church established Paul Quinn College in Austin, Texas, in 1872. The school was named to honor Bishop William Paul Quinn, a.m.E. Bishop of the Western States. Several years after its founding the school relocated to Waco. In 1990 Paul Quinn College moved to Dallas, Texas.

Prairie View Agricultural and Mechanical University. Prairie View. Founded 1876. Public, no religious affiliation. Enrollment: 6,200.

Prairie View A&M University is the second oldest institution of higher education in the state of Texas. The school began in 1876 as the

Agricultural and Mechanical College for Colored Youth. Today, Prairie View A&M boasts of many achievements and distinctions in minority higher education. It ranks among the nation's top producers of African American engineers and it is home to an exceptionally strong ROTC program.

Texas College. Tyler. Founded 1894. Religious affiliation: Christian Methodist Episcopal. Enrollment: 617.

Texas College is one of the oldest historically black private colleges in Texas. Leaders of the Christian Methodist Episcopal Church founded the college in 1894 to educate African Americans. Hence Texas College is evidence of the role African American themselves played in creating educational opportunities for their race.

Texas College aims for the overall development — intellectual, social, physical, emotional, and spiritual — of each student. Its graduates have made immense contributions to the nation and the world at large.

Texas Southern University. Houston. Founded 1947. Public, no religious affiliation. Enrollment: 8,934.

Texas Southern University began as the Houston College for Negroes. The institution adopted its present name in 1947.

Texas Southern University claims a distinctive record in the education and training of African American professionals. The Texas Southern University Thurgood Marshall School of Law has trained more than half of all African American attorneys practicing in Texas and a significant percentage of African American pharmacists in the state graduated from the School of Pharmacy.

Wiley College. Marshall. Founded 1873. Religious affiliation: United Methodist. Enrollment: 552.

Bishop Isaac Wiley of the United Methodist Church started Wiley College in 1873 to provide the education and training necessary for newly freed blacks to transition into freedom. The college holds the distinction of being the first black college west of the Mississippi River. Over the course of its more than century of operation, the college has served as a gateway to higher education for generations of underserved minorities. Wiley College remains committed to providing students with a broad liberal arts education in a Christian environment and atmosphere.

Virginia

Hampton University. Hampton. Founded 1868. Religious affiliation: Independent. Enrollment: 6,000.

In 1868 General Samuel Chapman Armstrong, the son of missionary parents, established the Hampton Normal and Agricultural Institute to educate newly freed blacks. Several institutions and organizations, including the American Missionary Association, the Freedmen's Bureau, and northern philanthropists supported Armstrong in this endeavor. Like many school established for African Americans after the Civil War, for many years Hampton Institute emphasized preparatory education, and as such the majority of its early students were enrolled in the high school department. Postsecondary-level programs were introduced in 1922 and the first bachelor's degree was awarded in 1926.

Given its history as an institution founded to uplift former slaves through education Hampton University aims to educate students to be socially aware and willing members of the team working to solve problems affecting our nation, and indeed, the world. Hampton prides itself on being able to maintain a research orientation while at the same time being student-centered.

Hampton's campus, considered one of the most beautiful campuses in America, is home to many historic structures. The "Emancipated Oak Tree," one of the first places where the Emancipation Proclamation was read in the state of Virginia, is located on the Hampton campus. The tree towers as a symbol of the important link the freedmen saw between freedom and education. Five of Hampton's buildings are national historic landmarks.

Hampton's current president, William V. Harvey, has led the University since 1978. Under Harvey's leadership, Hampton's student population, academic programs, physical facilities, and financial base have grown substantially. Moreover, Harvey has received national distinction for his leadership model, which has been responsible for numerous Hampton University administrators rising to college presidencies at institutions throughout the nation.

Norfolk State University. Norfolk. Founded 1935. Public, no religious affiliation. Enrollment: 7,710.

Norfolk State University began in 1935 as the Norfolk branch of Virginia Union University. It then became independent and over the years operated under several names including Norfolk Polytechnic College,

Norfolk Division of Virginia State University, independent Norfolk State College, and finally Norfolk State University. With a student body of more than 7,000 students, Norfolk State University is Virginia's largest historically black college, and one of the largest traditionally black higher education institutions in America. The school is located in Hampton Roads, a major metropolitan area.

From 1938 to 1975 Norfolk State University was led by Lyman Beecher Brooks. It was during the Beecher administration that Norfolk State grew from a small junior college into a full-fledged four-year institution.

Today, Norfolk State is a diverse institution, drawing students from all geographic regions of the United States and 38 foreign countries. The school's record of excellence places it among the best institutions in the land. Norfolk State boasts a ninth ranking among schools graduating African Americans with bachelor's degrees. The University is fully accredited by the Southern Association of Colleges and Schools.

St. Paul's College. Lawrenceville. Founded 1888. Religious affiliation: Episcopal. Enrollment: 474.

St. Paul's College was founded in 1888 in Lawrenceville, Virginia. A liberal arts-focused institution, the school has historical ties to the Episcopal Church.

Since 2002, John K. Waddell has served as president of St. Paul's College. One of the youngest college presidents in America, Waddell has infused St. Paul's with energy and vision. He has introduced new academic programs and expanded services to students. Moreover, he has carried out major campus and building renovation projects, including the construction of a new student center and plans for the construction of new dormitories, a new library, as well as classrooms and science laboratories. And under Waddell football returned to St. Paul's following a 15-year absence.

Virginia State University. Petersburg. Founded 1882. Public, no religious affiliation. Enrollment: 4,974.

In 1882, Alfred W. Harris, a black delegate to the Virginia General Assembly, petitioned the state legislature to establish a public institution for the education and training of African Americans. The General Assembly responded favorably to Harris' appeal and on March 6, 1882, passed a bill to charter the Virginia Normal and Collegiate Institute in Petersburg.

In 1920 Virginia Normal Institute became the state's designated land-grant institution for African Americans. The school grew substantially in the 1920s when the college program was initiated and the name subsequently changed to Virginia State College for Negroes. From 1944 to 1969 a two-year branch of Virginia State operated in Norfolk. In 1979, after continued expansion, Virginia State was elevated to university status. Since its inception, African American men of distinction have held the Virginia State University presidency. John Mercer Langston, a prominent nationally recognized African American leader of the late-nineteenth century served as the first president. From 1888 to 1968, four presidents—James H. Johnston, John M. Gandy, Luther H. Foster, and Robert P. Daniel—led the University. The period 1968 to 1992 witnessed six presidential administration: James F. Tucker, Wendell P. Russell, Walker H. Quarles, Jr., Thomas M. Law, Wilbert Greenfield, and Wesley Cornelious McClure. In 1993, Eddie N. Moore, Jr., the former Treasurer of the Commonwealth of Virginia, assumed office as the twelfth president of Virginia State University.

Virginia Union University. Richmond. Founded 1865. Religious affiliation: Baptist. Enrollment: 1,548.

Virginia Union University was founded in 1865 as the Richmond Theological Institute. The sponsoring organization of the school was the American Baptist Church USA. In 1899, following a merger between Richmond Theological and Wayland Seminary in Washington, the name of the school changed to Virginia Union University. Several years later, Hartshorn Memorial College of Richmond and Storer College of Harper's Ferry, West Virginia, two other institutions for the education of blacks, also merged with Virginia Union.

Virginia Union has produced many graduates who have gone on to meet achievement and distinction in various fields. L. Douglas Wilder, the first African American governor of the United States, and Samuel Lee Gravely, Jr., the first black admiral of the United States Navy, are both graduates of Virginia Union. Moreover, numerous college presidents, and one out of every ten African American ministers graduated from the University.

Virginia Union University continues to grow in programs and student diversity. The University is a member of the United Negro College Fund and is fully accredited by the Southern Association of Colleges.

West Virginia

Bluefield State College. Bluefield. Founded 1895. Public, no religious affiliation. Enrollment: 2,405.

In 1895 the West Virginia Legislature established Bluefield State College as a teacher-training institute for African American teachers. The school grew and evolved over the years and by the 1960s the college had become a comprehensive four-year school offering programs in teacher education, arts and sciences, and engineering technology.

After the Supreme Court *Brown v. Board of Education* ruling in 1954, Bluefield became integrated. Today, Bluefield has more white than black students.

West Virginia State College. Institute. Founded 1891. Public, no religious affiliation. Enrollment: 5,100.

West Virginia State College was founded in 1891 for the higher education of African Americans. In the mid–1950s, an era define by desegregation in public education, West Virginia State became racially and culturally diverse, attracting significant numbers of non-black students, faculty, and staff.

Today, the College offers strong baccalaureate and associate degree programs in the arts and sciences and in professional studies.

Sources of Information: HBCU Institutions

BIBLIOGRAPHY

Interviews

Brown, Carlton E. Interview with author, 13 March 2003.
Francis, Norman C. Interview with author, 16 October 2002.
Lomax, Michael L. Interview with author, 26 August 2002.
Lowe, Calvin W. Interview with author, 2 April 2002.
Mason, Ronald F. Interview with author, 7 March 2003.
Massey, Walter E. Interview with author, 29 August 2002.
McDemmond, Marie V. Interview with author, 11 September 2002.
Ponder, Henry R. Interview with author, 26 February 2003.
Tatum Daniel, Beverly. Interview with author, 28 February 2003.
Wallace-Reid, Carolynn. Interview with author, 12 September 2002.

Secondary Sources

Adair, Alvis. *Desegregation: The Illusion of Black Progress.* Lanham, MD: University Press of America, 1984.
Altbach, Philip G., and Berdahl, Robert Oliver, eds. *American Higher Education in the Twenty-First Century: Political, Social, and Economic Challenges.* Baltimore: Johns Hopkins University Press, 1999.
Anderson, James D. *The Education of Blacks in the South, 1860–1935.* Chapel Hill: University of North Carolina Press, 1988.
Bacote, Clarence A. *The Story of Atlanta University: A Century of Service, 1865–1965.* Atlanta: Atlanta University Press, 1969.
Bailey, Ruby C. "Proud Past, Uncertain Future: Some Historically Black Colleges are Fighting for their Lives." *Detroit Free Press Online,* 21 February 2003.
Banks, James. "The Canon Debate, Knowledge Construction, and Multicultural Education." *Educational Researcher* 22 (June/July 1993): 4–14.
Bond, Horace Mann. *Education for Freedom: A History of Lincoln University, Pennsylvania.* Princeton: Princeton University Press, 1976.

Bowen, William G., and Bok, Derek. *The Shape of the River: Long-Term Consequences of Considering Race in College and University Admissions.* Princeton: Princeton University Press, 1998.

Bowles, Frank, and DeCosta, Frank A. *Between Two Worlds: A Profile of Negro Higher Education.* New York: McGraw-Hill, 1971.

Brint, Steven, ed. *The Future of the City of Intellect: The Changing American University.* Stanford: Stanford University Press, 2002.

Brown, M. Christopher. *The Quest to Define Collegiate Desegregation: Black Colleges, Title VI Compliance, and Post-Adams Litigation.* Westport: Bergin & Garvey, 1999.

Browning, J.E., and Williams, J.B. "History and Goals of Black Institutions of Higher Learning." In *Black Colleges in America*, eds. Charles V. Willie and R.R. Edmonds. New York: Teachers College Press, 1978.

Campbell, Clarice Thompson. *History of Tougaloo College.* Ph.D. dissertation, University of Mississippi, 1970.

Carter, Lawrence Edward. *Walking Integrity: Benjamin E. Mays, Mentor to Generations.* Atlanta: Scholars Press, 1996.

Collins, Donald Earl. *"A Substance of Things Hoped For": Multiculturalism, Desegregation, and Identity in African American Washington, 1930–1960.* Ph.D. dissertation, Carnegie-Mellon University, 1997.

Davis, Leroy. *A Clashing of the Soul: John Hope and the Dilemma of African American Leadership and Black Higher Education in the Early Twentieth Century.* Athens: University of Georgia Press, 1998.

Drake, St. Clair. "The Black University in the American Social Order." *Journal of the American Academy of Arts and Sciences* 100(3) 1971: 837.

Drewry, Henry, and Doermann, Humphrey. *Stand and Prosper: Private Black Colleges and Their Students.* Princeton: Princeton University Press, 2001.

Duderstadt, James J., and Womack, Farris W, eds. *The Future of the Public University in America: Beyond the Crossroads.* Baltimore: Johns Hopkins University Press, 2003.

Dyson, Walter. *Howard University, The Capstone of Negro Education, A History: 1867–1940.* Washington, DC: The Graduate School of Howard University, 1941.

Eddy, Edward Danforth, Jr. *Colleges for Our Land and Time: The Land-Grant Idea in American Education.* New York: Harper & Brothers, 1956.

Fairclough, Adam. *Teaching Equality: Black Schools in the Age of Jim Crow.* Athens: University of Georgia Press, 2001.

Foster, Michelle. *Black Teachers on Teaching.* New York: New Press, 1997.

Gallot, Mildred D.G. *A History of Grambling State University.* Lanham, MD: University Press of America, 1985.

Garibaldi, Antoine. *Black Colleges and Universities: Challenges for the Future.* New York: Praeger, 1984.

Gasman, Marybeth. *Charles S. Johnson: Leadership Beyond the Veil in the Age of Jim Crow.* Albany: State University of New York Press, 2003.

_____. *Fund Raising from Black-College Alumni: Successful Strategies for Supporting Alma Mater.* Washington, DC: Council for the Advancement and Support of Education, 2003.

Hale, Frank, Jr., ed. *What Makes Racial Diversity Work in Higher Education.* Sterling: Stylus Publishing, 2004.

Hanson, Joyce Ann. *Mary McLeod Bethune and Black Women's Political Activism.* Columbia: University of Missouri Press, 2003.

Harlan, Louis R. *Booker T. Washington: The Wizard of Tuskegee.* New York: Oxford University Press, 1983.

Holmes, Dwight Oliver Wendell. *The Evolution of the Negro College.* New York: Teachers College Press, 1934.

Irvine, Russell, and Irvine, Jacqueline. "The Impact of the Desegregation Process on the Education of Black Students: Key Variables." *The Journal of Negro Education* 52(40) 1983: 410–422.

Jones, Edward A. *A Candle in the Dark: A History of Morehouse College.* Valley Forge: The Judson Press, 1967.

Jones, Lee, and Scott, LeKita. *The Storied Past and Relevance of Historically Black Colleges and Universities.* Sterling: Stylus Publishing, 2005.

Jones, Maxine D., and Richardson, Joe M. *Talladega College: The First Century.* Tuscaloosa: University of Alabama Press, 1990.

Kluger, Richard. *Simple Justice: The History of* Brown v. Board of Education *and Black America's Struggle for Equality.* New York: Vintage Books, 1975.

Lewis, David Levering. *W.E.B. Du Bois: The Fight for Equality and the American Century, 1919–1963.* New York: Henry Holt, 2000.

Litwack, Leon F. *Trouble in Mind: Black Southerners in the Age of Jim Crow.* New York: Knopf, 1998.

Logan, Rayford W. *The Negro in American Life and Thought: The Nadir, 1877–1901.* New York: Dial Press, 1954.

Mays, Benjamin E. "The Black College in Higher Education." In Charles V. Willie and Ronald R. Edmonds, eds., *Black Colleges in America: Challenges, Development, Survival.* New York: Teachers College Press, 1978.

_____. *Born to Rebel: An Autobiography.* Athens: University of Georgia Press, 2003.

McGrath, Earl J. *The Predominantly Negro Colleges and Universities in Transition.* New York: Teachers College Press, 1965.

Preer, Jean. *Lawyers v. Educators: Black Colleges and Desegregation in Public Higher Education.* Westport, CT: Greenwood, 1982.

Read, Florence M. *The Story of Spelman College.* Princeton: Princeton University Press, 1961.

Richardson, Joe M. *A History of Fisk University, 1865–1946.* Tuscaloosa: University of Alabama Press, 1980.

Roebuck, Julian B., and Murty, Komanduri S. *Historically Black Colleges and Universities: Their Place in American Higher Education.* Westport, CT: Praeger, 1993.

Rovaris, Dereck J. *Mays and Morehouse: How Benjamin E. Mays Developed Morehouse College, 1940–1967.* Silver Spring: Beckham House, 2004.

Rudolph, Frederick. *The American College and University: A History.* New York: Random House, 1962.

Sims, Serbrenia J. *Diversifying Historically Black Colleges and Universities: A New Higher Education Paradigm.* Westport, CT: Greenwood, 1994.

Sowell, Thomas. *Black Education: Myths and Tragedies.* New York: McKay, 1972.

Thompson, Daniel. *Private Colleges at the Crossroads.* Westport, CT: Greenwood, 1973.

Tollett, Kenneth. "The Fate of Minority-Based Institutions after *Fordice*: An Essay." *Review of Litigation,* 13(3), pp. 447–493.

Washington, Johnny. *Alain Locke and Philosophy, A Quest for Cultural Pluralism.* Westport, CT: Greenwood, 1986.

Williams, June Audrey. "Man with a Mission: On the Eve of His Retirement, the President of the United Negro College Fund Reflects on the Purposes and Challenges of Black Institutions." *The Chronicle of Higher Education,* 7 November 2003.

Williamson, Joel. *The Crucible of Race: Black/White Relations in the American South since Emancipation.* New York: Oxford University Press, 1984.

Willie, Charles V, ed. *Black Colleges in America: Challenge, Development, Survival.* New York: Teachers College Press, 1978.

_____, ed. *The Education of African Americans.* New York: Auburn House, 1991.

Wilson Mbajekwe, Carolyn O. "Black Colleges after *Brown:* Benjamin E. Mays, Frederick D. Paterson, and the Quest for a Cultural Pluralism-Based Definition of Collegiate Desegregation." Ph.D. dissertation, Emory University, forthcoming.

Wishnietsky, Dan H. *American Education in the Twenty-First Century.* Bloomington: Phi Delta Kappa Educational Foundation, 2001.

Woodson, Carter G. *The Mis-Education of the Negro.* Washington: Associated Publishers, 1933.

Woodward, C. Vann. *The Strange Career of Jim Crow.* New York: Oxford University Press, 1955.

Wright, George C. "The Founding of Lincoln Institute." *Filson Club Quarterly* 49:57–70.

INDEX